POWER, POLITICS,
AND THE MISSOURI SYNOD

POWER, POLITICS, AND THE MISSOURI SYNOD

A Conflict That Changed
American Christianity

James C. Burkee

Fortress Press
Minneapolis

POWER, POLITICS, AND THE MISSOURI SYNOD
A Conflict That Changed American Christianity

First Fortress Press paperback edition 2013

Unless otherwise noted, Scripture quotations are taken from the *New Revised Standard Bible*,
copyright © 1989 by the Division of Christian Education of the National Council of Churches of
Christ in the USA. Used by permission. All rights reserved.

Holy Bible, New International Version®, copyright © 1973, 1978, 1984 International Bible Society.
Used by permission of Zondervan Publishing House. All rights reserved.

Photos courtesy of Concordia Historical Institute, Department of Archives and History, the
Lutheran Church—Missouri Synod, St. Louis, MO 63105.

Cover design: Joe Vaughan
Interior design: PerfecType, Nashville, TN

ISBN 978-1-4514-6538-9

The Library of Congress cataloged the hardcover edition as follows:

Library of Congress Cataloging-in-Publication Data
Burkee, James C.
  Power, politics, and the Missouri Synod : a conflict that changed American Christianity / James
C. Burkee.
      p. cm.
  Includes bibliographical references (p. 239).
  ISBN 978-0-8006-9792-1 (alk. paper)
  1. Lutheran Church—Missouri Synod—History—20th century. 2. Conservatism—Religious
aspects—Lutheran Church—Missouri Synod—History—20th century. 3. Preus, Jacob A. O. (Jacob
Aall Ottesen), 1920–1994. 4. Otten, Herman, 1933– I. Title.
  BX8061.M7B87 2011
  284.1'32209045—dc22   2010044874

Manufactured in the U.S.A.

15   14   13   12   11   1   2   3   4   5   6   7   8   9   10

Contents

Foreword

Did a subject of one of his poems, William Wordsworth asked, sing of "old, unhappy, far-off things and battles long ago" or of something else? "Something else" will never come up as an alternative in this book.

Begin with Wordsworth's first word, "old." The drama of *Power, Politics, and the Missouri Synod* sounds old, since it climaxes in a story from the middle of the previous century. Yet, as James Burkee tells it, the aftershocks and ripple effects of the trauma remain vivid in denominational culture wars today.

Secondly, as for "unhappy," this mini-epic of a church battle certainly evokes that adjective. This story of conflict within one denomination has not a happy beginning, middle, or ending. Even those who claimed victory never sounded happy. But the unhappy character of the tale does not detract from the value of the book.

The poet wondered also about "far-off" things. To combatants in these battles and to their heirs, the plot may remain "too near" for comfort. To everyone else the story of a church body, a synod called "Missouri," might appear to be insignificant, a distant matter of concern only to those involved. As he addresses the larger culture, Burkee is able to draw previously uninvolved readers to care about strategies, personalities, issues, and outcomes that find parallels beyond Missouri.

While the names of almost all the characters and the details of the events described in this book may be strange to most, there are good reasons for them to read on. The first reason has to do with the intrinsic value of this type of human story. All kinds of publics read tales of drama in gypsy camps, Hasidic Jewish congregations, Shaker colonies in Kentucky, or the lives of Basque shepherds. There are far more Missouri Lutherans than there are participants in any of these just-mentioned communities, but all of their struggles can illuminate aspects of the human story. So here, readers patiently will learn the names of Lutheran characters, many of whom would be forgotten apart from their place in this story.

To sell it, the author has to write well and, to build confidence, has to demonstrate that his work is well grounded in research *and* that he can write well. The research is more than satisfying. While previous histories of this conflict were partisan documents, often based on personal experience, author Burkee doggedly pursued long-neglected, seldom-noticed, and even guarded communications. The best example of this is his attention to anti-hero Herman Otten Jr., a peeved and persistent irritant to all sides in the debates and intrigues. The characters Burkee calls "moderates," their self-chosen name, tried to ignore Otten. They disdained him as a Holocaust-denier and plagiarist, someone who purloined and published copyrighted materials. Ethically, he was to them beneath contempt. Why dignify him, they reasoned, by admitting that they paid attention to him as he editorially gunned them down, or, for that matter, even by paying attention in the first place?

Why? In Burkee's telling, by disdaining and avoiding Otten, the moderates misfired in their responses to "the other side," while more credible leaders of "the other side" were playing along and using Mr. Otten to their presumed advantage, especially as he reached over the heads of leaders to reach the otherwise bypassed laypeople in the synod. To see those who had first been in surreptitious alliance with Otten later noisily breaking with him introduces an element of pathos in Burkee's tragic story.

A third reason for reading *Power, Politics, and the Missouri Synod* is because it demonstrates how much effort a historian can put into being fair-minded when dealing with controversies like the one featured here. Until now, most of the narratives dealing with the Missouri breakup were written by partisans in both parties. Some of these authors display qualities that can be alluring, but their mixed tones of defensiveness and aggressiveness can lead to a questioning of their legitimacy as historians. What about Professor Burkee? I met him first when I was an invitee to his dissertation examining committee at Northwestern University, joining a company of well-regarded historians who had been largely unfamiliar with this scene. They invited me in as an "expert witness." (Burkee also invited me in later, as can be seen, to be glimpsed in a couple of cameo roles and as a bit player in several scenes.) If I was identified as a "moderate" observer, though having no personal stake as an employee of the synod or its congregations, Burkee himself might appear to some readers as having an investment in the camp of conservatives.

And why that? First, because he is conservative in his mien and manner and his commitments. Since "politics" is in the title of this book, readers may want to check out his own politics. He polished his credentials as a moderate conservative by running as an unsuccessful but educationally rich primary candidate for a Congressional seat from Wisconsin. As for his biography and the investment of his career and the risks involved, he is well thought of as a professor at two of the Missouri Synod schools. Tarnishing the denomination's image would be neither his mission nor a strategically cunning move. As far as I can tell, he was guided by what he heard from the secretly taped conversations of the conservatives and from what he read in many documents that he helped discover.

What strikes the reader, or at least this reader, is how in the course of his hearing and reading, Burkee first evidenced a confidence-shaking suspicion and finally a firm rejection of the winning party. He did so as he came to view the demonstrably unethical actions of the synod president, Dr. J. A. O. "Jack" Preus, and so many others who were at his side or who were rivals in power-seeking acts against the moderates. If he found an admirable actor among the conservatives, he paid attention. Similarly, if he found something to criticize on the moderates' side, he did not hold back. Admirers of Concordia Seminary president John Tietjen, the main foil and target of the Preus-Otten connection, cannot use this story as an enhancement of the moderate cause and course.

Professor Burkee did find some "admirable actors" among the moderates, but he spent little time on them, their theology, or their motives. They saw themselves as witnesses to the Christian gospel over against legalists, but, since his book is mainly about the "Preus-Otten" connection—a link referred to in the title of his original dissertation—he concentrates on the theology, motives, and strategies of the conservative party. His range is wide, but what will be striking to the reader is how little gospel, good news, or anything positive shows up in the documentation on their side. I have asked some readers of the dissertation and asked myself with this book in hand, is there, even once, a paragraph or a couple of lines that could be described as "spiritual," "evangelical," or "positive"? Burkee had no motive or reason to exclude such lines. Their presence would have added color to his story. Instead, the nearest a reader comes to "doctrinal" discussion occurs in conservative references to their chosen front line, the doctrine of the inerrancy of the Bible as the Word of God and their interpretations of it as also being inerrant.

Their tactical choice was wise, since they were bidding to the largely off-stage (in this book) laity in a time when fear dominated participants in a changing culture and church. Moderates could proclaim the wonders of the gospel, but the militant conservatives could always minister to the fears by advertising the absoluteness of their position: "*They,* the moderates, are errant compromisers, while *we* can assure you of absolutely assured truth in biblical interpretation." So they "won."

Burkee's plot suddenly shifts as he pays attention to the fate of those who had the votes and thus gained and then used the power. He shows what they wanted and gained—including the power to impose as binding truth even the most recently voted-on synodical doctrinal resolutions, plus presidential power in nominating members of all boards, a kind of autonomy the pope might envy. Yet he has to tell of the patent joylessness of their victory and subsequent of power. To the surprise of no one who follows plots like this in religion or politics, Burkee follows the parties and plotters *in statu nascendi* as they gain in power through unitive activity that almost instantly gives way to factions fighting over division of the spoils. It is not a happy story; there are side-glances at the divorces, alcoholism, perhaps abuse that colored the biography of significant participants, though Burkee does not exploit his knowledge of these.

Perhaps most devastating of his findings has to do with the decline of the denomination after its largely uncivil war. During the peak years of the controversy, a major book of sociology of religion appeared and was noticed: Dean M. Kelley's *Why Conservative Churches Are Growing*, which was useful to the Missouri conservatives. They used it as an advertising lure and strategic map. In effect, they were saying, with an envious glance at gainers like the Southern Baptist Convention, which had a concurrent upset of moderates and winner-take-all takeover by fundamentalists: "Look, fellow Missourians, as we purge the 'libs,' the moderates, and send them into exile, we will then be free to ride the church-growth bandwagon." So they cleaned house, said good-bye to much of the leadership, muffled the talent of most who stayed, and, to their surprise, saw drastic decline and devastations that paralleled the course of both in the "mainline" Protestant denominations.

Burkee leaves the second part of the story there, a story that finds Missouri's two parties still struggling for advantage, still engaged in the denominational "politicking" that they had abhorred before this conflict began. What use Missouri's parties and those beyond Missouri who side with either will make of the story is up to them. For now, be assured that reading the Burkee account of "old, unhappy, far-off things and battles long ago" will be a primer and a prompt for fresh thinking on urgent topics in churches and cultures.

—Martin E. Marty

Preface

Sunlight is the best disinfectant.
Justice Louis D. Brandeis

In late summer 2004, my dear friend and coworker Jeff Walz and I set out on a twenty-church tour of Lutheran congregations in Milwaukee to debate the coming presidential election. Jeff, a Democrat who heads the Political Science Department at Concordia University Wisconsin, advocated for Senator John Kerry, the Democratic presidential nominee. A Republican, I took incumbent president George W. Bush. We each made the case for our respective candidate, debated, and fielded questions from congregation and community members. Our objective was to foster a healthy and necessary political dialogue in area churches and to show our fellow Lutherans how we can agree in a civil and fraternal manner to disagree.

Our very first debate at a Lutheran Church—Missouri Synod (LCMS) congregation set the tone for the next several weeks. Reporting the next day on the three-hour event that drew about a hundred participants, *Milwaukee Journal Sentinel* reporter Tom Heinen likened Jeff to the biblical prophet Daniel, indicating that Jeff, like Daniel, now knew what it was like to have spent time in a lions' den.[1] I spent much of my time defending Jeff, who argued with an emotional and often disagreeing crowd that one could be both Christian and Democrat. The evening ended with a pastor telling Jeff of his genuine concern that Jeff was risking eternal damnation for supporting a Democrat. At another LCMS church we polled those in attendance and found seventy-eight Republicans and two Democrats (one of whom was not a member of the church). The pastor reported that after the debate two people left the congregation. One was the only Democrat and the other was a conservative outraged that the congregation would let a Democrat like Jeff speak. We found slightly more balance in ELCA (Evangelical Lutheran Church in America) congregations, but Jeff spent a good deal more time defending me in these more left-leaning congregations than I did him.

We inhabit an age of rigid partisanship that has transformed society and our churches. Today about eight in ten Missouri Synod Lutherans self-identify as "conservative" and vote Republican. ELCA clergy, conversely, tend to self-identify as "liberal" (while ELCA laity divide more evenly).[2] Our churches have become as politically polarized as our Congress.

But it wasn't always so. My LCMS grandfather was more likely to vote Democrat than Republican and perhaps support woman suffrage while belonging to one of the country's most traditional church bodies. Sprinkled across other Lutheran denominations was an equally mixed bag of social and political beliefs. Conservatism then didn't mean what it does today. Church members and church leaders shared essential beliefs but accepted a degree of ideological diversity often absent in today's churches. Where they disagreed, they often agreed to disagree.

The story I tell in this book describes a conflict that reshaped the landscape of American Lutheranism and fostered the polarization that characterizes today's Lutheran churches. But it's about more than just Lutheranism. The remaking of the Missouri Synod took place alongside conflicts elsewhere in American Christianity and the formation of the "Religious Right." Since 1970, Americans have been increasingly switching religious denominations, selecting churches that share their theological *and political* attitudes. There may have been predominantly Republican or Democratic churches forty years ago. But what was then the exception is now the norm. This is the story of how it happened in one small corner of American Christendom.

Those of us who grew up Missouri Synod Lutheran during the 1970s knew little to nothing of the civil war that had torn the thriving church body apart earlier that decade. Thirty years later, those who endured it still evinced the demeanor of divorced parents: one got the house and custody of the kids, but no one really won. Many today look back on the period with a mixture of embarrassment that things got so ugly and melancholy for what might have been.

So when I first began to examine the period Missouri Synod Lutherans refer to simply as "Seminex," I found two things: the wounds of Missouri's partition still fester and run deep, and few want to talk about it. This makes for at once a scholar's dream and nightmare. It is rare that a researcher comes across a topic of such significance that has been left relatively untouched. But it also makes for difficult research, particularly when so many are so unwilling to talk, be it for personal or professional reasons.

Those who would talk were of tremendous help, among them some of the men I was warned to fear, often with good reason. Herman Otten not only granted me hours of interviews but allowed me unsupervised access to his files and copy machine for several days in July 2000. He endured several phone interviews and almost always answered even my most probing questions. Waldo Werning, one of Jack Preus's closest confidants and arguably the leader of the organized conservative movement after 1965, also endured hours of interviews, provided documentary evidence, and read portions of my dissertation. Although he objected to the direction of my dissertation and is criticized in it at times, he was pastoral, if fervent, in his detailed evaluations and always accommodating. Ralph Bohlmann, one of the "Faithful Five" who remained at Concordia after the 1974 walkout and became Preus's successor to the synod presidency in 1981, provided sage counsel during my research and volunteered hours of interviews.

The undersized staff at the Concordia Historical Institute (CHI) in St. Louis, on the campus of Concordia Seminary, was of tremendous assistance during and after the summer of 2000. Marvin Huggins, Associate Director for Archives & Library at CHI, worked miracles. He provided constant encouragement during my weeks of research, pointed me in directions I had not considered, granted me access to Jack Preus's unprocessed files and interviews, and went on a successful scavenger hunt for Executive Office Records from the Harms administration, mislaid records that had been sitting for decades in a storage garage. He was subsequently prompt and courteous in reply to dozens of my pestering e-mails. Mark Loest, Reference Director, also provided valuable support.

Finally, I was exceptionally blessed to have had a "dream team" of scholarly eyes review my manuscript. My graduate advisor at Northwestern University, Michael Sherry, provided sometimes frustrating but always sage guidance. Josef Barton and Nancy MacLean, also at Northwestern University, read early drafts and provided helpful direction. Martin E. Marty, himself a participant in and product of the Missouri Synod schism, advised me in my dissertation studies and has since encouraged me to publish. Rev. Fred Reklau meticulously edited early drafts. I am grateful to have so many hands helping me through this process.

My mother, Jan, who met my father for their first date, of all places, at a lecture by Herman Otten at her San Diego church, has been a lifelong source of inspiration and encouragement. So too has my wife, Susan, for over twenty years.

But this is for my children, Christian, Grace, and Lydia. Let your faith, not faction, guide and define you. *Let your light shine before men, that they may see your good deeds and praise your Father in heaven.*

Introduction

In late 1958, a brash young seminarian from the Bronx, New York, named Herman Otten stood before the faculty of Concordia Seminary in St. Louis, Missouri, to answer charges that he had "violated the law of love" as expressed by Jesus in the New Testament. Earlier that year, Otten had leveled accusations of heresy against several seminarians. Later, in a secret meeting with synod president John W. Behnken, Otten charged that members of the Concordia faculty were teaching heresy, denying the veracity of cherished Bible stories, and questioning Scripture's inerrancy and infallibility. Faculty members, soon confronted by Behnken with Otten's charges, were incensed. They demanded not only that Otten admit that he had sinned in making charges without first confronting the accused—a clear violation of the principle of Matthew 18[1]—but that he retract his accusations. Otten refused. And so the faculty stood in judgment: After years of study and a graduate degree, Herman Otten would not be certified by Concordia Seminary for service as a minister in the Lutheran Church—Missouri Synod (LCMS). In effect, he was blackballed from the church.

Fourteen years later, in October 1972, many of the same men who had sat in judgment of young Otten were marched, one at a time, before a similar committee in St. Louis. This time, they were on trial. Each man was now forced to answer the charges first raised by Otten in 1958: Were Adam and Eve real historical persons? Was Jesus' mother, Mary, a virgin? Is the Holy Bible infallible and inerrant?[2] Within three years, all but five would be out of a job, fired after a series of political defeats, tactical errors, and self-exile.

1

Their fall bookended a decade of hope, political conflict, and spiritual struggle. And it ushered in a new age in the Missouri Synod, which now took its
place as a champion of American evangelical conservatism, while entering
an era of chronic decline.

Missouri's story is modern church history writ large. It is yet another
tale of epic struggle between the forces of modernism and conservatism
in American religious life. It is also the essential story of modern history
in the life of a great American religious denomination, then the country's
eighth-largest church body, and its nearly three million members. Most significantly, it is the story of a small but dedicated group of men, their relationships, their behaviors, the ideologies to which they were committed, a
movement they created, and a church they forever altered.

Unchartered Waters

I began my circuitous route to this story from a distance. A child of the Missouri Synod, I spent all but one of my pregraduate educational years in its
schools and churches. After four years of graduate study in history, I began
to look at the modern phenomenon of organized political activity among
Christian conservatives—the "Religious Right." Only then did I come across
a sound I may have heard once or twice in passing as a child and teen:
"Seminex," the word that has come to embody one of the most convulsive
periods in the short history of the LCMS, a civil war that split the church in
the 1970s.[3] My curiosity was roused when a historiographical survey turned
up but a handful of accounts of the period, mostly emotional, partisan, or
triumphalist works written by participants in the struggle. Mary Todd, in
her 1996 dissertation (and subsequent book), tells why: Concordia Publishing House (CPH) in St. Louis, the synod's official publishing enterprise,
subjects all submissions to a process of anonymous doctrinal review.[4] The
manufactured flaw, she recognizes, is that the church writes its own history,
leaving only filtered works that present a glorified past. Moreover, almost all
of what little has been written about the period addresses the theological
debate that divided the church, as if the schism happened within a contex-
tual vacuum. Was it mere coincidence that the synod had rapidly liberalized

during the 1950s and 1960s just as the nation moved forward on civil rights and a "Great Society"? Or that it, like the rest of America, fought with itself during the 1970s over the changes produced by those earlier decades? That J. A. O. "Jack" Preus, the conservative candidate for the LCMS presidency, narrowly won election in the same year that Richard Nixon first took office? Or that conservatives in the Missouri Synod had organized into a political movement just as the Religious Right in America was taking form?

In 2000, I contacted the Concordia Historical Institute (CHI), the synod's Department of Archives and History, to ask about the status of records from the period. Executive Office records from the Behnken and Harms administrations (through 1969) were accessible. Better yet, the files of Jack Preus, the synod's president from 1969 to 1981, which had been sealed for nearly two decades, would be open to me the following summer. Jim Adams's 1977 book, *Preus of Missouri and the Great Lutheran Civil War*, raised significant questions about the man.[5] To synod moderates, particularly the ones who had left Missouri in the late 1970s, Jack Preus was the great villain of modern church history, together with kingmaker Herman Otten. (Former Concordia professor Frederick Danker referred to the schism as "the Preus-Otten Purge of Missouri."[6]) To conservatives, Preus was the champion who recaptured the seminary and saved the synod from the forces of liberalism. I wanted to know more about the man and the movement that brought him to power. I resolved to spend the summer of 2000 in steamy St. Louis, working through the musty Preus files and interviewing those still alive who led the warring parties.

It was then that my journey took a disturbing turn. Several people, many who had lived through the period, cautioned me to back off. These are dangerous people who might make my life miserable, I was warned, particularly if I wanted to teach at one of the synod's colleges or universities (which I now do). I went to St. Louis just the same. As I worked my way through Preus's files and the files of his brother, Robert, I collected names, phone numbers, and e-mail and mailing addresses of dozens of men who knew or had gone to Concordia with Otten; men involved with various movements to combat liberalism in the church; men who helped elect Preus and served in his administration. When I began calling on those

still alive to request interviews, I often found something completely unexpected: silence. Many were unwilling to talk. The reasons were diverse. For
some, the emotional wounds were still fresh. Some were embarrassed by
their involvement. Others had professional reasons, wanting to stay "neutral" while serving in official capacities in the church. Some were afraid of
reprisals. The most unsettling, however, was the stonewalling from men
who did not want the truth exposed; who did not want aired the details
of a veiled organization that, it was implied, still rules the synod. Richard
Koenig had dubbed the "conservative reaction" in Missouri a gathering
of "fearful" men: I fully expected allusions to Nixon, but I did not expect
this cloak-and-dagger, Deep Throat dynamic, surely not in a conservative
Christian church.[7] But here they were, Lutheran ministers engaging me in
the most juvenile of conversational acrobatics: "What are you, conservative
or lib?" "I can't tell you that." "Those who know will take these secrets to
their grave." "There are no Dick Morrises [former political advisor to Bill
Clinton turned tell-all journalist] in our organization." "Men of integrity
will never reveal" who is in the inner circle. Or better yet, "Why don't you
ask me the questions, and I'll tell you if you are getting warmer or colder."
It was this researcher's journey—these unforeseen interactions and the
surprising nature of the documentation—that moved me to unforeseen
conclusions.

I argue here what I believe everyone knows but few will confess: the
schismatic history of the Lutheran Church—Missouri Synod is about more
than just theology. I readily concede that theological language dominated
the conflict as the synod polarized in the postwar years around questions
of truth: those who saw biblical truth in part as subjective, through historical and cultural lenses, and those who viewed it as definable and untouch-
able, transcending time and interpretation. But as James Davison Hunter
suggests in *Culture Wars*, this worldview and this language were neither
specific to the Missouri Synod nor exclusively theological.[8] By the 1960s,
the emerging progressive and orthodox poles in the LCMS were defined
as much by their social and political views as their religious beliefs. Most
of the major accounts of the conflict revolve around the 1969 election of
Jack Preus.[9] The war that followed was a war of ideologies, primarily but

not exclusively theological in expression. And, lest we forget, the war's great battle was fought over a seminary. So yes, it was about theology.

But it was also about the cultural and political contexts in which these men lived. "Religions," writes Martin Marty, "have always engaged in dialogue with their environment."[10] Missouri was no different. Lutherans of all stripes struggled to define their churches in an age of weakening ties to denominations. To say this seems superfluous, but it is not: Missouri Synod Lutherans voted, shopped, and went to the movies just like other good Americans. Missouri liberals often called themselves good Democrats and cultivated deeper relationships with like-minded people outside the denomination, as did many good Republican conservatives. They had opinions in an age of resolute opinions: during the sixties they held views of the civil rights movement, Vietnam, the welfare state, or the communist menace. They called themselves "conservatives" and "liberals" (later "moderates"), self-denominating with words that intentionally transcended the synod's boundaries and embracing ideologies that increasingly consisted of both secular and religious elements.[11] The events of the 1960s and the reactions they generated opened a window in time, creating space for change. Conservatives and their champion, Jack Preus, stormed through that window.

Those disagreeing, insisting that the conflict was solely theological, must ask themselves this: Would the schism have happened in the absence of the great, convulsive events of the 1960s? Would America's conservative "silent majority" have been so frightened of "liberals" had there been no civil rights and antiwar marches, no riots, no black radicalism, or no welfare state? Jack Preus's resonant call for order in the LCMS in 1969 paralleled what most conservatives, Lutheran and secular, were saying: liberalism had gone too far.[12] And liberalism meant more than just theology.[13]

Finally, this was about the men. Individuals shape history, particularly in elitist polities. And the Missouri Synod, like many mainline church bodies, is a clerical oligarchy, an organization dominated by elites—male, typically white, clergy. As Mary Todd writes, "This is a church body in which clerical hegemony has been the rule." It is a church body with a long history of "strong pastors" and "clergy-dependent people."[14] Its officers, with the exception of treasurer, must be clergy, and fully half of all delegates to synodical conventions must be clergy. Clergy, for those purposes, equates only with ordained LCMS ministers.[15] And LCMS ministers must be male. Missouri Synod conventions, held every two to three years, elect all of the church's leaders, control the bureaucracy, decide doctrinal issues, and make a variety of pronouncements. Herman Otten's great epiphany, developed sometime in the mid-sixties and perfected by the seventies, was that to control the LCMS you had to control the convention. Conservatives also recognized that organizing the clergy meant controlling the church. Jeffrey Hadden, in his 1969 study of Protestant churches (including the Missouri Synod), warned of a growing ideological gap between Protestant ministers and church laity. His survey was significant in defining lines between Missouri clergy and laity. But more significant, I believe, was a widening generational gulf he identified separating older, more conservative clergy from younger, more liberal clergy.[16] The synod's St. Louis seminary was producing the next generation of clergy, and before long, its graduates would dominate the synod. It is for this reason that the major confrontation in Missouri's "Great Lutheran Civil War" was fought over Concordia.

The movement's progenitor was Herman Otten. While pockets of grumbling dissenters did protest liberalism in the church throughout the 1950s and early '60s, Otten made it a *cause célèbre* among some Missouri clergy. Herman Otten's mouthpiece, *Christian News*, was the movement's mouthpiece in the years following its launch in 1962. He defined conservatism for the Missouri Synod, created a sense of crisis, and, through *Christian News*, turned a handful of anxious pastors and laymen into a movement. Dubbed "Jacob's Ladder" after Preus's 1969 election, *Christian News* became a steady source of discomfort to LCMS leaders. Conservatives either loved Otten or hated him, but all relied on him. Otten and those who loved him were often relegated by those who hated him to the far-right fringe of Missouri sentiment. The pages of *Christian News* were filled with diatribes as often against communism, feminism, and civil rights protest as against theological liberalism. More "centrist"[17] conservatives likely saw those issues as distractions from what they believed the gravest threat to the synod, namely, theological liberalism. But for all their talk of grassroots distress over theological issues, these conservatives used *Christian News* to their advantage, far more so than any of the theology-laden publications others produced. The *Christian News* archives are filled with articles ghost-written by the same men who verbally minimized his influence and excluded him from the conservative inner sanctum. These conservatives, too, tried to compete with Otten, and almost always failed.

In their zeal to moderate, many conservatives struggled to write a history that excluded Otten. Their conservative reaction, the story goes, was a divinely inspired, grassroots, lay-led movement that spontaneously materialized and unified. Here is how *Affirm,* a publication that competed with *Christian News* after 1971, wrote its own history:

> But God caused events to occur which they [the liberals] may not have imagined possible. In one way, they might have seemed odd and unthreatening events. For example, in one part of the country a few clergymen met to express their dismay over what was happening to their church, their beloved Missouri. They met again, perhaps with an enlarged group.
>
> In another city others met—unaware that concerned people were meeting in groups elsewhere. Some groups in the main were not the church's clergy, but members of its laity. They decided to meet again. The groups multiplied. So did the meetings. The common concern grew. It didn't take long before these groups began to find out about each other's work. Soon they no longer merely talked at their meetings; they began to decide on a course of action.[18]

Others tried to manufacture a story that isolated Preus from his conservative partners. Concordia's Board of Control, then headed by Preus ally E. J. Otto, wrote in 1977 that liberals tried "to create the impression that the crisis in the Missouri Synod had been originated and been fostered by conservatives under the leadership of Balance Incorporated (publishers of *Affirm*) and the editorial position of *Christian News*."[19]

Again, it is necessary, given such revisionism, to state the obvious: Herman Otten was the single most influential conservative in the synod before 1969.[20] Serious questions can produce no acceptable answers in Otten's absence. How did so many Missouri Synod Lutherans come, by 1969, to view liberalism as so dominant and threatening, and Concordia Seminary as less than orthodox, if not for Otten's unrelenting assault on the synod's administration and faculty? By Preus's election, a large minority of LCMS pastors questioned the seminary's commitment to "sound Lutheran principles."[21] If not for Otten's *Christian News*, how can such sentiment be explained? The historian has few other means to measure popular opinion than simply to read what people were reading and draw conclusions from its contents. *Christian News* is what conservatives were reading.

Herman Otten is the Missouri Synod's great pitiable figure. Time and again, he was exploited by conservatives too cowardly to publicly associate their respectable names and clerical collars with his ethically questionable actions. Several times during his career as the synod's chief antagonist, Otten led crusades that began with scores of professing supporters in underground gatherings, only to find himself alone and abandoned when the campaign reached daylight. Otten's long march was both directed and devastated by these men—aging professors in the 1950s, "movement" leaders in the sixties, and a synodical president and his cronies in the seventies—who often encouraged, exhorted, and supported him in private, only to renounce or denounce him in public. An odd dynamic emerged during interviews with conservatives, one that exists now as then: no one admits to reading *Christian News*, but everybody does. Perhaps the great tragedy for both Otten and the synod was that his determined campaign for seminary certification failed, largely for personal reasons. It failed because he had attacked the fundamental values of men who had dedicated their lives to Christian ministry. It failed because most conservatives, declaring sympathy for his cause, deserted him when it counted. Most of all, it failed because Otten made the crusade about much more than theology.

Herman Otten is also the Missouri Synod's most infamous figure. Otten saw himself, as others still see him, as the "Martin Luther of the Missouri Synod," standing firm for truth regardless of the cost.[22] But as *Christian News* developed in the 1960s, it came more to reflect Otten's truth than biblical or even religious truth. Before long it had become his child, a manifestation of his own beliefs and idiosyncrasies (he primarily uses the editorial "we" in *Christian News*'s pages). *Christian News* made it crystal clear that this was about much more than just the Missouri Synod. Otten's paper covered a lot of ground, blasting liberals in other church bodies, social movements, secular politics, and foreign countries, always in the name of conservatism. By the 1980s, he was taking on secular history and becoming active in the Holocaust-denial movement (the Anti-Defamation League called *Christian News* an "anti-Semitic tabloid").[23] Otten was consistently conservative but ideologically inconsistent. He claimed a respect for journalistic standards but reprinted articles without securing appropriate consent. He professed honesty and openness at all costs, but published ghost-written articles, anonymous accusations, and even personal letters—so much so that by the 1970s, personal letters from friends at times opened with "NOT FOR PUBLICATION." He complained about the conservative movement's secretive tactics but attended clandestine meetings and frequently communicated through back channels. Herman Otten's sprawling conservatism and problematic methods gained him unmatched influence. They gained him a strong and loyal following. And they gained him enduring infamy.

The other figure central in the Missouri Synod's conservative movement was Jack Preus, though he was neither its founder nor its most faithful contributor. A newcomer from the "Little Norwegian" Evangelical Lutheran Synod (ELS),[24] during the 1960s Preus associated with conservatives erratically. When he did meet with them, he entered through the back door, careful not to leave a record of his presence. But he was, many soon judged, conservatism's most attractive, articulate, and politically able member. In short, he was the most electable. The son of a Minnesota governor, Jack Preus seemed to many conservatives the ideal synthesis of theologian and politician. A back-slapping good old boy who could skillfully trade locker-room expletives, he was just as comfortable jousting over theology with brainy professors. He was good in front of the microphone, photogenic, and, most important, he reasoned like a politician.

Conservatives hoped for the theologian but got the politician. In 1969, Preus took charge of a movement that seemed unified. Humbly accepting nomination by his backers and election by delegates, he quickly distanced himself from the first by reaching out to the second. That Preus was a master of duplicity is the one point on which nearly all those I interviewed (who were willing to talk) agreed. He seized control of the church and built a decade-long career by constructing and fueling a fraudulent leadership dynamic in the church, consistently showing one face to the public and another to his cronies. From the day of his election in 1969, Jack Preus openly and repeatedly condemned the men who elected and kept him in power, only to backtrack with them in private, encourage extralegal exploits, and coordinate organized political activity through a mysterious "pipeline." He gave conservatives what they wanted—victory against the liberals. When it was achieved, the tenuous coalition collapsed and turned on him while conservatives turned on each other. The same men who crowned him in 1969 dethroned him in 1981.

Finally, there are the men who built and became the conservative movement. The movement was made up of two tiers. Atop sat a small but increasingly organized cabal of elites, mostly clergy but also some wealthier laymen, who shared important commonalities. Some were refugees from the war against liberalism in other Christian denominations. Among the most powerful, the group to which Preus would attach himself, were those who considered themselves more mainstream or less radical conservatives, men who believed they were focused intently and solely on the *sine qua non* of synodical survival, doctrinal purity. Another, more radical wing openly embraced secular conservatism and operated relatively independently of the first. This group, considered by the first to be less than legitimate, was comprised of men impelled by another agenda. These were the synod's John Birchers who decried the advance of communism, civil rights, and bureaucracy. But lines between them were fluid, with several powerful personalities like Otten maintaining ties to both. Most of them were men who had the time, resources, and commitment to their diverse agenda to organize, momentarily unify, and lead a movement against their one common enemy.

The second tier was comprised of elites of a different stripe: pastors, mostly graduates of Missouri's two seminaries, and a smaller number of laymen. They looked a lot like first-tier conservatives. They were white, often suburban, theologically and socially conservative, likely to vote Republican, and probably held antagonistic or prejudiced views toward the socially active, Jews, and blacks. For all the significance of the men at the top, these were the movement's foot soldiers, the ones who proved a receptive audience for *Christian News*, organized local campaigns at the behest of movement leaders (often circumventing the established structures and elected leaders within their local districts), and funneled information to the men at the top. Before 1965 they gave increasing portions of their local church budgets to the synod; after 1965 they withheld more and more.

This was, however, no lay groundswell. It took a full decade to generate enough suspicion of the "liberal" church leadership to bring about a change in 1969, and even then it happened only by a razor-thin margin, often with only a bare majority of convention delegates. Some conservative leaders again and again carped about the lack of passion and interest on the part of so many "neutralists" on the local level. But there were just enough conservatives to capture the presidency and ram through conventions the conservative agenda.

Missouri and the Religious Right

The challenge for any book is: Who cares? The schism in the Lutheran Church—Missouri Synod was a traumatic and triumphant experience for many of nearly three million Missouri Synod Lutherans. It tore apart families and churches, leaving scars that, in many cases, have never healed. It did not have to happen that way. This book points to the personalities and ideology that turned disagreement into an all-out war that has not yet ended and whose outcome is still uncertain. The LCMS has also assumed a place in America's emergent Religious Right, if not in so public a way as others. (In 2004, President George W. Bush gave one of three election-year commencement addresses to an enthusiastic audience at the synod's flagship university in swing-state Wisconsin.) The LCMS's presidents and conventions regularly issue proclamations on issues like abortion, homosexuality, sexual abstinence, and stem cell research. Its 2001 convention urged participation in the Republican Party's "Faith-Based and Community Initiatives."[25]

This book helps explain the transformation from a church that rarely took such positions to one that, during the 1960s, supported many liberal political positions, to what it has become today. For much of its history, the LCMS enjoyed "fellowship" with one or more of the nation's major Lutheran church bodies. Today it is routinely censured by the one minor body to its right, the Wisconsin Evangelical Lutheran Synod (WELS), while it censures the big brother to its left, the Evangelical Lutheran Church in America (ELCA).[26] Finally, the synod is today as politically managed and charged as ever. Among the first orders of business at its 2001 convention were efforts to limit the orchestration of party-bloc votes through the use of wireless devices.[27] The opening sermon of the convention contained a surprisingly frank condemnation of "noisy minorities" on the "right and the left," singling out "liberal" political groups critical of synod leadership.[28] These dramatic changes in the life and direction of the Lutheran Church— Missouri Synod were not inevitable but contingent on the exploits of a few driven and powerful personalities and the hidden dynamic of a movement shaped by those men.

This story is now, as it was then, of great interest to other American Lutherans, as well as secular and religious communities. With considerable curiosity, the story was followed in spurts during the 1970s, in the pages of *Time*, *Newsweek*, national and local newspapers, television stations, and religious periodicals. Conservative evangelicals look proudly to Missouri's tale of victory over liberalism,[29] a distinction few other mainline churches can claim, while liberal critics have disparaged "Pope" Preus and the shift in the church.[30] Moreover, while the schism in Missouri may have ended that body's hopes of generating unity in American Lutherandom, it did have a determinative role in the formation of the nation's largest Lutheran church, the ELCA.[31]

Finally, this book speaks to the history and nature of religious conservatism. Religious conservatism as an ideology was not a new phenomenon in 1969; an "Old Christian Right" of religious conservatives skillfully fused theology and politics as a countermovement to Roosevelt liberalism in the 1930s.[32] The Old Right spied in modern liberalism a Marxist conspiracy, adroitly exploited forms of mass communication, organized parachurch parties, and was visibly anti-Semitic.[33] McCarthy's Red Scare, the attenuation of denominational loyalties, postwar growth in government, and secular (primarily judicial) challenges to religion in public life in the 1950s generated what Richard Hofstadter called a "paranoid style" in American religious conservatism.[34] A decade of ideological polarization (1965–1974) found religious conservatives increasingly comfortable in the public political sphere; Alabama governor George Wallace called on religious conservatives in his 1968 presidential bid, while evangelist Billy Graham endorsed Nixon for president that same year.[35]

Herman Otten belongs on any list of the most significant leaders of the "New Christian Right."[36] Otten and the movement he helped create bridged the gap between old and new movements. While Missouri's religious conservatives were more hesitant than others to fuse politics and pulpit openly (and not at all hesitant to criticize the theological failings of their conservative brethren for doing so), they often marched lockstep with American fundamentalism and evangelicalism. Leo Ribuffo writes of the latter:

> While theologically and politically liberal social gospelers campaigned for racial equality and against the Vietnam War, many evangelicals and Fundamentalists not only rejected their specific stands but also charged that social activism in general distracted attention from saving souls. Similarly, the ordination of women and gays was worse than bad policy; it was sin that might provoke God's judgment on the United States. Conflict between theological liberals and conservatives over these issues reopened half-healed wounds from the past, and Protestant denominations once again debated biblical inerrancy and the legitimacy of Pentecostalist practices.[37]

Before there was conservatism, there were conservatives. Missouri conservatives complained, rightfully so, that they were at a disadvantage in the public ideological war.[38] With tolerance established as an essential principle, they argued, liberalism easily united people of diverse backgrounds and ideas while diluting intensity of conviction. But their view of liberalism was inaccurate; liberalism and conservatism were both ideologies that shared commonalities. Ideologies, for all their historic mutability, often degenerate into prideful, intense, and zealous self-assurance.[39] Richard John Neuhaus, LCMS liberal who became a Catholic neoconservative, lamented the drive to ideological "positioning" that left him a stranger in a civil rights movement he helped build.[40] Conservatism dominated the LCMS because more of its people were conservative. Even so, given the diversity of background, experience, and interest even among so homogenous a group as Missouri Synod Lutherans, conservatism was a perpetually fractured movement.

It was, and had to be, a movement of common denominators. Unity was attainable only with a shared, easily identifiable, and threatening adversary. In its absence, conservatives easily relapsed into parochial interests and insistence that "my" brand of conservatism is "purer" than yours. For all the Lutheran talk of *adiaphora* (practices that are neither expressed nor forbidden by Scripture, and therefore not a basis for sectarianism), the ideology of conservatism is distinctively at home in the Missouri Synod, which so often in its history rejected visible forms of unity for insularity.[41]

Missouri's modern history is about conservatism because Missouri conservatives made it so. They voluntarily appropriated the language of a movement bigger than Missouri, calling themselves "conservatives" contra "liberals." In personal correspondence they complained about the frustrating nature of conservatism. They could hardly agree with each other, much less non-Lutheran conservatives. But they recognized and frequently articulated that with their religious and secular counterparts they shared common characteristics and a common enemy.[42]

Clarifications

A few clarifications and definitions are in order. In this book I rely heavily on quotation. While I make no claims to impartiality and certainly make clear my thesis, my hope is to let the actors tell the story as much as possible. I also rely heavily on quotation because, particularly after 1969, conservatives were doing so with each other as evidence of duplicity or even as threats.

Categories like liberal and conservative are relative newcomers to our political lexicon. They are politically charged designations, frequently meaning one thing when used pejoratively and another in self-identification. Within the broader polity they remain historically very fluid terms.[43] Conservatives in Missouri have never been ashamed to refer to themselves as such; it was a badge of honor rather than a scarlet letter. Accordingly, I will freely use the term in reference to a conscious movement within the church of (predominantly) men who were at once theologically and politically conservative. Theologically, this translated into a literalistic view of the Bible and a belief in the binding nature of official church doctrine on all members.

Politically, this same group typically stood against ecumenical relations with bodies not in complete agreement with LCMS doctrine, against most forms of social activism (especially integration), and against communism, big government, and woman suffrage.

Defining liberalism is trickier. By the mid-1960s, many of those to the left of Missouri's center took to calling themselves "moderates," in part to quash criticism by conservatives that they were "liberals." I argue that many Missouri moderates can properly be called liberal. Liberals in Missouri as elsewhere were commonly proponents of social action (particularly with respect to race relations), champions of ecumenism, decidedly less than literalistic in their theological postures, and open to a greater—if circumscribed—diversity of views within the synod. Like conservatives, Missouri liberals saw themselves as part of a broad if undefined movement. Yet many of their views were outside the mainstream of grassroots synod thought. Because of this disconnect, many liberals called themselves moderates to hide the fact that they were liberal, particularly as liberalism became a political liability by the 1970s.[44] In the interest of consistency, I will use the word "moderate" primarily to depict those who self-identified as such, although the term will be used interchangeably with "liberal."

I also make two modifications to lend this book consistency and readability. Otten's publication was known as *Lutheran News* from its inception in 1962 until 1968, when it was renamed *Christian News*. Here, however, you will see it referred to only as *Christian News*. To avoid confusion I also on occasion refer to J. A. O. "Jack" Preus as "Jack," and Robert Preus as "Robert." Finally, the Lutheran Church—Missouri Synod will be referred to interchangeably, as it is within synodical circles, as "synod," "Missouri," "Missouri Synod," and "LCMS."

1

Change and Reaction in the LCMS: 1938–1965

In 1964, John Stormer, chairman of the Missouri Federation of Young Republicans, published his best-selling *None Dare Call It Treason*, reopening charges of "subversion from within" leveled by McCarthyites with such effect a decade earlier. Published to coincide with Barry Goldwater's presidential bid, Stormer's book aimed to reawaken an indifferent nation to the expansion of communism abroad and at home, asserting that America's battle in the Cold War was thus far a losing one. At the core of a movement of internal subversion, wrote Stormer, was a cadre of religious liberals bent on undermining America's Christian traditions. Leading the charge were communist-front groups like the National Council of Churches (NCC), the editorial staff of *Christian Century*, and liberal seminary intellectuals bent on undermining the authority of the Bible. Through use of code words like peace, ecumenism, and tolerance, he claimed, many church liberals served as unsuspecting pawns in neutralizing clerical opposition to communism.[1] Stormer's book was advertised on a grassroots level among conservatives of all stripes by groups like the John Birch Society. Within eight months, six million copies had been sold.[2]

Liberalism Ascendant

Across the religious spectrum, choir groups, quilting groups, youth groups, and groups for men and women proliferated as denominations grew in

17

the midst of a religious awakening in the 1950s. During the 1960s and early 1970s, parachurch organizations grew in membership at least one-third faster than denominations. The growth can be attributed in part to heightened degrees of professionalism in an America that was becoming increasingly white-collar, higher levels of education and affluence, and the availability of new technologies. But the growth also reflected the expansion of special interest groups in secular politics, a growth appreciated and imitated by activists within the church. Dragged along by a budding civil rights movement, liberal Christians struck first in the special interest wars. Natural competitors within these denominations then arose, again in imitation. And so liberal groups begat conservative foils, and vice versa.[3]

Liberalism, at least as we understand it today, seemed ascendant in the 1950s. Louis Hartz argued in 1955 that America has a dominant, liberal tradition rooted in a consensus (often unconscious) about values ranging from individual property rights to a social contract based in equal access and participation.[4] We are all liberals, Hartz argued, and our disagreements are little more than family quarrels. Hartz's sentiments echoed those of Lionel Trilling, who argued in *The Liberal Imagination* that America's tradition is not conservative, but liberal. Liberals were dominant, if not arrogant: Trilling claimed in 1953, "There are currently no conservative or reactionary ideas in general circulation today."[5]

The perceived dominance and excesses of liberalism created a reactionary movement in the form of a revamped conservative ideology. In 1955, William F. Buckley launched his effort, a promise to "stand athwart history, yelling Stop, at a time when no one is inclined to do so, or to have much patience with those who do."[6] Buckley resurrected and reshaped a conservatism that had been in the political minority since the New Deal. This conservatism was intensely anti-communist and a defense of localism in the face of intrusive government. Buckley took up arms in response to the Supreme Court's 1954 *Brown vs. Board of Education* decision, creating a movement born in and sustained by reaction. But Buckley's was a secular conservatism. Other elements were yet to be added to the conservative formula.

The big distortion among some Christian conservatives was that ecumenism was the province of liberals. Conservative evangelicals in 1942–43 responded to the growth of liberal ecumenism and special interest groups in kind, founding the National Association of Evangelicals (NAE) to rival the liberal activism of the Federal Council of Churches (FCC), later the National Council of Churches.[7] The "revival of revivalism" in the 1950s, sparked by evangelist Billy Graham, gave Christian conservatives a new identity and confidence characterized by militant anti-communism and anti-modernism.[8] This identity defied denominational boundaries. Intra-denominational journals, like *Christianity Today*, worked to draw conservative Christians together in opposition to a liberalism seemingly entrenched among denominational bureaucrats and seminary professors.[9] Christian conservatives might not worship and pray together, but they now saw themselves as part of a movement, one created and defined more by what they stood against than by what they stood for.

Missouri's Heyday

The years bracketing World War II had been glory days for the Lutheran Church—Missouri Synod. A small church body founded over a century earlier by a few hundred Saxon Germans had grown up and was poised to take its place among America's mainline Protestant churches. Between 1935 and 1960, membership in Missouri nearly tripled.[10] This remarkable growth was the axis on which all revolved in the modern history of the LCMS. For with new blood came new ideas and new relations with the very culture Missouri had strived so long and hard to avoid, to be "in" but not "of." No longer could it sidestep the ideological battle brewing in America. Missouri would embrace it and be consumed by it.

From World War II to 1969, as society moved to the left, the LCMS moved toward the ideological left, becoming more liberal during the "years of liberalism."[11] Liberalism during those decades came to be defined less by those who wore the badge than by those who disparaged it. Barry Goldwater's 1964 presidential campaign helped circumscribe liberalism by defining his brand of conservatism as a populist and anti-intellectual "Dime Store New Deal." Juxtaposed with Goldwater conservatism of limited government and nationalistic anti-communism was sixties liberalism, characterized by an openness to change and an aggressive promotion of individual liberties and government-directed equal opportunity. Tolerance was the watchword of the liberal, tolerance for alternative worldviews and tolerance for challenges to long-standing norms.

The Missouri Synod, by 1964, had become more liberal.[12] It was more advocatory, more aggressive in the growth and use of its bureaucracy, and more tolerant of new social and theological ideas. Most Lutherans were happy with the direction of their country. In 1964, the Missouri laity voted overwhelmingly for Lyndon Johnson, but nearly half of LCMS clergy were more taken with Goldwater.[13] The country and the synod had grown more liberal, and a significant minority of clergy were discontented.[14]

For Richard Koenig, onetime editor of *Lutheran Forum* and Missouri moderate, the roots of the schism were found in 1938 at the synod's triennial convention. It was there, in St. Louis, that delegates first bucked the church's isolationist legacy by voting on steps to bring about full altar and pulpit fellowship with the American Lutheran Church (ALC). Led in part by Walter A. Maier, a Charles Lindbergh supporter, leader in the America First movement, and rising star on radio's *Lutheran Hour*, delegates decided that minor divergences in interpretation should not be "regarded as a cause for division." It was, in effect, a directive to President John Behnken to bring the two churches together.[15] Although the convention approved the measure, Behnken never implemented the order.

The 1938 move toward ecumenism gave birth to the granddaddy of modern Missouri conservatives, Paul Burgdorf. Burgdorf, a small-town preacher in Iowa, founded the *Confessional Lutheran*, a thin repository of conservative news and views that railed month after month against the "liberal" forces of "unionism" that threatened to strip the synod of its confessional identity. Burgdorf's paper was the first of its kind in Missouri, an extrasynodical venture to keep conservatives informed and active. Circulation, which was limited to subscriptions, remained small,[16] but Burgdorf's paper helped create enough backlash to all but kill the ecumenical momentum by 1945.

Less than a month after the United States bombing of Nagasaki, a group of prominent moderate pastors and laymen dropped a bomb on Missouri by publishing "A Statement," which criticized the church's traditional resistance to fellowship with other Christians and its exaggerated fear of "unionism."[17] Bemoaning the "horrible theological climate" of "fault-finding [and] innuendo" created by Burgdorf's "unofficial, partisan, polemical periodical,"[18] the "Forty-Four," as they soon became known, endeavored to halt the forces of authoritarian and parochial conservatism in Missouri. Condemning the "loveless attitude which is manifesting itself in Synod," the Forty-Four reasserted the 1938 convention's mandate to reach out in fellowship while deploring "the tendency to apply this non-Biblical term ["unionism"] to any and every contact between Christians of different denominations."[19]

Synod president John W. Behnken, a gentlemanly Texan with a plodding, southernized German baritone, would have none of it. Behnken, a "babe in Academe," was no admirer of the intellectual types, among them professors at Concordia Seminary in St. Louis, who put their names to "A Statement" and caused him no end of grief.[20] In January 1947, Behnken convinced the Forty-Four to withdraw "A Statement" as a basis for discussion with vague promises that he as president would facilitate the dialogue with Missouri's pastors and congregations.[21]

Yet for all Behnken's success in suppressing the Forty-Four, something new had taken place in the LCMS. On both right and left, well-organized, if diminutive, extrasynodical special interest groups had arisen by 1945 to fight for Missouri's center. For all the "politics" that may have existed in the synod since its inception in 1847, this was new because it became a public battle. Burgdorf would become somewhat of a pariah in official circles, but he began to create a perception among vulnerable laymen and clergy that something was rotten in St. Louis. And he and the Forty-Four, through public challenges to synod leadership, set precedents that would be exploited to a greater degree by their progeny.

Mission and Money

The remarkable growth of the LCMS, by 1950, had generated an atmosphere of optimism and excitement in the church. The dry years of depression and war now yielded to a torrent of new construction and record expansion as

Missouri poised to capture new souls in America's burgeoning suburbs.
New mission fields were established in the Americas, Europe, and Africa.
Mission efforts were intensified in Asia and in the South Pacific.[22]

America's postwar era was characterized by the rapid growth of bureaucracy in government and religious organizations. The expansion of government in the United States between 1940 and 1960 far outpaced population
or even economic growth.[23] Yet growth of denominational bureaucracy in
Missouri outstripped even the growth of secular government, bulging by
over 550 percent between 1940 and 1960.[24] The mounting liberal consensus
in America reached deep into the church, and new functions and agencies
added new dimensions to Missouri polity. Each year brought requests from
church activists for more funds for ministries to the deaf, to the mentally
retarded, or for world poverty. In 1951, President John Behnken relocated
from Oak Park, Illinois, into the synod's new headquarters in downtown St.
Louis. From the "Lutheran Building," Behnken led a "Building for Christ"
effort to raise funds for new ministries that netted some $4.7 million dol-
lars in 1955: the synod's budget increased by $3.8 million between 1955
and 1956, to $12.9 million.[25] Lutherans were happy with their church, and
their offerings reflected it. In 1951, giving for synod's budget averaged
$3.62 per communicant; in 1961, it was $10.93.[26] Like most, Behnken associated the growth of church budgets with the success of the church and of
its missions.[27]

The synod's new money and missions led to a flurry of proposals and
steps to centralize organizational polity and authority. The challenge for
pro-growth Lutherans was to build a powerful and efficient central structure
based in St. Louis while preserving Missouri's tradition of congregational
autonomy, a shaky and always-shifting equilibrium.[28] In 1953 at its Houston
Convention, synod delegates approved a resolution augmenting the power of
the bureaucracy, modifying its role as an advisory body by granting it official
power to exercise authority.[29] Delegates also expanded the Church Exten-
sion Fund, "God's Bank" for the construction of new buildings.[30] A Department of Social Welfare was created in 1956, and a powerful "Commission to
Survey the Organizational Structure and Administration of Synod" (Survey
Commission) was established to review and revise organizational polity. The

Survey Commission's findings and proposals in 1959 led to the creation of new synodical boards, a centralized Council of Administrators, and a powerful executive secretary.[31]

Bureaucratic expansion translated into organizational professionalization in the LCMS. An atmosphere of "upward social mobility" existed in certain sectors of Missouri as in the country, where colleges and headquarters desperately needed professional staff.[32] This was the perfect time for outsiders to join and influence the growing church, a time when the "Almighty Ph.D. was the passport to mobility."[33] In 1958, two young brothers named Jack and Robert Preus would exploit Missouri's great need. Both were professors from the tiny Evangelical Lutheran Synod (ELS), but checking their passports at the door, they would take on new identities in the LCMS as professors at the synod's seminaries in Springfield and St. Louis.

But this growth and upward mobility meant a certain accommodation, even theological accommodation, with the secular world, particularly the secular academy. The synod's top theologians were now going outside the synod to complete their education. Bright young minds were pulled into the seminary from the ranks of prestigious but secular graduate schools: Yale, Harvard, and dozens of other secular institutions. Concordia professor Arthur Carl Piepkorn was making a name for himself and the institution in deliberations with the Roman Catholic Church. Concordia Seminary was blossoming, in the opinion of many, into a world-class institution. But not everyone was happy.

The Ecumenical Sixties

By the mid-1960s, the ecumenical movement in Protestant America was reaching its zenith. The explosive growth of denominational organizations and the concomitant boom in construction of home and foreign missions meant that increasingly church workers of all stripes from suburbia to Africa were crossing paths.[34] A stronger secularism brought people of faith closer together for mutual support and strengthened American "civil religion," identified by Martin Marty in 1959 as a new "relativist, pragmatist, common-creed religion-in-general."[35] Gravitational forces increased across the social

spectrum in America during World War II and remained strong during the
early years of the Cold War.

These forces, with increasing levels of higher education and a rapid
influx of new ethnicities during the church's period of expansion through
1960, combined to lessen denominational loyalty among Missouri Lutherans.[36] Increasingly, Lutherans were marrying outside traditional denominational boundaries. More and more church leaders, seminary and college
professors, and even pastors were learning outside the traditional boundaries of the Missouri Synod's cradle-to-collar education system. While the
impact of education and the liberalizing pressures of the civil rights movement did widen the gap between laity and clergy on social issues, a majority
of Lutherans by 1969 did not see themselves as different from other Christians. Moreover, a significant minority of the laity favored a merger of all
Lutheran groups in the United States into one organization.[37]

As the LCMS became more modern, its theologians became more theologically modernist and politically liberal. Publicly, this took shape in a new
openness of thought and action among professors at Concordia Seminary,
who were growing more sympathetic to ecumenism and issues of social justice and action.[38] Privately, students took note of a more dramatic shift. German higher criticism, out of which confessional movements like the Missouri
Synod were born in the nineteenth century, was making its way back into the
church through its classrooms at Concordia Seminary. At issue in Missouri
as in earlier modernist-fundamentalist battles, was the use of methods of
historical criticism of the Bible. Increasingly, church scholars were using the
tools of modern biblical scholarship, ending matters of biblical authority with
question marks where there had been periods. Students and faculty openly
challenged Franz Pieper's *Brief Statement*[39] and questioned "inerrancy."[40]

Three essays symbolized the shifting winds at Concordia. In 1958, Martin Scharlemann, military chaplain and seminary professor, wrote an essay
entitled "The Inerrancy of Scripture," which was intended to spark internal
debate among faculty members by challenging static views of biblical interpretation. In his essay, Scharlemann, who had completed his postgraduate
studies at Union Theological Seminary, proposed to "defend the paradox
that the Book of God's Truth contains 'errors.'"[41] In 1963, Norman Habel,

professor of biblical studies, argued that the "fall narrative" (the Genesis account of Adam and Eve) could be legitimately considered as a "symbolical religious history."[42] And in 1965, Arthur Carl Piepkorn challenged the synod's growing infatuation with "inerrancy," warning that belief in the Bible's inerrancy could too easily become belief that the Missouri Synod is inerrant.[43] These were controversial proposals, but they were in keeping with similar discussions taking place in Missouri's sister churches, the American Lutheran Church (ALC) and United Lutheran Church (ULC).

New ideas in Missouri manifested themselves in sympathy for ecumenicity and new efforts to reach across denominational lines. In 1953, LCMS pastor and civil rights activist Andrew Schulze founded the Lutheran Human Relations Association of America (LHRAA), a pan-Lutheran organization dedicated to integrating Lutheran churches.[44] In the years that followed, a growing chorus of liberal voices in Missouri called on the church to explore participation in budding ecumenical movements, from the Lutheran World Federation (LWF) to the World Council of Churches (WCC). By the time of President John Behnken's retirement in 1962, plans were afoot to push for fellowship with the nation's other dominant Lutheran bodies, the ULC and the ALC.

The civil rights movement accelerated these changes and empowered liberals inside and outside church doors. The Supreme Court's *Brown vs. Board of Education* decision in 1954 opened floodgates for Missouri moderates, most visibly those on the Concordia-supervised editorial staff of the synod's official organ, the *Lutheran Witness*.[45] The prospect of black students in the white public schools of Cleveland, Milwaukee, and St. Louis brought the civil rights movement home to Missouri. Andrew Schulze wasted no time in reminding his spiritual siblings of the historical missteps and responsibilities implicit in *Brown*. "The Church," he wrote, "has trailed the conscience of the courts too long. Here is a chance to remedy the weakness of our witness."[46] *Witness*, LCMS's official newsletter, editors issued a "Plea for Patience," an acknowledgment of the turbulence faced by many white Missourians confronting the prospect of racially integrated schools.[47]

The *Brown* decision exemplified Missouri's penchant for reconfiguring social and political beliefs into theological expression. Integration was now the law of the land. Missouri liberals could now turn the tables on synod conservatives, using the church's historic doctrinal emphasis on unconditional obedience to government to further the cause of integration.[48] This gave some doctrine-minded conservatives fits and demonstrated how theology and politics were not so easily separated. At Concordia Seminary, Dr. Richard R. Caemmerer introduced "practical field-work experience" to the curriculum, a social-welfare emphasis that forced students out of the parochial confines of the Clayton campus for the first time.[49] Soon dozens of students were championing the "Caemmererian Gospel."[50] By the 1960s, many were heading to inner cities on an "urban plunge."[51] Most of the synod's churches and schools still would not accept black members, but at its 1956 convention, the LCMS passed its first resolution in favor of integration. The decision left Andrew Schulze singing the church's praises for a decision on fellowship "which transcends all racial and ethnic barriers."[52]

Loosed by the Supreme Court and their synod's own convention, Missouri moderates now looked back in regret to the inner cities the church was fleeing. The *Witness* published a series in 1956 called "The Church in a Changing Community," an assessment of the church's abandonment of urban centers and America's blacks. Author William Drews suggested that flight to the suburbs had altered the face of American Protestantism. He praised the small "minority" in the church who had "made heroic efforts to adapt their ministry to a changing environment and thus remained true to their divine charter and commission," condemning those who did not stay.[53] Drews had no kind words for Lutherans who restricted their interests to "our kind of people."[54]

A Young Conservative Takes Shape

In the fall of 1952, as Dwight Eisenhower cruised into the White House and McCarthyism gripped the nation, a young upstart from the Bronx, New York, entered Concordia Seminary in St. Louis. Herman Otten, the son of German Lutheran immigrants, was excited about his first year at the seminary and quickly noted the "new spirit" on campus. He considered it a "healthy corrective for the dead orthodoxy and scholastic dogmatism" that he had come to associate with the synod's past and that he regarded as dangerous to Missouri Lutheranism.[55] But Otten's early optimism and excitement did not last. "Before the ink was dry on his final exams," writes James Adams, "Otten was accusing professors of heresy."[56] Otten the student became Missouri's most vocal critic. But Otten, says his younger sister, Marie, was "the way he is long before he ever got to the seminary."[57] For Herman Otten was a product of both a moderating seminary faculty and a crusader mentality shaped by his perceptions of family and history.

Otten's grandfather, Herman, had been a pastor in the Lutheran Free Church of Germany, one of several conservative sects opposed to the state-supported Lutheran church, and had served as a chaplain in World War I. At gatherings of their extended family, the Ottens recounted with pride the tales of their German ancestors, of Grandfather Otten and his unique mixture of patriotism and orthodoxy, and of resilient Grandmother Oma Tibke, who, according to family legend, defiantly refused to say "Heil Hitler."[58] The Otten legacy of religious independence and patriotism was taken up by young Herman, who added to it his own perceptions of family ultraorthodoxy and self-righteousness.

His father, Herman Otten Sr., was a different story. From an early age, Herman Sr. was a "black sheep" in the Otten family. He married Louise Tibke, a Lutheran but of the wrong persuasion; she was from the state church in Germany. While his brother, Bill, spoke out against such vices as dancing and roller-skating, Herman Sr. believed that rules were "made to be broken."[59] He worked as a painter for his brother-in-law, Henry, a well-off property owner and manager. Once Herman Sr. shocked his brother-in-law by paying his young nephew and apprentice, Paul Behling, five dollars and a bottle of whiskey.[60] Herman Sr. was a complex man. He grew to hate Franklin Roosevelt and doubted the scale of the Nazi holocaust, but he was also interested in "social justice."[61]

Young Herman, already well versed in the family ideology, began early on to believe that his father was "slightly pink." The Otten family church, St. Matthew's Lutheran on the north end of Manhattan, regularly hosted vicars,[62] seminarians who in their third year serve in churches to gain practical experience. St. Matthew's, where Herman Sr. served as congregational president, was a revolving door for the best and the brightest of young, often liberal pastors-in-training, including future LCMS leaders Oswald Hoffmann, Ralph Klein, Walter Bouman, Art Simon, John Damm, and John Tietjen.[63] Herman Sr. enjoyed the company of these men, sharing with them, in his German accent, a love for people and an interest in social justice.[64] Bouman remembers him still as an "expansive, beer-drinking conversationalist and raconteur."[65] One summer, he turned the family apartment over to Walter Bouman while the family was away in Europe.[66] Nearly every week one or more of these young men broke bread at the Otten dinner table. When Herman Jr. was away at seminary, they often took his place. And while he spent his summers upstate, sweating to earn money on a dairy farm, they sat in his cool home, drank his father's beer, and talked of peace and justice.

Early on, Herman Jr. took his father's conservatism and discarded the rest. At Concordia prep school in Bronxville, he developed a friendly but adversarial relationship with Professor Carl Weidmann. Herman spent many evenings at 2 Concordia Place arguing with his advisor about theology and politics. One night it might be Weidmann's predilection for liturgy, the next, Otten's contention that Roosevelt was responsible for World War II.[67] Before long, however, Weidmann began to receive confrontational letters, sent anonymously. He attributed them to Herman.[68] There is no question that Herman was capable of writing such letters—and worse. His sister, Marie, tells of a time when Herman's younger brother, Walter—who, like Herman, was an athlete—got caught drinking beer at a postgame celebration. According to Marie, what Walter got from his father was nothing compared to the vitriol from his older brother.[69]

Matriculation at Concordia Seminary in 1952 shaped Otten's curiosity, his confidence, and, eventually, his confrontational temperament. This was an exciting time for the seminary. Most seminarians had come from the synod's feeder schools,[70] where they were steeped in Missouri tradition and tutored with the same techniques. In St. Louis they encountered a massively different version of Lutheranism than they had known at the Concordia prep schools and colleges. Professors like F. E. Mayer and Jaroslav Pelikan pushed them into biblical texts and contexts and challenged the long-standing assumption that Franz Pieper had accurately interpreted the Lutheran confessions in his *Brief Statement*.[71] Some students became hard-core defenders of Pieper and of the traditional Missouri story. Others, feeling betrayed by LCMS, came to hate the old orthodoxy and stormed out of the synod. Still others, heavily influenced by a new breed of professors, began to believe that Bible texts had been taken out of context by the church. Among the supporters of the seminary's new direction was Walter Bouman. The upperclassman took young Otten under his wing, convinced that, with patience, he would catch up and join their ranks.[72] But Bouman and his friends were sorely overconfident.[73]

By 1953, Otten's curiosity upon coming to Concordia had changed to concern about the direction the seminary seemed to be heading. Having grown up hearing horror stories at family gatherings about the Forty-Four, an already cautious Otten chafed at faculty and student attacks on biblical "inerrancy," which Franz Pieper had introduced to the Missouri canon two decades before. As early as 1953, students were arguing with Otten over the traditional doctrine of the inspiration and inerrancy of the Scriptures, even questioning the Genesis creation account. Otten fumed.

In the spring of 1953, Herman returned home determined to tell all. The whole family was excited about his return as he was scheduled to give his first sermon at St. Matthew's. Herman chose as his text John 8:31-32: "Then Jesus said to the Jews who had believed in him, 'If you continue in my word, you are truly my disciples; and you will know the truth, and the truth will make you free.'" At the first of three services, Herman climbed into the pulpit and immediately tore into the Concordia Seminary faculty. Alfred Trinklein, pastor at St. Matthew's, was in shock. After the service, he dragged Herman into his office and shouted, "Herman, you are going to revise that sermon, or you are not going to preach the next two services." Unwilling to risk humiliation in front of his father, who was attending a later service with his family, Otten yielded to Trinklein's threat.[74]

Otten returned to the seminary and, in the fall of 1954, received backup for his position. One ally was Kurt Marquart, a scholarly young refugee from Estonia classically schooled in Austria whom Herman met through a college friend named David Scaer. While Marquart was a year younger than

Otten, he was light-years ahead of him in intellectual gifts.[75] A connection going back to his school years in Bronxville was more important, however, for Otten found a patron in Arnie Petterson, a wealthy conservative living just down the hill from Concordia in Tuckahoe.

Petterson fancied himself a player in church politics and rewarded the young men handsomely for the information they funneled him from St. Louis. One summer he purchased a bulky and expensive mimeograph and asked them to take it to St. Louis to copy evidence of seminary liberalism. Petterson would take the insider information provided him and fire off letters to the seminary's academic dean, Arthur Repp.[76] Herman's first public appearance as conservative crusader happened entirely by accident. In 1954, Petterson urged Otten to speak with church administrator Walter "Pat" Wolbrecht about liberalism in the church. Otten misunderstood Petterson's request and assumed that Wolbrecht was Petterson's friend and a conservative. Thirty seconds into his private tirade to Wolbrecht, Otten realized his mistake. The brief conversation exposed Herman's radical conservatism to Wolbrecht and others and set him on a path he would follow for the rest of his life.

That same year, Otten raced through a copy of E. Merrill Root's *Collectivism on the Campus*, a book widely circulated among conservatives. Root claimed that "professors have been increasingly dominated for two decades by militant collectivists, and even betrayed by a small but potent group of outright subversives." He praised the "intensely loyal small minority" of conservatives who were doing their best to stand up to "collectivist uniformity" in academia. Root's work was an elaborate conspiracy theory, conveying a tale of brave, conservative students and professors stamped out by "brutal, violent, and well organized" means.[77]

Otten read with rapt attention Root's description of Robert Andelson, a seminarian at the University of Chicago Divinity School. Andelson had founded a conservative group called "Students for America," written numerous articles, and even testified before the House Committee on Un-American Activities about "leftist" activities among the faculty at Chicago. He was attacked in print and expelled from campus clubs. Finally, despite having completed all required coursework, Andelson was denied advancement to candidacy for his master's degree. The faculty committee felt that Andelson "had evidenced the kind of mind and outlook it could not condone or put its stamp of approval on" and proposed to award him a degree in exchange for an apology.[78] Andelson refused. He left the school, his conservative conscience intact, and worked elsewhere for the conservative "movement."[79]

Herman was sold: principles first, above all other considerations. After all, this was the way of Luther, who put his convictions above his very life when he stood before Charles V in Worms and announced, "Here I stand, I can do no other." Yet Otten managed to secularize the conflict, imagining Luther as capitalist, Charles as Stalin—and himself as Joe McCarthy.

Taking Aim at the Faculty

In the winter of 1954, Otten and Marquart turned up the heat at Concordia. They began with written protests. The previous fall, Marquart had complained to Repp about liberalism in the student-run paper, *The Seminarian*.[80] Next, Otten and Marquart turned on William Schoedel, a fourth-year student. Marquart and Otten pulled Schoedel into Repp's office and confronted him: "Do you accept Adam and Eve as real historical persons? Do you accept the doctrine of the plenary inspiration of Holy Scripture as it has been taught traditionally in the Christian Church?"[81] Schoedel fudged. Knowing that he would be certified soon and on his way to teach at Concordia prep school and college in Milwaukee, Wisconsin, he had no interest in rocking the boat.[82] Otten and Marquart complained again to Repp, who assured them that district authorities would handle the situation from that point forward. No one ever did.

Otten and Marquart, their confidence buoyed, went after bigger game. Otten ran into trouble first for criticizing faculty outside the classroom. Classroom teaching is private, they countered, so Otten did not have the right to reveal what was being taught.[83] Then in March 1957, Otten, Marquart, and others in their camp debated the inerrancy of Scripture, its verbal inspiration, and even theistic evolution with a contingent of students who didn't share their views.[84] Otten took notes.[85] Tempers flew. Letters followed. Paul Heyne wrote Otten in one, saying, "I accept the reliability of Scripture, but

I refuse to accept the inerrancy of Scripture, which is a philosophical deduction posing as a theological one."[86] Soon, Otten, Marquart, Scaer, and five other allies filed formal charges of false doctrine against Heyne and eight others.[87]

Academic dean Arthur Repp was distraught at receiving the accusation. "For heaven's sake," he chided Otten, "why did you put it in writing? That is the worst thing. . . . Now that you've put it in writing I have to do something." The next morning, remembers Otten, Repp brought the accusation to the student body in chapel. Students sat on the edges of their seats in the packed chapel and listened to Repp speak. "A terrible thing has happened at our seminary," he announced. "Eight men have charged eight others with false doctrine. And now we have to do something about this."[88]

Seminary president Alfred Fuerbringer took steps to remedy the increasingly untenable situation on campus. He appointed eight faculty members to handle the situation and invited some of the accusers and accused separately to his home. Then Otten and his group were brought before the faculty. Martin Scharlemann, dean of the Graduate School and a military chaplain, opened the meeting by pounding his fists on the table. "Otten," he screamed, "what you need is love!" The faculty committee pressured the young fire-eaters to withdraw their statement, threatening to send them in for psychological evaluations. Otten's friend David Scaer appeared shaken. Another succumbed to the pressure and collapsed in tears. But all held fast. None would retract. Scharlemann quickly dismissed the charges, and the controversy ended—for the moment.[89]

Changing times and new blood upset more than just Otten's cohort of seminarians. Passing quickly was an old guard at the Concordia Seminary, including John Baur, who had raised the funds to construct the seminary; Lewis Spitz, a historian "dragooned" into teaching systematic theology, who boasted that he had bested liberals at the University of Chicago, his alma mater;[90] and Alfred "Rip" Rehwinkel, who, with Walter A. Maier, had been a founding member of Charles Lindbergh's isolationist America First movement.[91] This aging breed had learned from the likes of Franz Pieper and had struggled to plug the leaking dam protecting Missouri from the encroaching mainstream. Rehwinkel had shared the stage with Lindbergh, and, like

Lindbergh suffered from an anti-Semitic bent. He had been a critic of Nazi persecution of the Jews but believed as well that "the Jews brought it upon themselves." Rip protested that American Jews had enriched themselves "at the expense of the very lifeblood of the nation."[92] He despised Roosevelt, whom he believed a hypocrite for speaking against the bombing of civilians in 1939, only later to employ the tactic himself. He also thought that Roosevelt had sold out the nation to the communists at Yalta. Walter Bouman remembers that Rehwinkel was a popular teacher at Concordia, but as an almost "comic figure."[93] In his last years, Rehwinkel defied publicly what he believed to be a growing liberal consensus at Concordia. In his retirement speech, he scolded the assembled faculty:

> You younger fellows think you are the first ones to ever confront this new theology. Well, you are not. We fought these same battles long ago. And you older men, how can you sit idly by and say nothing when you of all people should know where this will lead us? You are misleading and giving offense and destroying the church for which generations before you have given their lives.[94]

Finally, there was J. T. Mueller, who was described by one student as an eccentric, neurotic, even psychotic teacher.[95] Mueller was past retirement age, his contract now reviewed on an annual basis by Martin Scharlemann. "If I complain," worried Mueller, "he'll [seminary president Fuerbringer] say, 'Dr. Mueller, your eyesight is getting bad. It's best for your health if you don't teach anymore.'" Politically weak among an increasingly youthful and modernist faculty, the septuagenarian was afraid to speak up for fear of being forcibly retired. In Herman Otten he believed he had found his protégé—or patsy. Early that fall, Mueller asked Otten to his office to discuss the growing controversy at Concordia. He then directed Otten to travel to Milwaukee for a visit with Mueller's friend, synod vice president Henry Grueber.[96] Otten jumped at the opportunity.

A few weeks later, Otten sat in an office with Grueber and detailed what he believed to be liberalism run amok at Concordia. He provided Grueber with a written summary of problems at the seminary. Then Grueber pulled out the *Lutheran Annual*, a directory of all LCMS pastors, and ran down the list of professors' names, asking Otten, one after another, "Where's this guy?

Liberal or conservative?" Beside each name he wrote "L" or "C," indicating where Otten believed each professor to be.[97] The meeting concluded and Otten returned to the seminary knowing full well the bee's nest he had just stirred.

A strange confluence of events now brought Otten to the attention of synod president John Behnken. First and foremost was Otten's recent discussion with Grueber, who passed along Otten's charges to Behnken. Next, Martin Taddy, Otten's roommate, and Otten's cousin Paul Behling conspired to play a practical joke on Herman. Taddy worked on the night janitorial staff at the Lutheran Building, home to President Behnken's office. One night he made off with some of the president's stationery. He and Behling used the stationery to forge a letter from Behnken to Otten that said, "I hear that you are familiar with problems with the professors at the seminary. I would like to hear about this." Unaware that it was a fake, Otten was excited to receive the letter. Bumming a nickel from his cousin Behling, Otten called Behnken's secretary and asked to speak with the president.[98]

Weeks later President Behnken did visit Concordia to confront the issue after a public dialogue on Missouri membership in the LWF. Speaking in favor of membership was a bright young graduate of the seminary named Martin Marty. Behnken, who opposed membership, was no match for the quick-minded Marty, and doubtless felt embarrassed by the visible tide of opinion among seminarians that Marty had won the debate.[99] After the debate, David Scaer, seminary professor Richard Caemmerer's nephew and seminary altar boy, approached Behnken and told him, "Some of us are concerned about what is going on here." Still stinging, Behnken proved a receptive audience. The group soon met with Behnken, who asked the students if they would be willing to share their concerns with the entire faculty. Only Otten agreed.[100]

In January 1958, Otten, Repp, Harms, and Behnken gathered before the seminary's Board of Control. Otten spent an hour detailing what he perceived to be the rapid advance of liberalism at Concordia, specifically criticizing professor Horace Hummel.[101] When he finished, Behnken asked Repp, "And what does the faculty have to say for itself?" Repp tore into Otten. "Who gave you the right to come down here like a bulldog?" he asked. Behnken jumped in, saying, "Anyone has the right to come knock on my door and share his concern." Repp then asked why Otten kept referring to himself as "we" in his written statements. In front of President Behnken, Otten modified his statement, changing "we" to "I," and signed his name. Then he looked around only to discover that his allies—friends and mentors alike—were nowhere to be found.[102] Otten was where he would remain—in front and often alone.

The Seminary Strikes Back

Herman Otten ushered in an ugly time at Concordia Seminary. Students took sides. They spied on each other and met in secret. Copies of personal faculty memoranda and letters turned up in public. Comments professors made in classrooms made their way in print to Behnken. Scharlemann's essay on inerrancy, written solely to foment debate among faculty members, somehow found its way into Otten's hands. Scharlemann confronted Otten and accused him of secretly taping conversations from outside his office window.[103] Otten claimed to have received the essay from a friend who "found it in Scharlemann's trash can."[104] But Paul Behling shed light on the dynamic of Otten's Concordia cabal, which allegedly included Kurt Marquart. Behling, then a disciple of his older cousin, lent his typewriter to Otten's group of friends, who, with the help of sympathetic students on the janitorial committee, raided faculty offices at night and typed copies of letters and essays.[105] Marquart disputed the story as a complete "fabrication."[106] How personal correspondence fell into the hands of Otten and his friends remains in dispute. That it happened is not.

Arthur Repp brought Otten's accusations to the faculty for review. Meetings were arranged between Otten and professors Piepkorn, Hummel, and Waetjen. In March, before the faculty took action, Otten filed formal charges with Repp against Herman Waetjen and included documents challenging Piepkorn.[107] When the seminary's Board of Control met soon after and decided to dismiss Hummel by refusing to renew his contract, the faculty turned its guns on Otten. On May 15, he was called before the faculty's Disciplinary Committee. The committee told Otten that he had "violated the law of love" by making accusations based only on hearsay and by contravening Christ's directive in Matthew 18 to meet individually with a brother who has wronged you before taking your charges public.[108] Otten's advisor, Albert Merkens, helped him craft an evasive apology to the faculty, which expressed regret only for circumventing proper procedures.[109] At a subsequent meeting, Repp told Otten, "We assume that this means that you admit that your reports were inaccurate." But Otten refused to retract his charges. Following his oral exams, Otten was awarded a master's degree (S.T.M.). Then Scharlemann handed down his final ruling. Otten was deemed ineligible to continue studies toward a Th.D. and would not be certified by the seminary as a pastor.[110] The faculty could not put its stamp on someone who could not "argue theology with an open mind."[111]

A series of appeals ensued, involving countless people and taking years to wend their way through the system. In late May, Otten asked the faculty in writing to reconsider the Disciplinary Committee's decision. He proceeded to attack Scharlemann and to dispute grades given him by "liberal" professors.[112] Scharlemann responded with a letter entitled "This I Expect," in which he demanded an apology. "The ability to distinguish between truth and fiction is a necessary qualification for anyone who wants to serve in the ministry," Scharlemann stated. Scharlemann doubted Otten could.[113] L. C. Wuerffel, dean of students, urged Otten to "repent and seek amends."[114] Otten refused.

Otten was rapidly developing a messiah complex, drawing parallels between himself and Andelson, McCarthy, and even Luther. When accused seminarians charged Otten with "McCarthyism" and leading a "witch hunt," Otten wore the badge with honor and used the moment to defend McCarthyism, not himself.[115] In his appeal materials, Otten compared himself to McCarthy, saying, "When you detect and start to expose a teacher with a Communist mind, you will be damned and smeared. You will be accused of endangering academic freedom." He included Root's account of the Andelson ordeal at Chicago as proof of academia's "collectivism." And he quoted William F. Buckley in *National Review* to prove the "Root thesis," that he was not alone in suffering persecution at the hands of communist sympathizers.[116]

Otten moved on while pressing his charges and his appeal. He secured an income when he was embraced by Trinity Lutheran in New Haven, Missouri, a congregation he had served as a student. He exchanged letters with Behnken, who, perhaps unwittingly, gave Otten encouragement to continue his crusade.[117] Otten traveled to San Francisco in 1959 to tell the synod's Committee on Doctrine about liberalism at the seminary. In early 1960, Behnken, too, abandoned Otten to his own devices. Telling Otten that he "would have been a witness" at the seminary and citing "administrative channels," Behnken, who had first brought Otten's charges so vigilantly to the Concordia faculty, now refused to serve as a witness in Otten's appeal.[118] When the Concordia Board of Control dismissed Otten's appeal, he followed channels to the synod's Board of Appeals.

Otten's stubborn congregationalism hurt his appeals case. In January 1961, Trinity Lutheran Church in New Haven called him to be its pastor. In doing so, Trinity was making a populist statement: It is the congregation that ordains, not elites in the synod or seminary. Within weeks, officials of the Missouri District, with the backing of the seminary, implored the congregation to rescind its call. Trinity refused. In February, Otten was ordained. The district moved to expel Trinity.[119] And John Behnken washed his hands of Otten. Responding to a final request from Otten for assistance, Behnken wrote, "There would not be any purpose in meeting you."[120]

As his case faded en route to appeal, so now did his support. Few backed Otten publicly. Kurt Marquart, with Dr. S. W. Becker and Rev. H. W. Nielwald, represented Herman before the Board.[121] Rehwinkel, too, testified for Otten.[122] J. T. Mueller hid at a nearby motel, hoping to provide moral support for Otten without associating with him publicly. Before the Board, Otten again recounted his conspiracy case. He refused to concede that "the repetition of disturbing quotes at second hand is always and under all circumstances (per se) a sin against love," claiming that the "case against me rests on the assumption that seminary instruction is not public doctrine." He again defended McCarthy and fancied himself a J. Gresham Machen, the "champion of Presbyterian confessionalism." Otten reported to the Board that the faculty had accused him of having a "messianic complex" and threatened him with a psychiatric evaluation. Building his conspiracy case, he charged:

THE ENTIRE CASE AGAINST ME IS AN EFFORT TO PREVENT
OR DELAY A THOROUGH INVESTIGATION OF THE ONLY REAL
ISSUE, WHICH IS THE COMPLEX OF THEOLOGICAL, DOCTRI-
NAL PROBLEMS AT THE ST. LOUIS SEMINARY.[123]

The Board, temporarily short one member, ruled 5-5. Both sides called it
a victory. No one would explain what the ruling meant. So the seminary's
refusal to certify Otten stood.

Big Government in Missouri

The 1956 LCMS convention in St. Paul, Minnesota, marked a turning point
in the development of LCMS polity. The surge of new missions and influx
of new money in the postwar years had put a serious strain on Missouri's
nineteenth-century bureaucracy. The Missouri Synod needed an overhaul.
So delegates voted to form a commission to study a restructuring of the
synod's administration. In the years that followed, the LCMS made "considerable alterations" to its constitution, ringing in a new era of efficiency and
centralization for the rapidly mainstreaming church.[124] In Missouri, as in the
secular political spectrum, moderates saw centralization as a sign of progress. But conservatives saw red flags. To them, centralization put money in
the hands of wasteful and liberal bureaucrats and threatened to destroy the
church's historic congregationalism. So it was that synodical centralization
begat a "new era of party political action," which emerged to "counter the
undesired aspects of centralization."[125]

In early 1956, a Lutheran businessman from Painesville, Ohio, named
Fred Rutz began sending letters to John Behnken, asking for permission
to examine the church's financial records. He was convinced that Missouri,
flush with funds, was wasting money. Rutz believed that he could help the
synod run more efficiently.[126] Moreover, he believed that the church had
no business keeping closed books. By the time of the convention, Rutz had
stirred up enough concern on the right to earn an appointment to the Synodical Survey Commission, which was created to restructure the church and
adopt the "best of modern administrative principles and practices" for the
synod's administration.[127]

Rutz was joined by an aging Missouri celebrity named John Baur. Baur had been a contemporary of Franz Pieper and was a master fundraiser who claimed credit for building much of Concordia Seminary in 1926.[128] He served briefly as president of Valparaiso University (a pan-Lutheran school supported by the LCMS) and fought alongside Roman Catholics in the 1920s to protect parochial schools from an encroaching public system. Where Rutz feared bureaucratic waste, Baur dreaded bureaucratic encroachment on Missouri congregationalism. Concerned by a move to replace parishes with electoral circuits in electing convention delegates, Baur, too, secured a seat on the Survey Commission.[129]

Over the next three years, Rutz and Baur proceeded to give commission chairman Arnold Grumm fits. By early 1959, most of the commission was prepared to recommend sweeping changes in synod structure, including the creation of an executive director position. But Baur argued that the synod's bureaucracy was already too large and that any alterations would result in the creation of a "vertical" rather than "horizontal," or decentralized, synod polity.[130] The synod was not, as the commission majority argued, "devoid of organization," but functioned as it should, with autonomous congregations.[131] Moreover, he warned, the commission's recommendations would lead to the creation of a "super-executive" who might someday trump congregational and district authority.[132]

By April, it had become obvious to Grumm that Baur and Rutz would not sign on to the "majority report" of the commission. So he stopped inviting them to meetings. Baur complained to Grumm, then to Behnken.[133] Grumm dealt diplomatically with Baur at first, finally snapping in May with a terse exchange that freed him from an escalating cycle of letter-writing. Baur, said Grumm, was "a very difficult man to deal with," a paranoid person who saw "something ulterior in everything that is written."[134]

Even as a minority of two, Baur and Rutz could not come to consensus. In June, they each submitted a separate minority report to the convention. Where Baur warned of centralization at the expense of congregational polity, Rutz found synodical spending spiraling out of control. Rutz noted that between 1947 and 1956, the synodical administration had grown six times as fast as synodical membership.[135] Worse yet, funding of synod missions had fallen during that period.[136] Rutz criticized the church's new fondness for deficit spending and even condemned the Synodical Survey Commission as "non-productive and costly."[137] He recommended that the synod scrap the commission altogether and start from scratch with members who weren't on the synod's payroll. Pastors and administrators, he believed, were not to be trusted.

Otten Builds a Movement

From its nineteenth-century origins, the Synodical Conference had bound Missouri to the smaller churches on its right: the Wisconsin Evangelical Lutheran Synod (WELS) and the tiny Evangelical Lutheran Synod (ELS). World War II tested the fraternity as the LCMS, ignoring the screams of its younger brothers, participated in the military chaplaincy. The bonds held until the mid-1950s, when Missouri's increasingly ecumenical vision led to protests and eventual desertion by WELS and ELS. In 1955, Jack and Robert Preus, then leaders in the ELS, talked their church into suspending fellowship with the Missouri Synod. Wisconsin soon followed suit. Behnken reacted "with shock and anger" to resolutions by ELS and WELS condemning Missouri liberalism, stating, "We do not admit the charges. On the contrary, we emphatically deny them."[138] For all his protestations, Missouri's brothers were right in one respect: the church was modernizing and leaving them in its wake. By 1963, the Synodical Conference was all but dead.

In response, Missouri conservatives began to organize. In late 1961, Behnken told a group of conservatives in Thiensville, Wisconsin, that he was growing worried about the situation in the synod. Maybe WELS was right, he speculated. Perhaps Missouri really had violated the principles of the Synodical Conference.[139] In May of the following year, hundreds of conservatives gathered in Milwaukee at the Hotel Schroeder to attend the first "State of the Church" (SOC) conference. At issue for SOC participants was the rising dominance of destructive "isms" in Missouri: Communism, ecumenism, and modernism. The SOC was a gathering place for Missouri's pious, discontent "dissidents and malcontents."[140] Nude statues in the conference room were draped to safeguard virgin Missouri eyes.[141] Herman

Otten, fresh from his battle with the St. Louis seminary faculty and ener-
gized for battle, organized the conference while his younger sister, Marie,
helped at the reception desk.[142] Behnken sent a "personal envoy," Dr. L. B.
Meyer, to attend and produce an "evaluation."[143] The *Confessional Lutheran*'s editor, Paul Burgdorf, and his son, Larry, were in attendance, as were
Otten mentors William Beck and Louis Brighton. And a young Jack Preus,
fresh from the Evangelical Lutheran Synod (ELS), attended the conference but refused to register. "We don't want people to know I was here,"
he said, hiding his nametag inside his jacket.[144] In the months leading up to
the synod's triennial convention, the conference produced a formal organization and placed Rev. Carl Hoffmeyer at the helm. Hoffmeyer and Otten
worked over the next year to churn out publications attacking liberalism in
the LCMS.[145]

Yet Otten was the engine driving the SOC. Already in 1962, his personal
and professional lives were beginning to merge, threatening to destroy relationships in both spheres. Following his wedding in August 1962, he took
his new bride on a whirlwind tour of the country, a "honeymoon" in name
only. Most nights were spent lecturing small groups at local churches, warning them of the inroads liberals had made in Missouri. At his sister, Marie's,
wedding reception (attended by her father-in-law, Adolph Meyer, editor
of the *American Lutheran* and a frequent target of conservative attacks),
Otten, never one for discretion, rose and read aloud greetings to the new
couple from the officers of the SOC, leaving guests and a groom flush with
anger and his sister humiliated.[146]

His backbreaking schedule and staunchness made Otten a minor celebrity in conservative circles. Throughout 1962, Otten maintained his speaking schedule and continued to produce materials for the SOC while tending
to his small congregation in New Haven. His publications were aimed
squarely at the synodical administration and the seminary. His three-part
series "What Is Troubling the Lutherans?" charged that a credibility gap
existed between synod and congregations and that the church was not communicating honestly through its publications.[147]

The hodgepodge group was geared up for the 1962 convention in Cleveland. Otten personally wrote nearly fifty memorials (statements to be voted

on by the convention) and had them signed and submitted by supporters. The SOC purchased a booth at the convention, for which it was charged ten times the going rate by Wolbrecht before its contract was rescinded altogether.[148] Before their expulsion from the convention, the SOC left little doubt that the growing civil rights movement and its emphasis on social activism were, in part, the spark that ignited this band of conservatives. Stretching across the back of the booth was a banner that advertised, "Saving Gospel Not Social Gospel."[149]

Still, allies in Cleveland struck a vindictive blow for Otten and his form of conservatism. It came against Martin Scharlemann, the professor who had denied Otten certification and so vehemently demanded of him an apology. Scharlemann's 1958 essay "The Inerrancy of Scripture," which Otten had somehow acquired and disseminated, had worked its way up the Missouri hierarchy to Behnken, who crafted a compromise. Scharlemann, humbled and humiliated, stood before the assembled convention, withdrew his essay, and apologized for the conflict it had caused.[150] Otten raced to the microphone and asked, "Does that mean that he recognizes that the essays contain false doctrine, and that he's retracting the false doctrine in the essay?" Scharlemann had already left the podium.[151] But the damage was done to both Scharlemann's and the seminary's public reputations in the LCMS.

Otten, already cross, was also driven to rage in Cleveland. With his case with the Board of Appeals on ice and Scharlemann gone, Otten refused to cede the microphone. George Loose, chair of the seminary's Board of Control, objected with a point of order, and Behnken, still chairing the convention, ruled against Otten. Loose walked off the floor and visited the men's room. In the hallway, he was confronted with a young, red-faced Herman Otten, who grabbed Loose by the lapels of his jacket and screamed, "You killed me! You killed me!" Loose responded, "Take your hands off me," then added, "I didn't kill you. You killed yourself."[152]

Tabloid Theology

Otten continued to hammer away at "liberalism" while making the SOC his own. Although he wrote several articles for Burgdorf's *Confessional*

Lutheran, Otten believed its circulation was too small and its focus too narrow. "I just didn't think that it was getting out to the people," he later commented.[153] Burgdorf, his son remembers, was "not the easiest man to work
with."[154] The SOC entertained several bids on a newspaper of its own, but
could not agree on the format or audience.[155] So Otten talked Hoffmeyer
into funding a six-month venture edited by Otten entitled *Lutheran News*
(henceforth referenced as *Christian News*), published first in December
1962. He charged a one-dollar subscription fee for six months and began
with a small distribution to SOC members. Membership soon grew as word
spread and like-minded conservatives fed Otten their mailing lists.[156] Week
after week, Otten published photocopied conference essays, journal articles,
and the text of lectures given by seminary professors.[157]

   The key to the success of *Christian News* was that it tackled much
more than just theology. Burgdorf's paper had adequately covered theological change in the church. *Christian News* gave Lutherans much more.
Before long, Otten's newsletter developed into a full-fledged church tabloid, complete with outrageous headlines designed to attract the eye. The
pages of *Christian News* were an editor's nightmare, containing unsigned
editorials published without comment, broad generalizations, and text taken
out of context. Otten would print the most "outlandish stuff" that liberals
would send him, usually without his own comment. This was something
that Burgdorf would not do.[158] Burgdorf gave readers theology, and Buckley's *National Review* provided the politics. Otten combined the two. The
motto for *Christian News* became "We Preach a Crucified Christ," but in
practice Otten preached also a militant anti-communism and social conservatism that smacked of John Birch Society extremism. Week after week,
Otten blasted civil rights leaders like Martin Luther King Jr. and activist
Christians, regardless of denomination. King was painted as a communist
and those who admired him as unwitting dupes. As he had before the Concordia disciplinary committee, Otten relentlessly referred to himself as "we"
in crafting a farcical identity as journalist crusader and impartial reporter.

   Yet there could be no mistake that Otten's brand of conservatism identified heavily with the secular sons of McCarthy. For much of 1964, *Christian
News* had written love letters to the Republican Party. For weeks Otten had

published articles sympathetic to Goldwater, making it clear just whom he supported.[159] But he made it a point to profess his impartiality after the 1964 presidential election:

> Which candidate does CHRISTIAN NEWS endorse for president of the United States? None of them. We have repeatedly stated that this is a Christian newspaper and we intend to keep it that way. We do not publish with the intention of influencing the elections. We have our preferences, but this is a private matter which is not for publication. As an editorial in the October 19, 1964 LUTHERAN NEWS at the time of the Johnson-Goldwater election stated: "Even though we consider it important that one certain candidate be elected, it is more important that churches and religious organizations should stay out of politics."[160]

Other pieces essential to the growing backlash fell into place by the end of 1962. For decades, the grand old man John Behnken had stood atop Missouri. Regardless of controversies or changes at the seminary, conservatives could find solace in that fact. Now Behnken was retiring, but not without firing a parting shot at liberals (and energizing conservatives). Shortly after his retirement, Behnken insisted that in his investigation of the St. Louis seminary, he had been misled by the faculty.[161] Some conservatives were also troubled by the perceived ideological leanings of the synod's new executive director, Walter "Pat" Wolbrecht.[162] Behnken's successor, Oliver Harms, was less well known. So with one exception, changes in the synodical administration in 1962 seemed to conservatives a total loss.

The Preus Way

That exception was J. A. O. "Jack" Preus. Preus, son of a Minnesota governor and a recruit from the ELS, had demonstrated his political skill by quickly working his way into the inner circle of Missouri's inbred hierarchy. His political instincts and malleability were exposed in an early skirmish over Scharlemann's essay on inerrancy. Behnken had convened a meeting in southern Illinois of "Ten and Ten," an ideologically balanced collection of Missouri elites, to find a middle ground on budget disputes and the issue of inerrancy. Scharlemann read his controversial paper and Preus countered with a defense of inerrancy. Someone then suggested to the group that the synod should not make doctrine of concepts not clearly rooted in Scripture. A shocked John Behnken turned to theologian Martin Franzmann and said, "Cite the Scripture passages for inerrancy." "There are none," replied Franzmann. Unsure after the brief theological discussion that followed "whether it was still 10 to 10 or 18 to 2" (himself and Behnken being the two), Preus retreated. When Behnken called on him for help, Preus cowered, "I didn't say I believed in what I read; my job was to give you Missouri's official position."[163]

By late 1962, months into his new role as president of the synod's smaller seminary in Springfield, Illinois, Preus's friends at the SOC increasingly pressured him to take a more active leadership role. Otten, in what became a modus operandi, sent Springfield professor Curtis Huber, an Otten "liberal," a simple questionnaire about his beliefs. Huber replied, "Drop dead."[164] So before he could get comfortable behind his new desk, Preus was fielding letters from Carl Hoffmeyer, who demanded that Preus fire "liberal" professors like Richard Jungkuntz and Huber. Preus responded to Hoffmeyer that neither Jungkuntz nor Huber was teaching false doctrine. But when Otten threatened to publish Preus's letter to Hoffmeyer in *Christian News*, Preus summoned Otten to Springfield. Preus first threatened to blackmail Otten by leaking Otten's association with the anti-communist Church League of America. But when Otten called his bluff, Preus quickly backtracked.[165]

Preus aimed for a middle ground: win over Jungkuntz while making it known that Huber's contract would not be renewed. "Help me gut [St. Louis professor Norman] Habel," Jungkuntz recalled Preus asking. When Jungkuntz refused, Preus employed a fail-safe method for eradicating rivals while keeping his hands clean, what Jim Adams called "doing it the Preus way."[166] "I know how to get rid of these guys" from experience, he later told Otten. "You give them the last class to teach in the afternoon, the first one in the morning, you don't invite them to faculty parties, you just make life miserable for them."[167] Preus was the master of duplicity. Having forced Huber out of Springfield, Preus called him to dinner and "got weepy and sentimental as he lamented the loss of Huber to his team."[168] When Jungkuntz's contract was up for renewal before the seminary Board of Control,

Preus assured Jungkuntz that he would fight for him. But when the doors closed, he demanded Jungkuntz's head. The gifted politico then left the meeting, wrapped his arm around Jungkuntz, and assured him, "I did all I could."[169]

The conservative circle was coming together, but not yet complete. Otten and Hoffmeyer, though not pleased with the methods, loved the results Preus rapidly produced in Springfield. Fred Rutz, now taking issue with the "monstrous" Missouri "hierarchy," showed Preus his appreciation by channeling funds from his Fred Rutz Foundation to the Springfield seminary.[170] By the time he was finished, Preus had forced six professors out of Springfield, men who left "the Preus way" because of the "heresy-hunting" atmosphere their new president had created among the faculty.[171]

By 1963, *Christian News* was providing conservatives with a public outlet for their frustrations and rapidly supplanting Burgdorf's paper in conservative circles. In March 1962, Richard John Neuhaus's brother, Frederick, complained to Behnken about the content of the *Lutheran Witness*, considering it work of "propagandists of the extreme left." Behnken could only reply that the *Lutheran Witness* was "very strong against communism."[172] But that was as far as it went. So conservatives like Neuhaus published their complaints with abandon in *Christian News*, creating far more pressure from clergy and laity on the synodical administration. Rutz also published and distributed his own pamphlet, "A Businessman Looks at His Church," warning of "inherent dangers" in the church's "drifting toward intellectualism" and financial mismanagement.[173]

This created headaches for the synod's leadership. In early 1963, Walter Bouman, who had interned under Otten's father, received a call to Concordia Teachers College in River Forest, Illinois. Otten quickly resurrected Bouman's seminary views to demonstrate rampant "liberalism" in the church.[174] Protest letters followed to St. Louis. Later, church leaders, Jack Preus included, traveled to Helsinki, Finland, to observe a meeting of the LWF. Otten secured funds for his wife, Grace, and Kurt Marquart to follow and protest Missouri involvement. Marquart's central concern was that the Lutheran churches of Lithuania, Latvia, and Estonia were to be accepted into membership, churches he considered pawns of the communist government. While Otten issued reports on the LWF in *Christian News*, his brother, Walter, embarked on a cross-country tour to stir the laity.[175]

Moderates in Control

Editors at the *Lutheran Witness* promoted racial progress and ecumenism with increasing frequency after 1960. The first cover in the new decade was devoted to race, with a bold headline asking, "Is the Church Retarding INTEGRATION?" The cover photo was of white and black children standing mixed in chorus; a vision, they hoped, of things to come. News from the synod's triennial convention the previous summer sounded taps to a church mired in social and theological isolation, augering entry into the religious "mainline." There, in black and white in the *Witness,* was a new party line from synod, acknowledging its "responsibility as a church to provide guidance for our members to work in the capacity of Christian citizens for the elimination of discrimination, wherever it may exist, in community, city, state, nation, and world" and officially instructing "the editors of the *Lutheran Witness* and other official publications and literature to give frequent expression to the stand which our church has taken on racial discrimination."[176]

At the 1962 Synodical Convention in Cleveland, Missouri, liberals flooded the church with proposals intended to develop a "synodwide mission approach to the American Negro." Delegates allocated two hundred thousand dollars for the Alabama Lutheran Academy, LCMS's only remaining black college. Several "inner-city responsibility" resolutions were fielded as well.[177] Finally, convention delegates passed a resolution stating that the church would officially take its share of "responsibility for injustices of the past," and apologized that "we have not always addressed ourselves in our Christian witness against open discrimination and vicious brutality often practiced toward Christ's brothers, our Negro members, and other minority groups."[178]

As Behnken's retirement neared, the *Witness* became increasingly vocal, even confrontational, in its advocacy of civil rights, social justice, and ecumenism. Overconfident moderates challenged synod conservatives with an "in your face" style of journalism, often provoking a reaction from readers.

But moderates in the church steamrolled forward, determined to convert conservatives to their agenda or leave them behind. In response, the staff was inundated with complaints and cancellations. "Please Cancel," read the lead article in the November 1961 issue. "If it revolts you to see whites and Negroes pictured together," answered the staff, "you'll just have to send in your cancellation notice as you say. . . . For there will be more pictures of whites and Negroes. It's unavoidable. It's life." In an open challenge to conservatives in the church, editors pledged that "the *Witness* will not be bought off, intimidated, or cajoled."[179]

Yet views among Missouri moderates were less than uniform. In contrast to the vision of *Witness* editors, Rosa Young—matriarch of black missions for the LCMS in the American South, long a worker within the synod's "black belt," and staff member at segregated Alabama Lutheran Academy in Selma—offered surprising resistance to the liberal vision. "Alabama," Young claimed, "is not ready for . . . integration." Using the hackneyed claims of segregationists, Young pleaded that moderates could not "legislate integration," even within the church.[180] In the next issue, the *Witness* was "jammed" by complaints from conservatives and moderates alike. Andrew Schulze, in a two-page letter to the editor, severely criticized what he saw as Young's obstructive stance, while conservatives protested the activist agenda of the *Witness*.[181] Moderates also were conflicted on the issue of interracial marriage. Marriage between people of the various races, asserted the *Witness,* is "not at all" unchristian. "On the other hand," the editors hedged, many obstacles exist for the interracial couple—obstacles nearly impossible for even Christian couples to surmount. Moreover, "if interracial marriages are forbidden by legal statute, Christians will have to obey the law." "It may be well to quote a sentence by Dr. Martin Luther King," the editors later referenced, that "we ask only to be the white man's brother, not his brother-in-law."[182] An ensuing article stated, "Miscegenation is almost as devastating socially as the nuclear bomb is physically," using the assertion of Robert R. Moton, former president of Tuskegee Institute, that interracial marriage constituted "active disloyalty to the Negro Race."[183] As with many whites of the time, interracial marriage was a step few Missouri Lutherans, even moderates, could yet stomach.

More intimidating yet to fearful conservatives was the strategy sponsored by young Martin Marty, purportedly urging church liberals to work "from within" their denominations "for constructive subversion, encirclement, and infiltration, until anti-ecumenical forces bow to the evangelical weight of reunion."[184] Depicted later by *Christianity Today* as Marty's theory of "ecclesiastical Machiavellianism," the proposal smacked to some of a communist stratagem, prompting fears that Marty and other young liberals were "founding Jacobin clubs behind the scenes."[185]

In 1962, John Behnken was succeeded as president by Oliver Harms. Harms was openly ecumenical, an advocate of closer relations with the ALC and LCA. Harms's ecumenical bent convinced many moderates that he was their ally. The kindly new president was anything but. Harms's ideology defied the new boundaries shaping conservatives and liberals in the 1960s. In an age of increasing ideological polarization, he transcended boundaries by remaining both theologically orthodox and socially progressive. It was Harms who, in the summer of 1962 and against the advice of moderate friends, appointed Jack Preus as president of the synod's seminary in Springfield.[186] Harms was worried even about the direction of Concordia Seminary in St. Louis and told Preus privately, "I want that school [Springfield] held solidly for Synod."[187] The last thing Harms needed was two seminaries to worry about.[188]

Meanwhile, social moderates pressed forward with their new agenda. Issues of "race, urban renewal, poverty, hunger, and war were placed on the synodical agenda and the leadership was forced to face those issues."[189] The Cleveland Convention voted into existence a new Commission on Social Action to define and apply the "social implications of the Gospel."[190] Moderates at the *Witness*, promoting synodical centralization, stated, "If local Christian congregations would act in accordance with national pronouncements on the matter of racial justice and equality, there would be a vastly improved situation in the nation as a whole."[191]

Civil Rights and the LCMS

As America advanced toward the long, hot summers of 1964–1968, moderates pressed their cause in the LCMS. No longer resting on traditional calls to "obedience" to government, moderates boldly stated that "integration is morally right" and that it was "morally wrong for a Christian to oppose it or refuse to promote it on social or economic grounds." The *Witness* continued to issue laudatory progress reports on the LHRAA, which took increasingly liberal and activist editorial positions. The LHRAA, based at Valparaiso University in Indiana, began in 1960 to endorse and participate in the civil rights movement's nonviolent protests. That year, the *Witness* reported on the LHRAA's endorsement of "Kneel-Ins."[192] Later, through the *Witness,* the association called on Lutherans to "participate in demonstrations and other non-violent means of protest against 'segregation and discrimination wherever they may exist.'" For habitually obedient Missourians, calls to protest one's government were not merely fresh or innovative but radical. And significantly, according to the *Witness,* active in the LHRAA were several professors from Concordia Seminary.[193]

Pressed to take stands on controversial issues and increasingly confident by 1964, many Missouri moderates openly committed to the dominant liberal political agenda. Richard John Neuhaus, recent seminary graduate and moderate leader, urged Lutherans to continue supporting and participating in demonstrations "precisely in order to 'antagonize'" conservatives in church and society.[194] In October, sixteen LCMS pastors participated in a "March on Washington for Jobs and Freedom."[195] In February, as the nation discussed a Civil Rights Act facing a vote on passage in Washington, the *Witness* seemed to give sanction to "freedom marches," sit-ins, and even anti-war protests. Calling demonstrations an "individual" choice, editors reminded Lutherans of their "responsibility as a church to try to change or remove the root causes of human misery, poverty, and strife."[196] Finally, in April, the *Witness* came out fully in support of the pending Civil Rights Act:

> Sorting through the arguments, thinking Christian Americans cannot easily blink aside that the ground which has swept the 55-page bill into the legislative process is—humanitarian. *The real subject of the bill is the dignity of man; it deals with God's body-soul-spirit creature for whose redemption He gave His only Son* [italics original]. It seeks for the large and long-deprived segment of our American society the same human dignity, privileges, and opportunities which free citizens of a lighter hue have always taken for granted.

The teeth in the Congressional law may seem to be too sharp for some. But for those who choose to disregard God's higher law, also in this rights-and-freedom issue, that selfsame Word of God (Galatians 5:15) presents a shuddering alternative: "If you bite and devour one another, take heed that you are not consumed by one another."[197]

When the Civil Rights Act passed, Missouri moderates again fused social views with theology, calling on Christians to obey their government:

Obedience to the Civil Rights Act . . . thereby becomes a moral as well as legal obligation, a matter of conscience for the Christian. . . . By going far beyond legal requirements in order to demonstrate Christian feelings and attitudes as well as legal obedience, those who are not Negroes can help make the American dream bright with promise for the future.[198]

As racial tensions flared in the summer of 1964, moderates turned up the heat on Missouri conservatives. Responding to conservative objections to proliferating riots in America's inner cities, moderates found ways to ratio-nalize black angst. In a mid-1964 article, the *Witness* urged Lutherans to understand the frustration that existed in America's "ghettos." Surely an offense to a significant minority of Missouri Lutherans who believed blacks responsible for their own problems, the *Witness* blamed white racism and called for "a better education and more job training for all Americans. A chance for Americans to live in respectable neighborhoods." America needed "a sincere acceptance of all Americans in political, industrial, com-munity and church life."[199] Finally, in its first-ever look at campaign issues in a presidential election campaign, the *Witness* seemed to scorn Repub-licans, calling on Lutherans to recognize "false issues" and to avoid "emo-tional responses," a thinly veiled rejection of growing conservative reaction in America.[200]

Moderate supremacy seemed a *fait accompli* by the time of the synod's 1965 convention in Detroit. There, delegates gave official synod endorse-ment of six Mission Affirmations. The most significant of the Affirmations, and most troublesome to synod conservatives, flowed directly from moder-ate involvement in civil rights activism, establishing within the LCMS the "principle of an interchurch approach to mission." With the Affirmations, conservatives worried, the synod seemed to be embracing a modified form of the modernist social gospel by affirming that "the church is Christ's mission to the total man and to the total society."[201]

Moderates followed up on their victory with other new departures. The convention voted to seek membership in the new Lutheran Council of the United States of America (LC-USA), which augured more cooperation with other Lutheran bodies not then in fellowship with Missouri.[202] The "principle" that women should be allowed to vote was adopted, provided that women held no authority over men.[203] Eighteen different social resolutions were also adopted, including one on race urging all congregations to "include in their missionary outreach all persons within their geographic area, without discrimination based on racial or ethnic grouping."[204] Finally, there was further movement in the direction of altar and pulpit fellowship with ALC.[205]

But moderate victories in 1965 exposed growing polarization in the church. Historian Bryan Hillis calls the Affirmations the "most damaging to the conservative cause" of all resolutions passed in 1965. The Affirmations, he states, affirmed that the LCMS is just a "confessional movement within the total body of Christ rather than a denomination emphasizing institutional barriers of separation." Phrases like "common humanity" and "universal redemption" smacked of unionistic or universalistic leanings.[206] These perceptions pushed delegates and even family members into opposing camps ideologically. Drama gripped the 1965 convention as Richard John Neuhaus publicly debated before the delegates his conservative father, a district vice president in LCMS Canada.[207] Moderate confidence was only slightly tempered by an increasingly visible conservative reaction and politicization. Conservative complaints compelled President Harms to decry "public accusations," "negative criticisms," and "impatience, suspicion, fear, and dissention" in Detroit.[208] Harms turned aside calls for an investigation of the seminary, promising that a newly established Committee on Theology and Church Relations (CTCR) would study the issue.[209] To some moderates in leadership, the best way to deal with conservatives was to simply ignore them.[210] Others were not so confident. Progressive churchmen meeting in New York voted in 1965 to adopt the word "moderate" to deflect conservative accusations they were liberals in a world where liberalism was fast falling from favor. Richard John Neuhaus objected, warning his friends that any term but "conservative" or "orthodox" implied a nonconfessional ideology that laypeople would associate with "liberal."[211]

Given license by their involvement in civil rights to enter the political "kingdom," Missouri moderates pushed for further reform of both church and state. In 1953, the LCMS still rejected outright the notion of universal women's suffrage. Less resolute was the synod's official line on women in the church by 1965. In preface to the 1965 convention, several editorials appeared in the *Witness* promoting woman suffrage, as well as convention statements on racial reconciliation and further political involvement and dialogue with other Christians. Views protesting the nation's involvement in Southeast Asia also surfaced. In June 1966, the *Witness* criticized the war in Vietnam. Americans were "taking casualties casually," wrote one author, who called United States involvement in the war a "matter of regret."[212] In another article entitled "I Stand Opposed," Lutheran Harvard scholar and LHRAA supporter Ralph Moellering took issue with the "domino theory," calling America's venture in Vietnam a "dubious battlefield."[213]

The Seminary Challenges Missouri Traditionalism

Missouri's new social activism was a product of the new blood and new ideas pouring forth from Concordia Seminary. Between 1964 and 1967, eighteen new professors were added to the ranks, eight of them from Concordia College in Bronxville, New York, Missouri's outpost of liberal thought.[214] At Concordia Seminary, social and cultural visions were translated into theological language, the result a new and heavy emphasis on Christian responsibility. In 1966, seminary professor Robert Werberig argued in the *Concordia Theological Monthly* that the LCMS must shed its parochial skin and enter the fray of politics. The church, he argued, is "a responsible political entity of . . . society" and should, therefore, work for the establishment of humane purposes and social justice.[215] Others, such as Norman Habel, were increasingly active in the civil rights movement.[216]

Ralph Bohlmann, on sabbatical to complete his doctorate at Yale between 1966 and 1968, returned to find a new attitude at Concordia, one that scared him.[217] He first had noticed changes at Concordia as a new professor in 1958. An aging John Behnken had walked Bohlmann around the seminary grounds and warned him that there were "serious problems" at the seminary, "dark clouds on the horizon."[218] Then, Behnken said, challenges to Missouri tradition were muffled; now they were openly advanced. "Sometimes," Bohlmann remembered, "the Missouri Synod was a word that was used derisively by professors. You were supposed to laugh when you heard the word 'Missouri Synod.'"[219]

Other new directions struck at the heart of synod doctrine and signaled moderate confidence and aggressiveness. Scharlemann's 1958 essay challenging inerrancy had sparked outrage among conservatives, who demanded and received a retraction. But seminary theologians were again openly challenging the notion that the Bible is "inerrant." Scharlemann's colleague Arthur Carl Piepkorn argued in 1965 that use of the term "inerrancy" was dangerous in that it put the stamp of infallibility on any and all synod pronouncements.[220] The following spring, Canadian representatives of the Missouri Synod teamed up with brothers in the ALC and LCA to clarify the inerrancy of the Bible on historical matters, stating that "a 'discrepancy' or an 'error of fact' can't affect the inerrancy of the Bible."[221]

This was problematic for Oliver Harms, president of a conservative church living in turbulent political times. Conservative pressure forced Harms in the spring of 1966 to ask the seminary for a "clear rejection of liberal errors regarding biblical interpretation." Alfred Fuerbringer, president of the seminary, evaded, arguing that factuality cannot be asserted where none exists, as in "any particular theory of the modality of creation."[222] He argued, according to Bryan Hillis, that such a clear-cut response "could not be formulated quickly; the matters were difficult ones not clearly discussed in the Scriptures or the Confessions, the only two documents that can be used as sources for doctrinal matters."[223] But time and again Harms would come away from meetings with the Concordia faculty assured that these professors believed in the same "inerrant" Bible he did.[224]

Missouri's presidents were consistently baffled by the Concordia faculty. In a dialogue in which theology became a matter of semantics and textual deconstruction, Harms, like Behnken before him, was poorly armed.

The silver-haired president was loved not for his theological acumen but for his pastoral, relational nature. His predecessor, John Behnken, had been equally ill at ease with Concordia's exegetes; he demanded little more from theology than an "unchanging constant, the clear-sounding 'Thus saith the Lord.'"[225] Behnken had been worried by the sweeping changes taking hold at Concordia under Alfred Fuerbringer, as now was Harms. Concerned about the seminary and the budding conservative reaction, an aging Behnken met with a young conservative named Waldo Werning. Behnken asked Werning to keep the meeting secret, lest others also request his intervention.[226] The old man told Werning that he had met repeatedly with the seminary faculty but was unsatisfied with their collective response, voiced through the seminary president. "Fuerbringer," he groused, "lied to me."[227]

Countering *Christian News*

Throughout 1963, Otten used the pages of *Christian News* to try his own case and others. A favorite target was seminary graduate and editor of *Christian Century*, Martin E. Marty. Otten filed charges of false doctrine against Marty, complaining that Marty was serving a publication that promoted ecumenism and stood outside Missouri discipline, an ironic charge, since Otten arguably did the same with *Christian News*.[228] Otten created enough pressure on Harms by March to force a meeting between Harms, Marty, and vice president Roland Wiederaenders, who assured Otten that the matter had been resolved.[229] When in April the Missouri District of the synod responded by again trying to oust Otten's home church, Trinity, from the synod for retaining Otten as its pastor, Otten painted a portrait of persecution in the pages of *Christian News*.[230]

Losing the public relations war, Harms struggled over how to respond. Wiederaenders saw the problem as one of integrity:

> Despite repeated efforts we have not dealt honestly with our pastors and people. We have refused to state our changing theological position in open, honest, forthright, simple and clear words. Over and over again we said that nothing was changing when all the while we were aware of changes taking place. Either we should have informed our pastors and people that

changes were taking place and, if possible, convinced them from Scripture
that these changes were in full harmony with "Thus saith the Lord!" or we
should have stopped playing games as we gave assurance that no changes
were taking place.[231]

Harms, struggling at first to respond as a gentleman to Otten's deluge
of letters, was losing patience. "Have you dealt with Martin Marty?" "Yes,"
Harms replied. "Martin Scharlemann's brother was just appointed to the
University of Southern California. Is our church body paying his way?"
"No," Harms answered softly.[232] In December, John Behnken wrote Harms
a three-page letter warning him about Otten and *Christian News*.[233] Harms
warned Otten in December that his tolerance was wearing thin: "Your last
Lutheran News leaves me wondering what you are trying to do."[234] He then
suggested that Otten might be throwing stones from a glass house and that
the SOC, by incorporating non-LCMS supporters, was practicing the same
"unionism" Otten denounced.

But Harms knew he was playing into Otten's hands and that he would
lose the battle unless he could find an answer to the growing power of *Christian News*.[235] In April 1964, Harms, Wolbrecht, and *Witness* editor Martin
Mueller acknowledged that influence and tried to combat it by printing a
public condemnation of *Christian News*. Already reaching some ten thousand Lutherans, *Christian News*, they worried, "may make it appear that
the publication speaks for 'conservative officials' of The Lutheran Church—
Missouri Synod." Their condemnation emphasized that *Christian News* "is
in no sense a synodical publication"; the editor "is not an ordained pastor" of
the LCMS; Otten's congregation "has been expelled from membership" in
the LCMS; and Otten was violating the "spirit and letter" of LCMS law by
sending *Christian News* "into congregations and homes unsolicited."[236]

2 Countermovement: 1965–1969

The year 1965 was a great time of transition for Missouri Lutherans as it was for all Americans. It was a year when great rifts appeared in the country's social fabric. It saw passage of the Civil Rights Act (the Voting Rights Act had passed in 1964). It also saw the full-scale introduction of American troops into Vietnam. As blacks in America's inner cities rioted and civil rights and antiwar demonstrations proliferated, suburban white Americans, like those in the LCMS, turned increasingly against the liberal agenda. Some former liberals were becoming "neoconservatives," as was the case with Alfred Rehwinkel, who was nauseated by rioting, particularly as it followed passage of two landmark civil rights bills in Congress. Rehwinkel, a Concordia professor who had founded the St. Louis Human Relations Association of America, now argued that history proved that blacks are intellectually inferior to whites and turned against the objective of the civil rights movement—integration—which he believed "ignored the real barriers between the races."[1]

Herman Otten exploited this turn to the right by turning up the volume against civil rights, antiwar liberals, and communism, linking them all to LCMS liberals. Martin Marty was a constant target in the pages of *Christian News*.[2] So was Andrew Schulze of the Lutheran Human Relations Association of America (LHRAA), whom Otten tied to "some Concordia Seminary" faculty who had "publicly prayed with Rabbis."[3] Civil rights leaders were hypocrites, charged Otten, for pointing to injustice in America while ignoring it abroad in communist nations.[4] One of his most effective tools in shaping an image of Lutheran liberals was to link them in photographs to their secular counterparts without printing a word. Seminary professor Richard Caemmerer was shown shaking hands with a Jewish rabbi.[5] Lutheran professors and students were shown in photographs marching with non-Lutherans for civil rights or against the Vietnam War.[6] In print he condemned clergy active in securing rights for black Americans. One editorial bemoaned the presence of "Those Preachers at Selma" who left many people shaking "their heads while viewing on television the role of so many pastors in behalf of the Negro."[7]

Marty aside, Richard John Neuhaus was in Otten's crosshairs for much of 1965. Neuhaus, a minister's son from Pembroke, Ontario, Canada, left home as a teenager before moving on to become a Lutheran pastor in Brooklyn, New York, in 1961. He was Missouri's revolutionary for civil rights, marching with Dr. King and tussling with delegates on the floor of the 1968 Democratic National Convention in Chicago. Neuhaus condemned America's Vietnam policy and, to the chagrin of conservatives, called on every Christian to "say yes to the city and to everything that takes place in the city, including the subway strikes, the picketing, the demonstrations, because this is all a part of what man is doing and therefore, what God is doing in the city."[8] He also knocked the "ideology of anti-communism," which he called an "idolatry."[9] Neuhaus was an oddity among Lutheran liberals, an intellectual without the degree.[10] He optimistically saw in the 1965 Detroit convention's adoption of Martin Kretzmann's Mission Affirmations a "BLESSED REVOLUTION in the Synod's thinking and practice."[11] Otten agreed, arguing now for the development of a countermovement, a reaction: "Yes, it is now an openly declared fact that a 'revolution' has taken place in the Lutheran Church— Missouri Synod. Only those who are asleep, those who have not done their homework, do not realize what has happened. The 'changeover' was completed at Detroit in 1965."[12] Elitist as were some other liberals, Neuhaus closed his eyes to what he believed an insignificant "handful of recalcitrants" who objected to his revolution.[13]

Otten gave several reasons for objecting to the civil rights movement. Primary was the same rationale the State of the Church Conference (SOC)

had been utilizing: "Saving Gospel Not Social Gospel." To Otten and his followers, one could not demonstrate the love of Christ through actions; it had
to be spoken (apparently, spoken only). He argued that Lutherans should
remember that "the primary work of the Church is to preach the saving Gospel of Jesus Christ." Reviving the pre–*Brown vs. Board of Education* doctrine
of obedience, Otten recalled, "Christians are to obey the laws of their government."[14] "Certain LHRAA leaders," he reminded his readers, "claim it may
be proper to break the law and practice civil disobedience." Also, true Christians were not to "pray with those who deny such scriptural doctrines as the
deity of Jesus Christ, His virgin birth and resurrection," charges Otten made
with increasing frequency against Dr. King. Finally, and most importantly,
Christians were to avoid the civil rights movement because of its affiliation
with "Communist front" groups like the Student Nonviolent Coordinating
Committee (SNCC), the National Association for the Advancement of Colored Persons (NAACP), and others that "have been substantially infiltrated
and influenced by fellow-travelers and dupes of the Communist Party."[15] An
April 1966 article in *Christian News* by August Brustat defended the police
in the wake of demonstrations turned violent, which he linked in part to
LHRAA president Clemonce Sabourin. Brustat called "nonsense" Sabourin's
claim that "these cops . . . beat our heads because we are black":

> It is to be noted, and regretted, that in the so-called Civil Rights marches
> and riots (as in Watts) the violences were in large measure due to Commu-
> nist agitation. . . . Do we want to follow the Civil DISobedience directives
> of such as Bayard Rustin, Hunter Pitts O'Dell, Martin Luther King, Augus-
> tus Hawkins, Don Smith, Mervyn Dymally, John Shabazz and others, who
> wittingly or unwittingly are playing the Communist take-over game?[16]

A civil rights activist, argued Otten, was a communist. Schulze, Neuhaus,
Caemmerer, and their kind were at best communist pawns. In this creative
and colorful way, Otten connected the dots from seminary professor to communist radical, "liberals" all.

Another Otten tactic was to link Oliver Harms to the rise of radical liberalism in Missouri. In December 1965, Harms organized a Chicago Conference on Racial Revolution to address the ever more fractious issue. The
conference, attended and steered by Richard John Neuhaus, resolved to

implement the dozens of resolutions "already on the books" from the 1962 and 1965 conventions.[17] Otten peppered Harms with questions through the mail: "Dear Dr. Harms: The report which appears in the January 1, 1966 LUTHERAN LAYMAN on the December 16–17 conference in Chicago on the 'Negro Revolution' gives the impression that you supported the statements of proposed action adopted by the conference. Did you support these statements?" In typical fashion, Harms's refusal to answer was equated by Otten in print with "Yes."

Lyndon Johnson's expansion of the Vietnam War in 1965 led to protests on the left, and protests of the left by the right. Service in Vietnam was the ultimate test of the Lutheran's mandate to obey his government, thought Otten. To refuse service is to repudiate the church. "Out of Saigon and into Selma," he editorialized, "has been the cry of liberal clergymen in recent weeks." Otten suggested that those calling for a withdrawal from Vietnam had "forsaken the real purpose of the Christian Church, preaching the Gospel of Jesus Christ."[18] Civil rights and antiwar protests were becoming one, allowing Otten to combine his attacks on each. Yet the mood in the country, and especially among his readers, meant that, most often, Otten did not have to say a word; the headlines said enough. "WCC [World Council of Churches] Urges Negotiations on Vietnam," read one.[19] Others reported on the work of the National Council of Churches (NCC), which challenged the Mississippi delegation to Congress in 1965. Most often, however, Otten allowed contributing authors to do his dirty work. "Again," wrote one *Christian News* epistler about the NCC, "we hear of the political activities of this monolith of ecclesiastical perversion."[20] And another noted rampant "Modernism within Lutheranism," claiming that the "main Lutheran denominations in the country (the American Lutheran Church and the Lutheran Church of America) have for many years hastened down the road of apostasy," smearing other Christians while leaving Otten free to claim journalistic privilege.[21]

Otten also made use of conservative aversion to ecumenism to target the civil rights movement. Otten was not erroneous in tying civil rights proponents to ecumenists. Sympathy for the plight of blacks in America's South and inner cities transcended denominational boundaries, uniting like-minded liberals from Lutheranism to Judaism. In May, he lambasted proposals in the workbook of the coming convention, citing problems with the Walther League, pacifism, overtures on civil disobedience, and potential membership in the NCC and Lutheran World Federation (LWF). How could the LCMS consider joining those liberal organizations, he asked, while refusing to consider membership in the International Council of Christian Churches (ICCC), a conservative (albeit ecumenical) organization?[22] Alongside, he again printed photographs of students and faculty at Concordia College in River Forest, Illinois, marching for civil rights in neighboring Oak Park.[23] No article, no complaints, just the photos. NCC here, civil rights there. Concordia Teachers College in River Forest nearby. It was a crude and dishonest, if effective, way of tying them together.

Commie Lies

While Neuhaus and Marty were Otten's targets inside the LCMS that year, one man outside the church absorbed the bulk of Otten's wrath, brought *Christian News* the greatest exposure, and served best to rouse and federate Lutheran conservatives: Pete Seeger. The father of modern folk music and civil rights activist of "We Shall Overcome" fame, Seeger was invited in early 1965 by leaders of the Walther League, the LCMS's thriving youth organization, to sing at its July convention. Seeger was Otten's dream foil, a former communist blacklisted during the McCarthy era, civil rights and antiwar protester, and purported tempter of innocent youth. Otten broke the news of Seeger's appearance in March and hammered away at the issue through the July youth convention. Seeger, warned Otten, was "identified by government witnesses as a Communist," and with LCMS "liberals" was working to brainwash Lutheran youth.[24] Rev. Elmer Witt, executive director of the Walther League, worked to refute the claims against Seeger.[25] SOC conservatives met in Detroit to formulate strategy.[26] Protests continued. "Identified Communist: Protests Mount vs. Seeger at Mo. Synod Youth Convention," blared one April headline; "Youth Officials Refuse to Heed Protest" in May.[27] Seeger was liberalism's evil archetype, a guitar-strumming commie, civil rights activist, and religious ecumenist. In Otten's Manichaean world, supporters of his appearance were no less evil.

Many of Otten's antagonists fraternized through the New York–based periodical *American Lutheran*. Controlled by Adolph Meyer, future father-in-law to Otten's sister, *American Lutheran* strongly supported the Walther League's stance against Otten. Editors praised the "courageous stand of the Walther League" against "the radical right, which has mounted the attack," and predicted that it would "spare us all a worse storm in the future."[28] Again, Otten saw conspiracy. In a May 1965 article, Otten tied *American Lutheran* support for Seeger to race and communist-inspired ecumenism: "*American Lutheran* Backs Youth Officials on Seeger, Urges LWF Membership, Supports Federal Aid and Race Demonstrations."[29] The list of editors and contributors to the *American Lutheran* was to Otten a "Who's Who" of Lutheran liberalism, and included several current and future faculty members from Concordia Seminary: John Tietjen (Editor), John Damm (Managing Editor), Oswald Hoffmann, Richard E. Koenig, F. Dean Lueking, Arthur Carl Piepkorn, Robert Bertram, Martin Kretzmann, Walter Bouman, Martin Marty, and Wayne Saffen. Few of these men would escape Otten's attacks in the years to come. Several had already been targets.

With the Seeger controversy, Otten managed to bring the secular battle brewing around the church home to the LCMS. He crossed the lines several times himself, hawking folk-singer Janet Greene, a right-wing alternative (of unknown religious affiliation), to Seeger: "The communists have been using FOLK-SINGING FOR YEARS. Now the tables have been turned," he boasted. Buy Janet Greene's music and fill your progeny's head with smash, conservative songs like "Fascist Threat" and "Be Careful of the Commie Lies":

> Be careful of the Commie lies;
> Swallow them and freedom dies;
> The U.S.A. must realize
> That she's the biggest prize.
>
> To find them is an awesome task;
> They always wear a different mask;
> But knowledge rips the mask away,
> And free forevermore we'll stay.[30]

Otten continued the assault through the July convention on the "Best Known of All Communist Party Entertainers."[31] In late May, he finally got the desired response when Oliver Harms asked the Walther League to reconsider its invitation to Seeger. Stating that the singer's presence would be "divisive" and would "not edify the body of Christ," Harms let his concern stand as a request.[32] Discarding his populist-congregationalism, Otten blasted Harms's "Shocking Administration" for not issuing a presidential edict.[33] Otten challenged the administration to a public debate on the Seeger appearance, and, as he was growing accustomed to, received no reply.[34]

Seeger sang and Lutheran teens cheered while conservatives seethed. Seeger, by now well used to hate mail and threats, blew off the concerns of conservative Lutherans. He recalls being quizzed before the concert by a small group of grayed Lutheran observers, angry that he and Ann Landers (both non-Lutherans) would be addressing their youth. "Ann Landers is here, along with 'a Catholic.' What exactly are you?" asked one. Another rose to inquire, "Who exactly do you intend to overcome?"[35] At concert's end, over four thousand teens gave Seeger a standing ovation. The newly formed *Lutheran Witness-Reporter*, recounting the concert, did mention "unproved charges that Seeger was a Communist." And Otten made hay with the *Reporter*'s note that "Dr. Harms described the convention as 'a magnificent thing.'"[36]

The Seeger controversy managed to do several things. First, it made Otten the undisputed public voice of conservatism in the Missouri Synod. It also helped secularize the conflict in Missouri, binding Lutheran conservatives to their secular, anti-communist counterparts. It also convinced many conservatives that Lutheran moderates really were the secular liberals Otten argued they were. Too, Otten was able to permanently link Harms, the theologically orthodox LCMS president, with liberalism and portray him as a cowardly and irresolute leader. Otten's powerful voice drove Harms in May 1965 to roll out a weekly synodical newspaper, the *Lutheran Witness-Reporter*, in a futile counter to *Christian News*'s monopoly as news- and scandal-monger. Many former Walther Leaguers lament that the Seeger appearance, and Otten's reaction, destroyed the Walther League. Finally, the Seeger controversy led to the development of a well-organized

conservative political movement in the LCMS. The conservative streams
were converging.

Baal or God?

For years Otten had been quoting conservatives whose books had influenced him. Now it was his turn to try his own hand at influence peddling
in book form. In 1965, John Stormer, author of *None Dare Call It Treason,*
visited Otten in Missouri and showed him how to publish his manuscript
"cheap," a case of one hundred books for twenty-five dollars. While Otten
objected strenuously to other Missouri Lutherans working and demonstrat-
ing with non-Lutherans, he suffered little moral angst at collaborating with
the non-Lutheran Stormer. The pair even traveled to Geneva, Switzerland,
to demonstrate in front of the United Nations, where "they let the communists in but not us." With Stormer's help, Otten that year published *Baal or
God?* elaborating on themes already well covered in *Christian News.*[37] His
chapter "The Law of God" attacked the liberal view of "civil disobedience,"
leaning heavily again on William F. Buckley and *National Review,* who had
editorialized:

> Who, in the last period, has defied law and order, has called for direct
> opposition to the law—if we are going to take the position that lawlessness
> leads to assassination? Is it just the universally condemned Ross Barnett?
> Let us look at others of the law-defiers. Martin Luther King. He has said
> that laws that are bad are immoral laws, and therefore are not really laws
> at all; and under his leadership, and that of his many followers, Americans
> have directly flouted the law.[38]

For good measure, Otten again reminded readers that he believed Martin
Luther King Jr. to be "a religious liberal" who rejected "the virgin birth," "hard"
preaching on heaven and hell, and even the bodily resurrection of Christ.[39]

By May, Otten's *Baal or God?* was making its way through conservative
circles. Branding himself a "spokesman for conservative Christianity," Otten
hoped the meticulously footnoted book would take him to the next level,
from tabloid journalist to serious theologian, a modern-day J. Gresham
Machen.[40] It did not. *Baal* contained little that Otten had not already said in

three short years of journalistic effusion. The social revolution was creeping into the Missouri Synod, a fact Otten sourly noted in *Baal*. Church youth were becoming estranged, sucked in by "America's Moral Revolution" and the "sexplosion."[41] Church liberals, he carped, were legitimizing homosexuality, pornography, and contraception. Most major Protestant denominations, he complained, no longer condemned the use of contraceptives:

> In 1956 the United Lutheran Church endorsed birth control for the first time in the church's history. The attitude of various denominations towards the remarriage of divorced members has also changed. *Time* reported that in 1956 the United Lutheran Church (now a member of the Lutheran Church in America) "abolished the group's long-standing restriction on remarriage of the guilty party in divorce, decided to permit Lutheran pastors to remarry any divorced person who shows repentance."[42]

In Machen's style, Otten condemned both Roman Catholicism and liberal Christianity—one being a perversion of Christianity and the other "not Christianity at all."[43] But *Baal* was more than just a work of theology; it was a treatise on modern liberalism, Christian and secular. Otten attacked neo-orthodoxy as a child of secular liberalism and argued that liberals had infiltrated denominations across the spectrum of American Protestantism. Conservatism, he argued, is a "matter of honesty." Liberals, either consciously or as communist dupes, are trying to deceive the public. They use the word "God" but do not believe that Jesus is God.[44] Look at Lutheran theologian Robert Scharlemann, he exclaimed, who actually argues that communism and Christianity share common values.[45] Tying it all together were members of the NCC, open collaborators with the Soviets, "supporters of Castro," atheistic in nature and wholly bent on undermining Christian, American values.[46]

1965: Detroit

Three years after the first issue of *Christian News* rolled off the presses and into the mailboxes of unsuspecting Missouri clergy and laity, conservatives were ready to act, a fact not even the *Lutheran Witness* could hide. In the *Witness*'s pre-convention issue, Karl Barth, a Milwaukee minister, published an editorial calling on the synod to address problems with "doctrinal purity" in the church.[47] Otten's unremitting bombardment of the Harms administration and Concordia Seminary had taken its toll. The Seeger controversy increased conservative dissatisfaction with church leadership. Protesting students and burning inner cities hardened contempt for liberalism in general. But it was the 1965 synodical convention in Detroit that triggered the insurrection. Passage of Martin Kretzmann's Mission Affirmations redefined the very identity of the Missouri Synod and was to moderates a welcome watershed. Yet it did more to unify conservative opposition than they could have imagined.

By 1965, political lines in the sand were yet being drawn, and present at the synod's Detroit Convention were hundreds of delegates still ideologically autonomous. These were men who believed that a Lutheran could be at once theologically orthodox and socially active, both conservative and evangelical, traditional yet ecumenical. They publicly affirmed that Jesus Christ is the only way to heaven, affirmed the infallibility and historicity of the Old Testament account of Jonah, and accepted woman suffrage in the LCMS. Like most Americans, who that year watched their country take its first big step into Vietnam and away from legalized discrimination at home, many Missouri Lutherans were religiously conservative, optimistic, socially moderate to progressive, and outreach-oriented. Many of the same delegates in Detroit who publicly declared that Jonah had literally spent three full days in the belly of a big fish also voted to commend the nascent Commission on Social Action; pushed the synod to reject racial discrimination; urged a more sympathetic approach to the divorced; and expressed a "radical commitment toward the poor." But the most powerful note they struck in Detroit was an ecumenical one. Delegates voted separately for each of the six Affirmations; to forge closer ties with the National Council of Churches and to "Continue Discussions with the American Lutheran Church and the Lutheran Church in America"; to establish a cooperative partnership with the LCA and ALC, the Lutheran Council in the United States of America (LC-USA); and to consider membership in the Lutheran World Federation.[48]

Unlike Otten, most Lutherans liked the new direction of the church and did not yet equate its new ecumenism with theological liberalism.

Consequently, delegates rejected several Otten-inspired resolutions, declin-
ing to appoint a fact-finding committee to investigate doctrinal matters in
the synod; to criticize the liberalism of synod publications; to order Harms to
remove seminary president Fuerbringer; to require the synod to discipline
Robert and Martin Scharlemann, Dr. Gilbert Thiele, Dr. O. P. Kretzmann,
and others; and to require the synod to fire Richard Jungkuntz, executive
secretary of the powerful Commission on Theology and Church Relations
(CTCR). They rejected conservative appeals to overrule the Concordia faculty by ordaining Otten and reinstating his parish, Trinity. They declined to
endorse an Old Testament translation by Otten's friend Dr. William Beck.
They rejected conservative overtures to make the pipe organ the "official
worship instrument" of the LCMS. And in a grand slap at Otten, delegates
repudiated months of *Christian News* assaults on the Walther League by
publicly affirming its leaders.[49]

While the main show attracted the attention of delegates and media, a
more significant battle was fought beneath the noise. Weary of Otten and his
exploitation of the populist and congregationalist machinery of synod conventions, moderate delegates responded by moving to strip the church of its
congregationalist nature. A progressive church needed an efficient bureaucracy. And that meant efficient conventions. Conventions would now be held
every two years, and procedures for electing delegates to the convention
were also changed. Otten fired off complaints to Harms, received a reply,
and, in what was becoming standard practice for Otten, printed the private
correspondence in *Christian News*. "Prior to Detroit," he told Dr. Harms,
"it was possible for laymen to submit memorials (overtures-petitions) as individuals to a convention of The Lutheran Church—Missouri Synod. They no
longer have this right." Now only congregations could. The end result, worried Otten, would be the stifling of conservative laymen by liberal clergy.[50]

Anti-Intellectual Conservatism

The Seeger controversy and Detroit Convention served as a clarion call for
the nascent conservative movement. In November 1965, a wealthy layman
from Missouri named Marcus Braun authored and widely circulated a tract

entitled "Why the Lutheran Church—Missouri Synod Has Lost My Further
Contributions (For Unaware Laymen)." Braun repeated in his tract Otten's
mantra that Lutheran leadership, like that of "other once Orthodox Christian church bodies," had become infected by "Marxist liberalism." Resolutions like 4-35 were evidence that Harms and Wolbrecht were manipulating
synod machinery to "grind protests away," close prestigious appointments to
opponents, and slander conservatives.[51]

Braun's argument smacked of an emergent anti-intellectualism in American conservatism. Liberals in Detroit used fancy language, he alleged, to
confuse and complicate while changing nothing. The synod had confronted
the Seeger controversy in 1965 with a resolution contrived to locate the
political center. To appease conservatives, Resolution 8-01 chastised Walther
League leaders for "poor judgment" and "faulty and inadequate communication." But the resolution also affirmed the Walther League's mission
to "equip youth as servants of God in His mission to the world in which
they live." The youth league, Resolution 8-02 confirmed, was charged with
speaking "to the human predicament in which modern man finds himself"
and training young Christians to work in "an indifferent or hostile environment."[52] Braun differed, complaining that under new synod guidelines even
"Satan himself" could speak to LCMS youth.[53] Like Otten, Braun warned
that synod liberals were conspiring to lead Missouri into Marxist liberalism
by couching their strategy in "doubt-creating" resolutions on civil rights,
discrimination, fair housing, and immigration.[54] Now, he urged Lutherans,
there was but one way to combat the "Marxist liberalism with which our
Synod has become infected": hold back your contributions.[55]

Braun's greatest emotion was reserved for what he believed conservatism's biggest adversary and liberalism's biggest aim, big government; in
this case, big *church* government. Resolution 4-35 had already taken power
from the hands of congregations and put it in the hands of district officers. Another resolution, less noticed but no less significant (and also aimed
at Otten), had "disfranchised" individual laymen, allowing only "pastors,
teachers and professors" to petition the synod individually.[56] With this new
resolution, Braun protested, "the President of Synod can exercise virtual
dictatorial control."[57]

And he was right. Resolution 5-38 allowed Missouri Lutherans to submit petitions to the synod, but made the process more difficult and gave the president veto power over submissions. "The President," read the resolution, "shall decide which of the matters [shall be] submitted for presentation to and consideration by the convention" in pre-convention materials.[58] The president also gained responsibility for deciding which committees would act on the proposals that he approved. That kind of power was neither Lutheran nor conservative, argued Braun. "What a tremendous weapon," he maintained, presciently, "in the hands of any power greedy administrator."[59]

Missouri anti-intellectualism, as embodied in Otten and Braun, signified the conflicted nature of a church body that was both populist and elitist. Wayne Saffen, Chicago campus pastor and later moderate activist, argued in 1966 that anti-intellectualism in the LCMS was a recent phenomenon, that Missouri's tradition conveys not anti-intellectualism but "superintellectualism." The backwater strain in Missouri signified the impact of modern conservative evangelicalism. Missouri Synod pastors demonstrated this contradictory state by prefacing statements, as they often did, with "I am no theologian, but . . ." Yes, countered Saffen, after all these years of education, you are a theologian! Otten attracted this inconsistent audience with articles that were "well reasoned" and written, yet appealed mainly to common sense in exposing "what is *really* going on in Synod, what we don't get in the 'managed news' of synodical publications." Captains of "yellow journalism," Saffen tagged them the "German mafia."[60]

But conservative populism was not simply manufactured. It existed and worked because its targets often were intellectual elitists. Walter Bouman claimed with pride that he was, and remains, an elitist.[61] And Saffen, railing against Otten and his ilk, made the case for intellectual elitism. *Christian News* and *Confessional Lutheran*, he wrote, were

> self-appointed censors, judges, self-appointed officials of rump 'synods.' Their court of appeal is popular opinion, appeal to 'what everybody knows.' What everybody knows, what the simple layman knows—whose sole theological training may have been Sunday School, Confirmation class, the pastor's sermons, and a few selected books and tapes—is superior in knowledge, and therefore in judgment to what a professor knows in the

field of his specialty for which he spent up to five years or more in post-graduate work to earn his Ph.D., what he has spent a lifetime doing in basic research, in which he may have done post-doctoral work, a field in which he may be an acknowledged authority among scholars, and in which he may have written books and articles published by reputable publishers.[62]

Anti-intellectualism resonated with some Missouri Synod pastors because until recently its seminaries had not encouraged intellectualism. But it was not the only strain in Missouri conservatism.

Harms Struggles to Respond

Moderate power was showcased at the synod's 1967 convention as conservative anger simmered beneath the surface. Dozens of moderate resolutions were offered to the delegates promoting inner-city housing and anti-poverty programs and critical of the war in Vietnam and continuing discrimination. But synod delegates and church laity were not as eager as moderate leaders to endorse liberal political programs or to take firm political positions, and could agree only to "study" and postpone many issues. Putting the best face on delegate intransigence, the *Witness* offered a post-convention article entitled "When Compromise Is Progress." The delegates did agree, boasted editors, to "support such poverty programs as are consistent with our faith" as a church, and to "endeavor to change the factors which create poverty." As if unable to hear the intensifying conservative opposition, the *Witness* spun the synod's "compromise" as incremental progress and predicted eventual synod adoption of more specific liberal positions.[63]

But as the synod continued to moderate, Harms struggled to shepherd restless clergy. By 1968, synod officials were wringing their hands over the "Ebenezer fiasco," a failed effort to raise millions of dollars for synod missions.[64] Some saw it as symbolic of Harms's leadership failures, others as a sign of growing lay discontent. Harms seemed to be losing his grip on the church. Time and again, Herman Otten's *Christian News* scooped the synod's archaic communication apparatus, leaving the impression that church leaders were either inept or had something to hide. Harms tried communicating directly to the church through a column in the *Witness*.

That failing, he recorded weekly messages for a full year in hopes that church leaders would call St. Louis to listen to the recorded message. Finally, in 1965, he established the *Lutheran Witness-Reporter*, a weekly foil to *Christian News*.

The problem, however, was not the medium but the message. Harms continually sounded an optimistic tone, discovering "how much zeal there is for getting God's Word out to our members and to all the world."[65] But he also advanced the moderate agenda, particularly his own pet, ecumenism. Harms wanted full fellowship with the ALC and drew the correct conclusion that most Lutheran congregations "generally support the concept of [the] Lutheran Council [LC-USA]."[66] Housing for the poor, membership in the World Council of Churches, woman suffrage, mission work, and racial reconciliation were also his concerns. But nowhere was Harms so personally and professionally invested as with the issue of ALC fellowship. Between the fall of 1967 and 1968, almost every one of his sixty-five recorded messages advocated the move. The message made him the darling of church moderates. But it also made him a chief target for *Christian News* and synod conservatives.

A Gathering Storm

In 1969, Jeffrey Hadden warned of a "widening gap" between clergy and laymen in America's churches. The educated clergy, he found, tended to hold more liberal views on social issues than most laymen, positions that increasingly came into the open and polarized during the turbulent 1960s.[67] The overwhelming majority of Lutheran pastors approved of the general objectives of the civil rights movement, thought that their church bodies had been "woefully inadequate" in facing up to discrimination, and believed that most members of their respective church bodies were at best ignorant and at worst hypocritical in applying principles of Christian unity to social justice. Half of Missouri Synod pastors supported those clergy who actively worked for civil rights. And most of them disagreed with the common belief that the problems faced by black Americans were often of their own making.[68] But in all areas, a significant conservative minority was at variance.

These beliefs reflected an expanding gulf between the laity and clergy elites in matters social and theological. The majority of Protestant church-goers rejected the views of their ministers with respect to the civil rights movement, Hadden asserted.[69] This chasm, warned Hadden, was leading to a "crisis of authority" in Protestant churches, where "laity, who have entrusted authority to professional leaders, have come to have grave doubts about how the authority has been used, and are beginning to assert their own influence." In clergy-heavy Missouri, the differences between pastors and laity in social and theological matters were less marked than in other Protes-tant denominations, but still significant. More importantly, the synod's most recent graduates from Concordia Seminary were among those most likely to reject the laity's conservative religious and social attitudes. Twenty-eight percent of Missouri Synod clergy under age thirty-five rejected a "literal or near literal interpretation of the Bible" in Hadden's survey, while only 16 percent of those over age fifty-five did.[70]

Of greater significance was Hadden's ability to bind theological and social issues, theological beliefs and political identification. Hadden demonstrated that Missouri's educated pastors were out of step with the laity less in mat-ters theological than in political matters. Moreover, highly educated clergy, more likely to self-identify as "neo-orthodox," were more than twice as likely to identify with the Democratic Party than their conservative counterparts.[71] Theological beliefs strongly correlated with political identification.

Intellectual moderates should have seen the ideological tide turn-ing against them. George Wallace had garnered support in the country's Midwest in 1968 while attacking "intellectual snobs."[72] Richard Nixon had won the presidency by exploiting growing conservative disquiet over Viet-nam, integration, and the welfare state and by mobilizing a "silent major-ity" against "nattering nabobs of negativism."[73] Many Americans wanted law and order, no less so in the Missouri Synod. Anti-intellectualism, a constant strain in American political culture, was experiencing a resurgence. This did not bode well for Missouri's liberal intellectuals.

This gulf was reflected in the months preceding Missouri's 1969 con-vention in Denver. Richard Nixon's 1968 victory might have forewarned church moderates. Instead, they fired additional salvoes in the *Witness* at

Missouri tradition and conservatism. A May 1968 article by Andrew Schulze promoted the use of "force" to bring about social and economic equality. Whites, he contended, had long used force to deprive minorities of civil rights. It was the church's duty, then, to use force in pursuit of equal opportunity. "When good intentions are expressed in nothing but silence," he wrote, "the silence itself becomes a force to bolster the segregational status quo."[74] The next month, ALC district president J. Elmo Agrimson urged Missouri Lutherans (in the pages of their own periodical) to work toward ecumenical action on racial justice.[75] *Witness* editors, moreover, had praise for growing student protests. "Youth must be credited," they wrote, "with having interest and spirit enough to want to do something about the world in which we live. Too many adults—as well as many students—prefer the easier role of apathy and noninvolvement. . . . Adults," they argued, "will do well to listen to the cries" raised by activist students.[76] A late 1968 article by Roger Fink blamed white racists, not rioters, for the four long, hot summers of rebellion in the nation's cities. Missouri Lutherans, he urged, "must admit racism. . . . Some of us," Fink complained, "love property more than people. Some of us feel black people are worth little more than animals. We should not be surprised that people begin to act like animals if you have treated them like animals. I marvel that it took so long."[77]

Mainstream Conservatives Organize

In August 1964, several young conservatives met in a motel outside Concordia Teachers College in Seward, Nebraska, to coordinate a response to a perceived leftward drift in Missouri. Among them were Gustav Lobeck, a district president from Iowa, Ellis Nieting, a pastor from Lobeck's district, and Nebraska pastor Waldo Werning.[78] All had been reading *Christian News* and believed that Otten was "absolutely right," even if they worried about a journalistic style that flirted with slander and violated Christian principles.[79] Lobeck, privy to discussions taking place among Harms and the other district presidents, convinced Werning of the urgency of the "dangerous situation" in Missouri.[80] Werning, an avowed and passionate conservative with an intense work ethic who rose early each morning to go "jogging for the Lord," took the meeting and turned it into an organized movement.[81] Within months, his movement would blossom into "Faith Forward—First Concerns" (FF–FC), the most significant conservative interest group in Missouri Synod history.

As the Seeger controversy persisted in early 1965, FF–FC gained momentum. In February, Werning gathered about twenty conservatives in Downer's Grove, Illinois, following an unsuccessful confrontation with the Council of Presidents (COP) the week before.[82] The group agreed to put pressure on Harms. A strategy meeting in April included Lobeck, Nieting, and Karl Barth, now a district officer in Milwaukee, Wisconsin. Also present was Jack Preus, whose name was already being bandied about as a conservative candidate to challenge Harms.[83] When Harms visited Nebraska, Werning met with him to inform him of the movement, which now included six district presidents. Meanwhile, he worked studiously to craft the documents that would become the organizing charter of the countermovement he founded.

As the Detroit Convention loomed, Werning circulated a letter and petition to hundreds of thousands of Lutherans. The petition, entitled "A Plea of Concern in Christian Love," immediately professed allegiance to President Harms and "other leaders who hold and teach the scriptural and confessional viewpoint of the inspiration of the Bible." But the tone of Werning's "Plea of Concern" was also threatening. Few could mistake that Werning's target was the faculty of Concordia Seminary, those "professors, pastors, and teachers" who were "propagandizing for their 'new system'" using the "new hermeneutic."[84] "WE EXPECT," he warned, that Lutherans in the teaching ministry faithfully reflect the public doctrine of the synod in their work. "WE EXPECT," he continued, that the source of unity in the LCMS and beyond be the "INERRANT WORD" of God.[85] Werning's concern, as elsewhere in battles between theological conservatives and modernists, was the slippery slope:

> If the story of Genesis can be demoted and reduced to a symbolic story of creation instead of accepting it as an historic happening, why should we dare to hope that the miracles narrated in both the Old and New Testaments, the story of the Virgin Birth, the resurrection of our Lord and the

ascension of our Lord will not be presented as non-factual but as symbols, allegory, or hallucinations. . . .[86]

Werning's petition was more than a simple expression of concern. With the accompanying letter to his brothers in Christ, Werning's "Plea of Concern" constituted a conservative manifesto, intent on creating a semi-permanent interest group among LCMS Lutherans to generate change from within. "Are you disturbed," he roused, "by the doctrinal unrest in our Missouri Synod?" Consciously or not, Werning sanctioned Otten's ideological paradigm. There are two sides, he argued, one liberal and one conservative (or "authentic"), both "singing the same hymn of adoration to the incarnate and crucified Savior, even though they are using different words and melodies." Citing conservative monthly *Christianity Today*, Werning encouraged his brothers by grouping Missouri Lutherans with Southern Baptists and other conservative Protestant bodies on the "growing edge" of Protestantism that lie "outside the circle of 'cooperative Protestantism.'" His call, "CONSERVATIVES UNITE! YOU HAVE NOTHING TO LOSE BUT THE MISSOURI SYNOD!" belied the "Plea of Concern's" criticisms of "independent groups within our church" who were "undermining the work of our synodical leaders!"[87] Werning later conceded, "We were building a separate movement. Synod needed the stability which this movement gave."[88]

Werning brought all of his connections, gifts, and abilities as a strategist to bear in building his movement. He felt a sense of urgency. Karl Barth and he agreed, he wrote to Bill Eggers, that "if this venture is not now successful, we will have lost for an indefinite period of time." Initially, Werning was inclined to combine his efforts with Otten's *Christian News*.[89] But he was worried about linking the movement with Otten, an association that might alienate moderates. Werning and Jack Preus, committed to run an article in *Christian News*, pulled the story at the last minute. Otten and Burgdorf agreed to keep their distance while it was politically expedient.[90]

The final document, "Faith Forward—First Concerns," was mailed to clergy and laity across the synod. It featured the signatures of several pastors, Werning included, and ten district presidents. The response was overwhelming. Almost 140,000 signatures were collected in the months preceding Detroit.[91] The message to Harms was clear. And loud.

Intended or not, Werning's "Plea of Concern" carried with it an impli-
cation that frightened Harms: take care of the seminary or else. If the language of the petition did not do the trick, those who signed it made sure
Harms understood. G. F. Barthel, a circuit counselor in Milwaukee, soon
told Harms:

> We who signed did not by such a signature wish to indicate that we were
> in complete agreement with your past policy in dealing with theological
> trends in our Synod, but it was rather to express to you our intent to sup-
> port you fully if you would take a positive and firm stand against every
> trend and teaching contrary to the historic position of our Synod.[92]

The pressure worked. Alarmed, Harms wrote to a friend, "Between you
and me, I am frightened about this and hope that it will not result in more
problems. Somehow I sensed that something like this could happen, and in
my meeting with the [Concordia Seminary] faculty a week ago I warned that
such a thing might happen."[93] By month's end he had crafted a memo to the
"Pastors, Professors, and Men Teachers of the Lutheran Church—Missouri
Synod." He addressed conservative complaints about Valparaiso University
and the Seeger controversy. Finally, he assured his conservative brethren
that charges and complaints of false doctrine were "being considered and
dealt with properly." For now, he hoped, he had bought some time.[94]

The Reactionary Movements Converge

Otten wasted little time convincing his readers of the need for continued
conservative action. For all his losses in Detroit, Otten found cause for optimism. "Seldom in recent years," he opined, "has such a high percentage of
true Missourians been elected to responsible positions. This is one of the
few times we can recall when so many of those nominated from the floor
were actually elected." Losses aside, conservatives had, for the first time,
coordinated their efforts and won some battles.[95]

The summer of 1965 gave Otten plenty of ammunition. The Watts
riots in Los Angeles in August led to a *Christian News* editorial on September 6: "That this is a negro-white problem is pure fiction. It is a matter
of Negro criminals getting out of hand and propagandists blaming it upon

race discrimination."[96] Among those propagandists was Dr. Martin Luther King Jr., activist and Christian "modernist." The "lawlessness" of Watts was encouraged by King and other "misguided" churchmen who, like so many liberals, were either conspirators or their dupes. "Communists," he again warned, "have been at work for years endeavoring to create class and racial hatred."[97] As a Christian, Otten had great difficulty attacking King's goals of equality under the law. So he attacked his theology. And again, Otten managed to work circuitously back to liberal Lutheran ecumenists: "The *Lutheran Witness* refers to Dr. King as 'a committed Christian' and even though Dr. King continues to remain one of the darlings of the Lutheran Human Relations Association of America, some of our Bible believing Negro friends reject both Dr. King's liberal theology and radical political views. So do we."[98]

By October, Otten was increasingly crying conspiracy. His anger in part may have stemmed from yet another rejection, this time in September, when the synod's Board of Appeals reinstated his congregation but refused to certify him.[99] The fury was palpable. Civil rights activist Richard John Neuhaus, now editing *Una sancta*, had announced the "victory" of the "new theology," which Otten tied to *Una sancta* contributors like John Elliott, Jaroslav Pelikan, Walter Bouman, and Arthur Carl Piepkorn.[100] "Pastor Neuhaus," he cautioned, "has boldly published his strategy for the liberal takeover of the Lutheran Church—Missouri Synod. . . . He confidently boast [sic] that the old Missouri Synod and its doctrinal position has [sic] died. Neuhaus, chairman of the Lutheran Human Relations Association of Greater New York, has been arrested for participating in an illegal school 'sit-in.' He has sought to have his synod support civil disobedience."[101] In December, Harms arranged a meeting with Neuhaus, Elliot, Lueking, and others to discuss the synod's stance on civil rights. Playing the journalist, Otten wanted in, but was rebuffed. "Why all the secrecy?" he asked. If Neuhaus and other Missouri liberals were the conspirators, then Harms and his subordinates were the dupes. "Frankly, we don't believe Missouri Synod officials are any match for the liberals who were scheduled to lecture to them" at the closed-door meeting. "These liberals, some of whom have been promoting civil disobedience and have been arrested, should be told in no uncertain terms that God's Word and the Lutheran Confessions condemn the kind of civil disobedience they have been promoting."[102]

In October, Concordia invited theologian Franklin Littell to speak to the seminary faculty. Otten dusted off his House Un-American Activities Committee (HUAC) files (published by the right-wing Church League of America in Wheaton, Illinois) and came out firing. HUAC had found in 1953 that Littell was an advocate of cell group activism. "Mr. Littell," Otten paraphrased, "it is plain to see, is a strong advocate of secrecy, on the part of the cell, in the adoption of a program leading to action. Why? Because the real motives behind the program can be hidden. The tactic of secrecy is followed by Communist cells in all movements infiltrated and in all front organizations." Littell was not at the seminary to discuss theology, Otten was certain, but conspiracy. "The cell form or organization, made up of small disciplined groups, bound by common ideology, meeting in secret closed doors, is what Mr. Littel favors and which the leadership of the Methodist Federation for Social Action endorses."[103]

Missouri's fifth column, believed Otten, was its propaganda mouthpiece, the *Lutheran Witness*. Not "known for its strong position of witnessing to the truth in recent years," the *Witness* was now under the influence of intellectuals like Martin Marty (appointed to the *LW-R* board in October 1965).[104] Next to a photo of Marty walking alongside Chicago's Archbishop John Patrick Cody, Otten reprinted, as he would do countless times in the decades to follow, Marty's supposed strategy for subversion. Marty's position on the editorial staff of *Christian Century*, which "consistently defends such Christ-denying modernists as Nels Ferré and Harry Emerson Fosdick," was proof enough of his leftish leanings.[105] Marty had even dared to criticize conservatism's champion, Barry Goldwater (who suggested in 1965 that Jesus Christ would have been the first one to volunteer to fight in Vietnam). Marty's writing, and what he brought to the *Witness*, was to Otten "cheap and tasteless journalism at its worst."[106]

The new movement was coalescing, and a clearer picture of its leadership was coming into view. Otten, emboldened and increasingly hopeful for change in the church and in his status as outcast, pushed on the fringes, always careful to support the more "legitimate," mainstream conservatives while allowing them distance from him. Werning, himself emboldened, continued to organize while utilizing Otten's populist reach through *Christian News*. Others joined their ranks, all with different agendas and ambitions. Many came from outside the synod's traditional leadership structure: Jack Preus, a refugee from the Norwegian Synod, participating furtively from his office at the Springfield seminary; his older and more staunchly orthodox brother, Robert, a professor at Concordia Seminary; the brilliant but abrasive theologian John Warwick Montgomery, a convert to Missouri Lutheranism and their intellectual gladiator; Chester "Chet" Swanson, a friend to German rocket scientist Wernher von Braun and a Proctor and Gamble executive with conservative ties and financial resources; Larry Marquardt, a Chicago area Buick dealer and former conservative Methodist; and Glen Peglau, a wealthy, conservative attorney who floated from denomination to denomination and provided financial support to Jack Preus in Springfield.[107] Joining them were other lay leaders and a host of conservative pastors steeped in Lutheran tradition and products of its educational system, each with his own view of what conservatism meant. Yet they were united by their disgust at the social and theological direction the Missouri Synod had taken in recent years, and determined to wrest control of it from the liberals.

Mission-minded Werning was particularly indignant over the direction of LCMS missions. In the wake of convention approval of Kretzmann's Affirmations in 1965, the synod's mission staff used every opportunity to implement its resolves. The result was that "Missouri Synod Lutherans now found official support for prayer with other Christians on the mission field and could go to the Lord's Supper with at least Lutheran non-Missourians."[108] Werning was appalled. Believing that liberals were using the Affirmations as a pretext for unionism, he wrote to Preus, "This may be an indication as to how far our ecumenists are stretching in order to convince one and all in Detroit that foreign missions groups should be completely untied from the home church (according to Mickey Kretzmann's suggestions) and also how wild some of our men are to go all out for everything in LC-USA."[109]

The success of Werning's movement finally animated Jack Preus to enter the fray, if tepidly. In July 1966, he published an article in the *Lutheran Witness*, "How Close Are Lutherans in America?" Preus warned that "Missouri

is beginning to participate in a thousand different fronts in various ecumenical and interconfessional activities." Ever the politician, Preus positioned
himself as a moderate and only indirectly criticized Oliver Harms, a proponent of LCMS entry into the LC-USA, by calling for "clarity" on ecumenical
issues.[110]

Dalliance with Montgomery

That same year, conservatives began a tight, troubled, and transitory relationship with conservative intellectual John Warwick Montgomery. Lawyer, philosopher, and theologian, Montgomery, referred to by Werning and
friends as John "Warlike" Montgomery, had gained recognition in conservative theological circles by publicly debating theological nonconformists
like death-of-God advocate Thomas Altizer.[111] The Missouri-Montgomery
romance, however, was brief.[112]

In 1966, Montgomery threw his considerable gifts to the conservative cause. The *Lutheran Witness-Reporter* stated in May, "Canadian representatives of the Missouri Synod, the American Lutheran Church, and
the Lutheran Church in America have agreed that a 'discrepancy' or an
'error of fact' can't affect the inerrancy of the Bible, according to a Canadian
Lutheran Council report."[113] Montgomery fired back:

> Whenever we reach the point of affirming on the one hand that the Bible
> is infallible or inerrant and admitting on the other hand to internal con-
> tradictions or factual inaccuracies within it, we not only make a farce of
> language, promoting ambiguity, confusion, and perhaps even deception in
> the church; more reprehensible than even these things, we in fact deny the
> plenary inspiration and authority of Scripture, regardless of the theologi-
> cal formulae we may insist on retaining. . . . I must—if only on the basis of
> common sense—protest the idea that 'error can't affect inerrancy.' This is
> like saying that the presence of corners can't affect a circle.[114]

A heresy hunt soon ensued, arranged by Werning and starring Montgomery.
Following a debate in River Forest in mid-1966, Werning warned Montgomery to restrain his abrasive style. "Don't do what you did with Altizer,"
warned Werning. "You took his theological ear and tossed it to the crowd.
Don't insult your public that way." In September, Montgomery headed up

an inquisition of Concordia Seminary theologian John Elliott. Werning had brought formal charges against Elliott, which led to a meeting between Werning, Repp, Fuerbringer, and other faculty members. Werning brought Montgomery along as a "theological consultant."[115] In the meeting, Montgomery, trained as an attorney, got Elliott to admit his belief that hell is "ontological."[116] "They were very glad to see our backs as we left," recalls Werning.[117] Within weeks, Elliott left Concordia for the University of San Francisco. Later that year, Werning and Otten opposed the nomination of Walter Bouman to tenure at Concordia–River Forest. When some of Bouman's papers were leaked to Otten, Montgomery took up the cause and opposed Bouman in print.[118]

Werning was taken with Montgomery. In October, he proposed creating a conservative intellectual journal to his expanding faction, the *International Lutheran Journal of Theology*. Intended as a foil to Marty's *Christian Century*, the journal was to be edited by Montgomery and backed up by Werning's Who's Who of LCMS conservative intellectuals: Robert Preus, Paul Zimmerman, Walter Roehrs, Walter A. Maier Jr., and Ralph Bohlmann. Chet Swanson would sit on the editorial board. To finance the journal, Werning proposed that Preus approach Fred Rutz, whose foundation already supported the Springfield seminary, Otten, SOC and other conservative causes, and other related (but not denominationally affiliated) conservative foundations like the Erickson Foundation, the American Economic Foundation, and even the Pew Charitable Trusts.[119]

But by then, Montgomery's relationship with Missouri conservatives was already fracturing. In February, Otten received a letter from a mole at Concordia Seminary in St. Louis warning him that Montgomery was badmouthing him and *Christian News*. During a dinner with "Lawrence and Celeste," Montgomery had railed against Herman's belief in a communist conspiracy and called Herman and his wife, Grace, "kooks who edit 'Lutheran News.'" He had also allegedly painted Otten as a racist, claiming that Herman was always careful when discussing "the Negro," but really believed, as did Grace, that there was biblical support for segregation. But Montgomery was not the only duplicitous one in St. Louis, they warned Herman. Jack's brother, seminary professor Robert Preus, also had "two faces—he also continues to make derogatory remarks about you and your work—so we find it hard to understand why you seem to think he is on our side. From our experience with him we have found that he is a two-faced fox!"[120]

Unlike Robert Preus, Montgomery was willing to criticize Otten in print and in person. In July 1967, he published an article aimed at Otten entitled "Down with Kookishness!"[121] In it, Montgomery asserted that Otten was "anti-fluoridation" and "anti-Negro."[122] Next, in personal correspondence, Montgomery censured Otten for conflating theological and political conservatism:

> I am dead against your assumption that to be conservative doctrinally means to be conservative in all areas of life—politically (right-wing Republican), economically (the free enterprise system can do no wrong), socially (integration efforts are questionable at best, Communist-inspired at worst), educationally (even the new math turns out to be a kind of liberalism), musicologically (folk singers are often Communist fronts), etc., etc., etc. Your judgments and innuendoes in these areas are as off base as are the liberal counter-arguments that one must be "radical" in all areas to be consistently Christian. . . . The result is that you drive intelligent Christians who want to be doctrinally conservative but who don't agree with your extra-theological judgments into the liberal camp.[123]

Soon Montgomery was hitting the whole movement. Critical of the "left" for believing that "all changes in doctrine or practice are harbingers of good for a sound union of separated churches," he also criticized the Lutheran "right" for "echoing the venerable cry of 'Jesuit regicide,' that suggests authoritarian religious conspiracies by Rome or by vast ecumenical units."[124] Where conservative ideology congealed in Missouri toward the end of the 1960s, Montgomery defied. His transitory flirtation with Missouri conservatism was coming to an end.

Kookishness

Otten, meanwhile, continued to define "kookishness" and conservatism for Missouri, even while embracing his own brand of ecumenism. In June 1966, he began hawking a book by Uriah Fields, *The Anatomy of Mutuality*, which argued, "Negroes cannot afford to follow Martin Luther King because he is surrounded with communists. A large percentage of last year's $500,000 budget of the Southern Christian Leadership Conference was contributed by redfront organizations and persons sympathetic to the communist's cause who are either red or bright pinks."[125] Later that year, Otten was a featured speaker at an ICCC convention at Carl McIntyre's Christian Admiral (a hotel attached to McIntyre's Bible College) in New Jersey.[126] Joining Otten on the dais that summer were several conservative politicians and evangelists, including South Carolina Senator Strom Thurmond and evangelist Bob Jones.[127] While Otten bashed liberal ecumenists out of one corner of his mouth, he rationalized his ecumenism from the other: Through his participation in the ICCC, he remembers, he "got readers in 60 different countries, see. Like going, in Geneva, when I was there, that was 1965, they put a copy of my book, *Baal or God*, into every delegate's packet, see. They all got a free copy. Then these delegates would take it home to their countries all over the world and that's how we got these international contacts."[128] The same reasoning led him to tout an Independent Board of Lutheran Missions, an offshoot of the dwindling SOC.[129] A supporter in Japan wrote Otten in 1966 to ask for his help:

> As you know, too, our greatest burden is for the 4,000 Japanese ministers and 4,000 leading Christian business men who have been "brain-washed" over here and we trust that your Independent Board of Lutheran Missions will consider sponsoring this. . . . After we complete the Japanese translation, then perhaps we might talk about Korea or Taiwan since Japan is much behind both of these countries. The Japanese are pro-Communist, pacifists and socialists while the Koreans are completely anti-Communist with a strong fundamentalist background.[130]

In 1968, hoping to broaden his conservative-ecumenical appeal, Otten changed the name of *Lutheran News* to *Christian News*.[131]

Otten kookishness included an unethical and often illegal tendency to violate basic journalistic standards. Otten's formula for prolificity in *Christian News* included reprinting articles from other publications, often without consent. In July 1966, Carl Braaten, editor of *Dialog*, demanded that Otten pay a permission fee. Otten complained that "we are not in a position to pay $200.00" and that "Missouri Synod Lutherans on your staff cannot hide behind copyright regulations when *Dialog* makes such an outright attack against the BRIEF STATEMENT."[132] Omar Stuenkel, managing editor of the *Witness*, took Otten to task for another of his predilections, publishing personal correspondence. "It is my understanding," he wrote to Otten, "that it is considered to be not only unethical but also illegal to publish private correspondence without the consent of the writer. Much of the correspondence, which you printed as deriving from me, was used without permission on my part. Furthermore it was not addressed to you or to your paper."[133] Richard John Neuhaus rejoiced when Otten finally relented. "That you now ask for permission before reprinting articles," he wrote, "is an encouraging sign. What neither elementary honesty or courtesy could persuade you to do in the past has apparently been achieved by force of United States copyright laws."[134] By the early 1970s, even Otten's friends and supporters, fearful that he would throw it on the cover of his paper, had to preface their personal correspondence with "NOT FOR PUBLICATION."[135]

By the late 1960s, as Otten's appeals to the synod met with opposition and avoidance and as enemies pressed their case against him, he grew increasingly unrestrained in print. In May 1967, the LCMS Board of Appeals ruled that synod's expulsion of Otten's church, Trinity, was invalid. Enemies in the district, with help from Concordia Seminary, appealed the decision (the case was thrown out in July). But while his congregation was readmitted to the synod, Otten was not. Appeals to the 1967 Synodical Convention were quashed. And in January 1968, the faculty at Concordia, still the ultimate arbiters of his fate, told the Commission on Constitutional Matters (asked to interpret an earlier Board of Appeals ruling) that "Mr. Otten's case is closed."[136] Only one thing could save Otten now—a full change in synod leadership. Otten pulled out all the stops to make that happen, targeting theological and political liberals, ecumenists, communists, civil rights activists, antiwar protesters, and Jews.

The United Planning Conference

Otten's doggedness in *Christian News* paid off. By 1968, many influential laity were convinced that the synod was rife with liberalism and Oliver

Harms could not stop it. Alvin Mueller and Carl Muhlenbruch, members of the synod's Board of Directors during the split, read *Christian News* as one of their sources for news in the church (although they denied being influenced by it). Mueller said of *Christian News,* "You can't believe everything you read, but you can repeat it."[137] Yet Otten had convinced them that the *Witness* was unreliable. He had also convinced them that Harms was not up to the job of confronting liberalism in the denomination. Both were frustrated by Fuerbringer's evasiveness when confronted by the Board. And Muhlenbruch, a businessman, was discouraged by Harms's inability to make a decision.[138]

Conservatives continued to organize. Otten's friend Carl Hoffmeyer echoed SOC supporter Marcus Braun, urging Missouri Lutherans to give their offerings not to the synod but to his organization.[139] What came to the SOC was then parceled out to Otten and his friends.[140] John Baur raised funds for Otten while Fred Rutz continued to pump money into the SOC.[141] The SOC, too, used hostility toward the civil rights movement to build support among conservatives. Carl Steffen, Pittsburgh conservative, formed the National Lutheran Soul Relations Association (NLSRA) in 1966, an offshoot of the SOC and an improbable foil to Schulze's LHRAA. The NLSRA's objective, wrote Steffen, was to "instill within the Lutheran Church—Missouri Synod that, as disciples of Christ, our lives are devoted to saving souls NOT bodies." Steffen's nastiness was characteristic of the SOC and accounts for the discomfort many mainstream conservatives had with the far right. He even compared President Harms to the Antichrist in a 1967 tract distributed to Missouri conservatives.[142] Yet much of what he said, mainstream conservatives found palatable. Steffen aimed to "place morality in its proper Christian perspective and, consequently, assist in raising the Nation's moral standards to their proper level." His final objective was to "expose, wherever they exist, liberal issues which are developing and promoting the social gospel and modernistic beliefs."[143]

But conservatism's most significant organization evolved from what Jim Adams called the "hard-core remnant" of FF–FC, led by Waldo Werning. In December 1966, Werning and others came together in what would be called the United Planning Conference (UPC) to formally organize in advance

of the 1967 New York convention. The UPC was to serve as a conservative political party within the synod, screening, nominating, and promoting candidates to church office. Their initial meeting brought together the
church's conservative heavy hitters: Jack and Robert Preus, Waldo Werning,
O. A. Gebauer, Herman Otten, Glen Peglau, Paul Zimmerman, Ellis Nieting, Karl Barth, Roy Guess, and others.[144] Montgomery spoke at their first
meeting on the third use of the Law.[145] The UPC met every other month
thereafter to discuss issues and collaborate; Werning and Gebauer were the
most faithful participants.[146] They worked hard to maintain secrecy. John
Lutze, a pastor in Downer's Grove, Illinois, and member of the UPC, was
told to hide his car when attending meetings.[147] Otten was invited to attend
only after consenting to keep his mouth shut. "I wasn't even supposed to
tell my wife," he recalled. When he confronted Robert Preus with his discomfort at all the secrecy, Preus responded, "We're in a war. And in a war,
you don't give the enemy your plan."[148] Otten kept quiet. Throughout 1967,
participants grumbled about the same issues Otten had been raising faithfully for years, including the LC-USA, the NCC, ecumenism, unionism,
church-state relations, and the growing church bureaucracy. Liberalism in
synodical publications, the "constant brainwashing" and "lack of conservative viewpoint among editors," was a serious complaint.[149]

Most significantly, members put in place a skeletal structure for organizing conservatives on a district level to work for the election of convention
delegates.[150] While Werning organized the show, Preus starred. Preus "asked
what should we do," recalled Karl Barth, but "didn't listen to what anyone
said."[151] Preus's biggest supporter, Glen Peglau, urged his allies to push for
Harms's removal by 1969 and to run Preus as their candidate.[152] Together,
they wanted action taken at the upcoming convention against what they
called "clear-cut cases" of liberalism like *Lutheran Hour* speaker Oswald
Hoffmann, the St. Louis faculty, and Concordia–River Forest. In preparation, Werning took phone surveys and secured lists of delegates, which he
shared surreptitiously with Otten.[153] Otten, in turn, sent copies of *Christian
News* to every delegate.[154] In their 1967 New York convention test case, the
UPC succeeded in having John Lutze and Larry Marquardt elected to the

Board of Regents of Concordia–River Forest.[155] While delegates at the New York convention continued to support resolutions on housing for the poor and social action, even resolving to support the work of the LHRAA, conservatives studied the machinery of the synod.[156] Their conclusion: control the delegates and you control the synod.[157]

Werning believed that conservatives had the numbers and needed only organization. The difficulty was that so many of the conservatives had their own beefs, agendas, and strategies. The diversity among conservatives was great and threatened to kill the movement from day one. "The problem [with] Fred Rutz," Werning wrote E. J. Otto in May 1967, "is that he was fighting his battle alone." Paul Zimmerman was so angry with Rutz that he went to Harms, complaining that Rutz was "not acting in a manner that reflects his Christian charity" by disseminating "misinformation" in his latest book (which Otten was selling through *Christian News*).[158] Others had concerns about Swanson, who was as interested in ending President Johnson's "War on Poverty" as he was liberalism at Concordia.[159] Werning's UPC aimed to change that.

> We will have many co-laborers and can win over any maneuvers [at the New York convention]. However, it is vital that you be present already on July 6th in order to attend open hearings of the committee on doctrine and also on church practice. Information will also be given in May on concerns that must be raised before those committees.[160]

While Werning and the UPC wanted theological reform, Otten, Rutz, Swanson, and others wanted to bring Buckley's conservative revolution to Missouri. But they could not agree on what conservatism meant. Even the theological conservatives were influenced by the secular battle. Karl Barth thought that historical criticism of the Bible or of the Lutheran Confessions paralleled liberal efforts to "rewrite and historicize the US constitution instead of interpreting it."[161] Otto, too, needed some convincing of the need to unite. "There will undoubtedly be attempts to white wash and brain wash at this convention," Werning warned, "but an informed delegate will not be fooled by this. . . . I can assure you that you are on an important fighting team."[162]

Tietjen Joins the Fray

In St. Louis, Harms was growing more deeply concerned. Marcus Braun's charge to conservatives to withhold funds from the synod was squeezing the church. Fresh off a fundraising fiasco, the "Ebenezer" project,[163] Harms was admonished in 1967 to exercise "economy" in running the synod.[164] While individual contributions in the LCMS had been rapidly rising for over a decade, increasing sharply between 1966 and 1967,[165] average giving to the church per communicant member in the LCMS had been slowly dropping since 1964.[166] Moreover, the synod's budget shrunk for the first time since Depression-era 1937.[167] Pat Wolbrecht estimated that Werning and Barth, now together in the South Wisconsin District, were partly to blame. He wrote to *Witness* editor Martin Mueller in 1968:

> P.S. Just on a hunchy basis, I have looked to see an analysis on a ten-year basis for the South Wisconsin District. In 1967, for example, there was an $89,000 increase in congregational remittances to the district treasurer. Meanwhile, there was a $40,000 decline for that district in total remittances to the synodical budget from the 1967 budget year to 1968 budget year. In both these fiscal years the district operations ran in the red respectively by $33,000 and $21,000. What would you advise?[168]

Mueller did his own survey and discovered that South Wisconsin, the synod's third-largest district in 1968, was withholding payment to the synod for the *Lutheran Witness*.[169] Rightfully so, remembered Werning: "It was a left-wing rag, so why should the district pay money for it?"[170]

Unlike most moderates, Concordia Seminary president Alfred Fuerbringer sensed something in the wind. In late 1968, in a preemptive strike, Fuerbringer moved swiftly to secure the seminary for moderates for fear of the unthinkable, a Harms loss at the synod's 1969 Denver convention. Martin Scharlemann, who had himself eyed the seminary presidency, testified:

> Dr. Repp one day suddenly announced to the faculty that we had better get a new president before the term of President Fuerbringer comes to an end. He suggested that the election of a new president ought to take place before the Denver Convention lest we get a man out of step with what was going on. . . . I think it demonstrates a determination to prevent any possible change in what was going on at the seminary.[171]

Fuerbringer abruptly and unexpectedly resigned just two months before the Denver convention, and in his place stepped John Tietjen, a solid, East coast intellectual and moderate. Tietjen was surprised by the decision, having considered himself an unlikely choice for the position because he was an easterner. "The East coast," he later wrote, "was a fringe area for the Missouri Synod and had a mind-set often out of touch with the Midwest, where LCMS members predominated."[172] Conservative professors Scharlemann and Ralph Bohlmann agreed that Tietjen was an odd choice for the position. Scharlemann had reportedly coveted the position for himself.[173]

Tietjen was a Harms man, ecumenical all the way. He had served as parish pastor, editor of the *American Lutheran*, and public relations director for the LC-USA. He was an accomplished scholar and journalist. He was liberal in ideology and bragged that his education at Union Theological Seminary had "challenged" his Missouri Lutheranism: "To pass the qualifying examinations I had no choice but to come to terms with biblical criticism."[174] But he believed God wanted him in St. Louis and that his mission was to divert attention from what he considered a "smoke screen" of doctrinal crisis to "real issues."[175] He was straightforward and determined to bring Missouri into the new world of biblical criticism. Bohlmann recalls that Tietjen "immediately began telling the church in a somewhat more accurate way . . . that this seminary believed in historical-critical approaches to the Scripture, that it was interested in more ecumenical opportunity for the church, and some other issues that sent signals to the grass-roots of the synod that this seminary was far from changing its course that was tending toward liberalism."[176] John Tietjen was just what Missouri moderates believed they needed. He was confident, loyal, and resolute—all qualities he would need in the tumultuous times that lay ahead.

Right Turn in Denver

By the time of the synod's 1969 convention in Denver, the conservative movement in the Missouri Synod had become a well-oiled machine. Herman Otten was at the height of his influence, furtively coordinating his efforts with the UPC while allowing the UPC to publicly portray independence.[177]

With John Baur's help, Otten planned to expand on the tactics employed at the 1967 convention. Having attended so many conventions, Otten and Baur knew that they were unlikely to have an impact *at* the convention. "You come to a convention," Otten remembered, "you get all these different booths, they give you this literature, this literature, you got this meeting you're going to and that thing, and that thing to go to, you stick it in your briefcase, and after you go home after the convention you read it."[178] So they resolved to influence delegates before the convention. Otten received lists of delegates by early 1969[179] and soon flooded them with his materials:

> You gotta know before convention starts, and that's where we came in. All the time. So at least 20, 25 issues before convention, we bombarded them, see. The delegates. And always start at ground one. Realize, you take a picture of the average member of your congregation, how much do you know? Probably very little. So you gotta look at that level, see. And then you gotta gradually build it up.

Week after week, Otten "hammered away," trusting that even those who might throw away the first free issue would be hooked after ten or twenty.[180]

Behind the scenes, UPC members refined their strategy for the 1969 Denver convention. Otten, Werning, and Swanson backed Ed Weber, a Michigan conservative with a deep, monotone voice and reassuring German tone, to oust Harms.[181] Weber decried Harms as a theological lightweight and, coldly, called for him and Wolbrecht to be "eliminated."[182] Peglau pushed for Preus, a more polished and attractive politician, who eventually became the party's nominee. Werning and Otten were concerned about Preus's commitment to conservatism, but held their tongues for the sake of conservative unity.[183] That spring, Otten's paper featured an "open letter" to Oliver Harms, ghost-written by Werning, calling on Harms to resign.[184] Three weeks before the convention, Otten endorsed Jack Preus on the front page of *Christian News*, earning it the nickname "Jacob's Ladder."[185]

The 1969 biennial convention of the Lutheran Church—Missouri Synod in Denver was as awkward and schizophrenic a gathering as Missouri Lutherans had ever seen. The UPC was ready. For the first time, an LCMS convention had "all the trappings" of a modern, secular political campaign.

Voters were met at the Denver airport with conservative "'hospitality' vans." Conservatives and their supporters wore fishhooks on their jacket lapels to identify party members. Slates of "approved" candidates for office were distributed to delegates. Heading that list was Jack Preus, who, as anointed son of the cryptic UPC, publicly played the modest churchman. "It is not my intent," he claimed, "to inject myself into an office which the church has not asked me to serve."[186] The convention floor was organized to "assure votes according to the will of the party leadership."[187] The UPC reserved rooms in the Albany and DeVille hotels to serve as headquarters while foot soldiers "stepped up the politicking."[188]

Harms and Wolbrecht were stunned by what they saw. Harms opened the convention on Saturday morning, July 12, with a report detailing the exciting business in the days ahead, including a final vote on his pet project, full fellowship with the ALC. Hours before the vote that would seal his fate, Harms gave the traditional presidential address to the delegates. Sensing the growing ideological rift, he implored his brethren one final time to heed his call to racial and ecumenical unity. But the message bore the fruit of his demise, a reference to the same civil rights movement so many white Americans were trying to forget. "Brethren," he pleaded, "let us not create obstacles where there are none." Harms pressed for a "Gospel-powered church" driven by Martin Luther King's message: "Not long ago our nation was awakened by a man who dared to tell of his dreams for his people. He dared to say: 'I have a dream.'" "How desperately," he counseled, "God wants us to bring to a halt this frantic race toward self-destruction."[189] He must have been comforted by the standing ovation that followed. Within hours, the delegates were prepared to vote on his presidency.

But then something happened to change the mood. As bartering on the floor intensified before the vote, executive director Pat Wolbrecht took the microphone, denouncing what he called "serious breaches in the democratic processes" by conservative politicos and admonishing delegates to carry out church business "properly."[190] It was an imprudent move for a man so often portrayed by conservatives as "Pope Wolbrecht," the power behind "Dupe" Harms's throne.[191] Conservatives rationalized that they were, after all, just taking the advice of synod liberals:

For one thing, the official position of the LCMS—spelled out in various
tracts, sermons, radio broadcasts and TV programs—was to encourage the
individual Christian to engage in secular politics. Getting informed, taking
thoughtful views, influencing others (citizens and political leaders) was all
a part of Christian duty.[192]

They rationalized that they were, as Werning later put it, "using political
means to a Godly ends [sic]."[193] After Wolbrecht's harangue, the vote was
taken and the results announced to a shocked convention hall. Oliver Harms
did not win a majority. The voting would continue. The next morning, Jack
Preus asked to take the podium. Ever the politician, the man who had
secretly maneuvered to oust Harms now, too, denounced the "politicking"
and pleaded with delegates to "demonstrate their love toward one another."
He received a standing ovation.[194] Another vote was taken the next morning and the final results were announced: On the third ballot, Harms was
defeated. Jack Preus would be the next president of the Lutheran Church—
Missouri Synod. Of 939 votes cast, Preus won by 80.[195] An exultant Preus
met Otten after the election and boasted, "We did it."[196]

His fate sealed, Harms used his last moments of power to seal his legacy. His report to the church on July 12 chided Missouri for its tendency to
isolate itself from the suffering of the world and from other believers. "The
church," he said, "has apparently forgotten the place and the power of the
Gospel. We betray our faith when we pass by on the other side in order to
avoid seeing or becoming involved. We betray our faith when we resort to
adoption of resolutions or the passing of laws designed to make Christian
people behave the way they ought."[197] American society seemed in 1969 to
be coming apart at the seams. Insisting that doctrinal differences were of
less significance than difficulties in other areas of common life, Harms asked
the delegates one last time to reach out in fraternity to other Christians.

> We are troubled at the tearing of bonds that hold us together in marriage,
> family, the community, and the nation. I hold that we ought to be dis-
> tressed when we seem too ready to dissolve or write off the fraternal bonds
> we have with those who share our faith.

His final words were reserved for the small band of conservatives who had
done him in. The Missouri Synod, he warned, was filled with a climate of

"rumor, suspicion, and competition of all kinds." He had tried since 1967, he explained, to combat rumor by creating "new and refined earlier devices for communicating and for implementing the work of the Synod." "As a result," he exclaimed, "I believe our membership is better informed and perhaps participates more promptly and more widely than in the past." But he knew better, for movements "generally do not emerge in large numbers until they are stimulated by some source."[198]

Christians believe that in death there is new life; so it was for moderates in Denver. Harms turned his razor-thin loss to Preus into a razor-thin victory on the issue of fellowship with the ALC, perhaps sacrificing his political life for what he believed a greater purpose. He urged delegates to approve Resolution 3-23, which resolved that "the Scriptural and confessional basis for altar and pulpit fellowship between The Lutheran Church—Missouri Synod and The American Lutheran Church exists," and urged the synod to make haste in implementing the decision.

Jack Preus may have helped him. Conservative euphoria over his victory was short-lived, because Preus took less than twenty-four hours to disappoint them. The morning following his election, July 14, Jack Preus took the podium to give his acceptance speech. Werning confidently told Preus that morning that conservatives had the votes to kill the resolution on fellowship with the ALC. Yet Preus refused to speak out against the resolution, stating instead that he believed that God had called him to the office of president of the synod and that he would carry out the will of the convention.[199] In an attempt to "win over some of the liberals" or "conservatives thinking with their heart," Werning believed, Preus was telling delegates, "Whatever way it goes, I'll accept it."[200] Now it was the conservatives' turn to be stunned. Larry Marquardt and others were "shocked" at the "apparent ease with which Preus 'capitulated'" on the ALC vote. The vote for fellowship, taken late on Wednesday, won by more than eighty votes—approximately the same margin as Preus's victory.[201] Delegates continued on to affirm woman suffrage in LCMS congregations, confirm the socially activist mission of the LCMS, and lend support to conscientious objection to military service in the Vietnam War.

❉ ❉ ❉

After the convention, Vice President Roland Wiederaenders met Preus and warned, "Jack, you're obligated [to Otten and other conservatives] up to your neck." Preus protested that he knew nothing about campaigning and smoothly claimed that his election was a complete surprise. Then, at a post-convention press conference, he tried to distance himself from his backers. Preus publicly denounced Otten's *Christian News* as "divisive" and pledged that there would be no "head rolling" under his leadership.[202]

Many conservatives were furious. Backtracking to rebuild his base, Preus apologized to Swanson:

> I hope that you understand that in the heat of things in Denver, I prob-
> ably did not always say everything exactly as I should. . . . What you say
> about "Christian News" is very true [Swanson's contention "that Christian
> News presented a more factual, honest, and complete narrative than the
> Lutheran Witness Reporter on given issues and occasions[203]]. I hope there
> is some way that this whole matter can be settled whereby Otten will sim-
> ply not [continue] to be looked upon as the arch-villain of the church.[204]

On the phone that evening, Preus also apologized to Otten and pleaded for his forgiveness.[205] Otten did not know whom to believe: Convention Jack, or this Jack. He accepted Preus's apology but, hedging his bets, secretly tape recorded the conversation.[206]

Herman Otten Jr. founded conservative tabloid *Christian News* following his rejection by Concordia Seminary. He shaped Missouri conservatism with an impact magnified by his freedom from church oversight. Otten was the most significant figure in modern LCMS history.

J. A. O. Preus, president of the LCMS from 1969–1981.

LUTHERAN NEWS, Inc.

421 Filmore Avenue • New Haven, Missouri 63068

publishers of *Christian News*
and other religious material.

March 19, 1977

Dr. Jacob Preus, President
The Lutheran Church—Missouri Synod
500 N. Broadway
St. Louis, Missouri 63102

Dear President Preus:

We've been having some difficulty reaching you. Yesterday we asked your assistant to pass a message on to you. We still hope that you will answer our letter of January 22. A top ELIM sympathizer told us that you shared this letter with others and have said that we were attempting to blackmail you. Is this correct?

If you continue your present policies, it appears to us that for the cause of the Gospel of Christ and the welfare of The Lutheran Church-Missouri Synod it would be best if you would not run for the presidency of the LCMS.

We intend to publish your record in a series of articles which will be sent to all voting delegates to the 1977 convention. The first in the series "A Closer Look at Preus" appears in the March 21 CN. We believe that when the voters study your record and statements the majority will conclude that it would be best if some honest, consistent conservative like Barth, Maier, Zimmerman, Merkens, Weber, etc. were elected.

If you should announce that you are not a candidate for the presidency, then it won't be necessary for us to publish your record which we have in our files. You have told us that you would deny some of these things if we ever published them. If you deny what we publish, you will only be caught deeper in lies.

Our major concern is the stand you now take on ALC fellowship, LCUSA, and disciplinary action against those in the LCMS who deny basic doctrines of Holy Scripture. There is no need for us to tell you about all our concerns. They'll gradually come out as we publish your record. Even your language shows that you haven't shown the kind of dignity necessary for a real churchman like Walther, Pieper, Behnken, etc. When readers read the kind of language you use, they should recognize that this is not the way they want the president of a great church body to talk. They may use such language themselves, but they expect more from the president of their church. Just recently you said that you wrote to Rev. Richard Neuhaus that you were sitting in the smallest room in your house with his paper before you and that in a few moments you would have it behind you. I have this statement and many others far more damaging on tape.

We have defended you many times all over the LCMS. We were probably the first in the LCMS to publicize your orthodox stand and commend you for it. Just check the past issues of CN. You probably know that we attend very few meetings of conservatives.

we preach a crucified Christ 1 Cor. 1:23

First page of a 1977 letter from Herman Otten to Jack Preus threatening to publish secret recordings if Preus again seeks the presidency of the LCMS.

Karl Barth, a Milwaukee pastor, district officer, and founding member of conservative "Faith Forward—First Concerns," a conservative group concerned about issues of "doctrinal purity" in the LCMS.

John W. Behnken, president of the LCMS, 1935–1962.

Ralph A. Bohlmann, one of the "Faithful Five" and president of the LCMS from 1981–1992.

Paul R. Burgdorf, a small-town preacher in Iowa and founder of the paper *Confessional Lutheran*. The first of its kind in Missouri, *Confessional Lutheran* was an extrasynodical venture to keep conservatives informed and active.

Oliver R. Harms, president of the LCMS until 1969, when defeated by J. A. O. Preus in Denver.

Roy Guess, geologist and founding member of the United Planning Conference, founded in 1966 to organize conservatives for the 1967 LCMS Convention in New York.

LUTHERAN NEWS, Inc.

421 Filmore Avenue • New Haven, Missouri 63068

publishers of *Christian News*
and other religious material.

May 17, 1977

Dr. Jacob Preus, President
The Lutheran Church-Missouri Synod
500 N. Broadway
St. Louis, Missouri 63102

Dear President Preus:

We have just received a report which comes from some of
your closest friedds and supporters that you are supposed to have
said that you are going to "annihilate" Fred Rutz and Chet Swahson.
Did you say this and are you out to silence these men?

We have also been told that you are really out to get us and
to xxxxxxxx break us once and for all. Adams in his book quotes you
as telling Martin Mueller: "Can't you print all the news so we can
put Otten out of business?" We've been told that your releasing
confidential information about the charges the Board of Control has
against me is part of your plan to "destroy Otten." Is it true that
you are out to "get us" and silence us? Could you please answer the
question I asked about the Seward matter in my letter of March 28:
"Do you believe the LCMS should have college presidents who defend
professors who hold to anti-scriptural notions?"

We've been planning an editorial on how you treat some of your
friends and opponents and want to make certain that you have been
properly quoted. Adams writes: "The main thing, Preus said, was
that Stegemoeller not get on a high horse and come riding out against
Preus. A 'pissing contest' would only result in both of them getting
wet, Preus said." You have used this phrase in conversations with me
but did you tell this to Stegemoeller?

Sincerely yours,

Herman Otten

Herman Otten

RECEIVED
MAY 17 1977
PRESIDENT'S
OFF CE

we preach a crucified Christ 1 Cor. 1:23

Another letter from Herman Otten to Jack Preus from Preus's 1977 "Blackmail" file.

Gustav Lobeck, a district president from Iowa and co-founder of "Faith Forward–First Concerns." In 1964, he warned of a "dangerous situation" in the LCMS.

Kurt E. Marquart, longtime Otten friend and ally. Marquart consistently advocated for the "regularization" of Otten's clerical status, which he considered key to "pacification" in the church.

Walter A. Maier II, theology professor and son of the famed *Lutheran Hour* speaker, was editor of the conservative publication *Affirm* and later a synod vice president.

New Haven, Missouri
February 17, 1965

The Praesidium of The Lutheran Church–Missouri Synod
c/o Dr. Oliver Harms
210 North Broadway
St. Louis 2, Missouri

Dear Gentlemen:

The February, 1965 issue of _Spirit_ has
announced that Peter Seeger is scheduled to be on
the program of the 1965 Walther League convention.

Since various documents by the House Committee
on American Activities refer to Peter Seeger as
a member of the Communist Party, could you kindly
inform us whether you will ask Walther League officials
to reconsider their plans to have Seeger on the convention program?

A good number of Missouri Synod Lutherans are
already disturbed about the Seeger announcement and
are wondering what action the Praesidium of their
church will take about this matter.

Sincerely,

Herman Otten

Herman Otten, editor
LUTHERAN NEWS

Letter from Herman Otten to LCMS President Oliver Harms warning him against allowing
Pete Seeger to sing at the 1965 Walther League convention.

John Warwick Montgomery, lawyer, theologian, philosopher, and author. Renowned for his debating skills, he was referred to by conservatives as John "Warlike" Montgomery.

J. T. Mueller, an aging professor at Concordia Seminary who spurred Otten to action but hid at a nearby hotel when Otten faced disciplinary action.

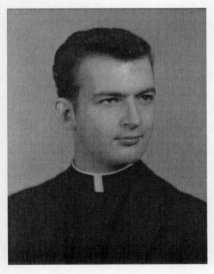

Richard John Neuhaus, son of a conservative vice president in LCMS Canada, was a Missouri moderate who gave public support for the civil rights movement and against the war in Vietnam. A pastor of a predominately black and Hispanic congregation in Brooklyn, New York, Neuhaus later joined the American Lutheran Church and, in 1990, was ordained a Roman Catholic priest.

Ellis Nieting, a pastor from Iowa and early member of both "Faith Forward—First Concerns" and the United Planning Conference. Jack Preus put Nieting in charge of the Constitutional Matters committee at the 1971 convention.

Glen Peglau, a wealthy attorney who supported Jack Preus but never fully trusted him. Peglau and Otten secretly recorded several phone conversations with Preus.

E. J. Otto, a Preus ally on Concordia Seminary's Board of Control and chair of Balance, Inc.

Robert D. Preus, first president of Balance, Inc., a conservative interest group founded after brother Jack's victory in 1969. "The key politician [in the synod]," remembers Ralph Bohlmann, "was Robert Preus, not Jack."

Waldo Werning, conservative pastor from Nebraska and leader of a movement that would blossom into "Faith Forward—First Concerns," the most significant conservative interest group in Missouri Synod history.

Martin H. Scharlemann, former liberal icon turned neoconservative who assumed control of Concordia Seminary upon President Tietjen's suspension in January 1973.

Edwin Weber, Otten's choice for LCMS president in 1969, called for President Oliver Harms and Executive Director Walter "Pat" Wolbrecht to be "eliminated."

Paul Zimmerman, a conservative convert from the Norwegian Synod, served as "special assistant" to Preus and headed the investigation of Concordia Seminary. He was later named president of the synod's college in River Forest, Illinois.

CONCORDIA LUTHERAN JUNIOR COLLEGE

4090 GEDDES ROAD
ANN ARBOR, MICHIGAN 48105

February 11, 1972

President J.A.O. Preus
The Lutheran Church - Missouri Synod
210 N. Broadway
St. Louis, Missouri 63102

Dear Jack,

Just a brief note to say that I rather believe that Chet Swanson is right
in saying that it is in the best interest of everyone concerned to settle
the question of what the 5-5 vote in connection with the Herman Otten
case really means. I believe that you can ask for a definite ruling on
this that will legally settle the question once and for all. I don't see
how you can lose. Those who favor Otten will feel that you are being
fair. Those who oppose Otten can hardly object to this that you say it
is high time that his cause for complaint of unfairness be settled
definitely so that the matter does not continue to be something used
to irritate the church. I believe you can take the position of being
very neutral about the whole thing and simply indicate that it is in the
interest of the church that a matter that has been unsettled for ten
years be finally laid to rest.

There are some other possibilities involved here, but I really see
nothing that would hurt you, particularly if you make it clear that you
are talking about it purely as an administrative matter.

Yours in Christ,

Paul A. Zimmerman

PAZ:sw

Letter from Paul Zimmerman to Jack Preus urging him to once and for all settle the matter of
Herman Otten's clerical status.

3

Power, Politics, and the Purge: 1969–1974

The months following Preus's victory in Denver set the stage for battles that would consume most Missouri politicos for decades to come. Conservatives wasted little time celebrating their conquest and soon moved to consolidate their power and promote their individual agendas. Yet the more secure Preus's power seemed, the less conservatives could identify common threats and remain unified. Infighting soon followed.

The situation was quite different for moderates. Preus's victory had blindsided them. While a conservative victory was something most thought possible, few found themselves prepared to handle the reality. Few doubted where the conservative victory would lead. A showdown over Concordia Seminary, the place where, at least for Otten, it all began a decade earlier, seemed inevitable.

Evidence that moderates little expected defeat is found in an article in *Lutheran Witness* previewing the upcoming convention. In an issue published in late 1968, the *Witness* predicted progress beyond what moderates had achieved in 1967 and called upon delegates to further acknowledge "social responsibilities." This, they argued, was a "time for boldness; we have the chance to pioneer."[1] After the convention, angry moderates wanted to expose the unexpected and blatant "politicking" at the convention. Pat Wolbrecht received a handwritten note in late July from Ray Holsten, executive director of the Lutheran Benevolent Association: "I have heard that

the L.L.L. [Lutheran Laymen's League] was involved in this effort [to elect
Preus]. Is this true? If not, could you tell me what group did initiate this
'underground' effort?"[2]

Shock and confusion characterized the initial reactions of moderates.
Some retreated into grief, others geared up for battle. Robert Preus recalled
the reaction of the Concordia faculty following Jack's election:

> The faculty was absolutely aghast. Right after Jack's election, I went up the
> elevator with one of the professors then by the name of Walter Bartling
> who was just weeping, profusely. I said, "Why are you weeping?" He said,
> "Your brother was just elected president of the synod. He'll destroy our
> church." The faculty immediately went into all sorts of meetings.[3]

Concordia professor Fred Danker, with others, worried for the future of
seminary intellectuals, conceding that Preus had the support of synod laity,
"especially those in the Middle West."[4]

Others remained in denial. The staff at synod headquarters made little
effort to welcome their new chief, settling only for a late-timed "Kool Aid
and cookies affair" (organized by Wolbrecht, who had invited Preus earlier
that year to a party to celebrate Tietjen's election as seminary president).[5]
In the months following the Denver convention, the *Witness* proceeded as
if moderate power was undiminished in the synod. Articles continued to
appear on race relations and ecumenical social action. A report by the synod's Commission on Social Action, detailed in the *Witness,* promised to study
"civil disobedience, smoking, tax exemption for churches, science, sexual
morality, Vietnam, and nuclear warfare," exploring all-new territory for the
LCMS.[6] One of only a handful of acknowledgments of Preus's election came
in the form of an arrogant lamentation of a "shift to conservatism" evident in
the results of the 1968 election of Nixon, paralleling what had happened at
Denver. Rather than accept the mood of synod laity (who not only resented
certain theological and social change but wanted church leadership to stay
out of politics), editors complained of a malleable churchgoing public. "The
quest for security," they reproached, "can easily make people suspicious and
inspire needless fear and prejudice. Then conservatism, instead of being a
form of political persuasion, is transformed into a reactionary, repressive
method of preventing change."[7]

In part, liberals' cautious optimism was bolstered by Jack Preus's early gestures of moderation. *Witness* editor Martin Mueller, having nervously assured Preus that "our columns will be open to you," was pleased with what he initially saw.[8] A February 1970 article in the *Witness* reported Preus's meeting with the New York Metro Mission Movement. Preus talked as if he, too, genuinely supported the synod's Mission Affirmations, speaking of Missouri's responsibility to "Mission to the Whole Society." When asked about an October 1969 *Newsweek* article about the conservative, white middle-class backlash, Preus responded, "This cannot take place for us as Christians. . . . Maybe the only voice the poor will have left is the church. It is time for the clergy of this area to stick very close together and resist what is apt to become a major trend in our country."[9] Also, in spite of backtracking privately, Preus continued to distance himself publicly from his conservative backers. In October 1969, Preus signed on to a statement issued by the synod's Council of Presidents that roundly condemned Otten's *Christian News*:

> We are of the conviction that the publication now known as "Christian News," disseminated with or without the prior consent of those who receive it, is an obstacle to the furtherance of the objectives of the Synod, breeds mistrust, creates unnecessary tensions, and disturbs God's servants in the performance of their tasks. We, therefore, unanimously repudiate this publication and caution against lending credence and support to it.[10]

In private, Preus tried to assuage moderates and avoid early conflict. During a November dinner meeting with seminary president Tietjen, Preus suggested that Tietjen appease conservatives by offering up a sacrificial lamb, Arthur C. Repp, Concordia's vice president for academic affairs, the same man who had overseen Otten's dismissal and non-certification. Tietjen adamantly refused.[11] A chance meeting with Martin Marty in 1969 highlighted Preus's gift for backroom banter. Marty, who was then on the editorial board of the *Lutheran Witness-Reporter*, was shifted by Preus to the synod's Committee on Social Concerns. (Some took to calling Marty "Preus's Moynihan," a reference to Daniel Patrick Moynihan, a Democrat who was an advisor to President Nixon.) After attending the committee's first meeting at synod headquarters in St. Louis, Preus struck up a conversation with Marty in a men's room and invited him to his office. Once seated, Marty volunteered to quietly resign his new posting, but Preus would have none of it: "No, Marty, you are exactly right for that job. I went over the whole clergy roster and picked the right person for each post. You are the first name that comes to mind for Social Concern." A minute later Preus displayed a chart on his plans for restructuring the synod. "Now, that Committee on Social Concern; we've got to redefine it," he pressed Marty. "It isn't worth a pile of shit."[12]

But Preus needed to show conservative backers that changes were in the works. So he set his sights on the editorial staff at the *Lutheran Witness* and *Lutheran Witness-Reporter*. Downward trends in subscription levels at the two periodicals continued even after Preus's election.[13] Initially wary, Preus distanced himself from the staff of the synod's mouthpieces. Editors at the *Reporter* complained that they knew less about Preus than did the *Lutheran Layman*, *Christian News*, and other publications. This reflected Preus's conscious decision to bypass Missouri's Public Relations Department. (For example, the PR staff did not know in advance about Preus's 1971 trip to North Vietnam.)[14] But conservatives weren't satisfied. They demanded quick action to axe editors. Preus expressed concern about Omar Stuenkel's "Flick Chart" column in the *Reporter*, which reviewed films that some, including Preus, considered "filthy" or "pornographic."[15] Edwin Weber complained publicly that the *Reporter* was "deficient."[16] Preus assured his conservative backers that change was coming, though it would take time:

> I believe that there are some changes on the Witness and Reporter staff in the works. Remember that I cannot fire such people, but rather that it requires the action of the Board, which has just now come into being. . . . I wish you would be a little patient. I am really quite optimistic about things, and I believe that before too long we will begin to show some improvement. However, the whole matter is going to take a very long time.[17]

Bringing change to his administration proved even harder for Preus. Under heavy pressure to let "heads roll" in St. Louis, Preus quickly backtracked from early promises to "take the axe to [First Vice President Roland] Wiederaenders,"[18] who was an associate and friend of Harms but a theological conservative.[19] With Harms gone, Pat Wolbrecht, the synod's executive director, was the focus of the conservative bull's-eye. Preus told Wolbrecht privately that he wanted to build a partnership: "Pat, you cooperate with me and we can run this church for a generation." In typical Preus style, he told Wolbrecht in September 1969 that he would fight those seeking the executive director's dismissal. But on October 9, the synod's Board of Directors met and voted 8 to 6, at Preus's urging, to ask for Wolbrecht's resignation. When Wolbrecht mentioned "legal counsel" and raised the specter of a fight, the Board reconsidered and, instead, slapped him with a gag order.[20] When Preus and Wolbrecht met later, Preus blamed the affair on the wishes of his wife, Delpha, who, like Herodias of John the Baptist fame, wanted Wolbrecht's head on a platter.[21]

Conservatives were furious that Wolbrecht was still around. In a letter to a supporter the day after the decision, Preus wrote:

> The report in *Christian News* is correct. The reason was that the Board, for
> . . . what it felt was the sake of peace in the Synod, decided that this would
> not be a wise time to take this step.[22]

Still, Preus continued on his slow and steady approach to cleaning house. Preus maintained later that the "Harms era will in many respects be known as the Wolbrecht era." Harms's biggest mistake, Preus asserted, was that "he allowed his underlings to get out in front and be too visible."[23] It was a mistake he would not make. In the months that followed, he continued to correspond with synod attorneys and finally succeeded in having Wolbrecht's position abolished by the 1971 Synodical Convention.[24]

Preus tried to maintain a delicate balancing act of avoiding a painful split in the synod while at the same time working to purge it of his adversaries—all the while holding anxious conservatives at bay. The edited transcript of a series of taped conference calls between Preus, Otten, and Glen Peglau (a wealthy attorney who supported but never fully trusted Preus) illumines the lengths to which Preus went in private to appease his most conservative backers (text is printed as in transcript):

> J.P. I think, Glen, we aught [sic] to think of two courses. If we can't drive
> the libs out then we may have to propose some kind of equal division or
> what do you call it—a proportionate division of the Church.

G.P. Wiederanders figures we're going to dump him.

J.P. I didn't realize he was that bright.

G.P. He's a real dangerous guy—he would crucify us for three cents.

J.P. Wiederanders would murder you.

J.P. I have given up the idea that you can ever heal the wounds. You can't bridge the Synod. It's too far apart. About all that we can do is just try to seize the control . . . that the liberals cannot get the property—then we'll just have to dump them. We are not going to make over these people. They are committed liberals. If conservatives can win some thunderous victories then we can be like the old Norwegians and give them six months where they want to belong. When it is all over count the hats and divy up the property proportionately. I believe the only way to bring about a settlement in this thing is to have a division. Do it in a legal and amicable way as you can. Don't talk about this.

J.P. I caved in on Herman. You are what the Russians call a holy man. Herman, you are an innocent soul, the way to succeed in this world is to be bad not good. Get the goods on them and tell them to beat it.

J.P. I'm going to tell Bert Frey: "If this is the way you guys are going to play it, buster, you're going to regret the day you were born." It's suddenly going to dawn on these guys that like it or not a new Pharaoh has arisen in Egypt.

[On ALC Fellowship]: J.P. I guess I shouldn't have said that. I could have used the ultimate weapon and said if you vote for this thing elect a new president. That would have killed it. But it would have split Synod. Was just about to do this but then got rising vote of confidence. Herman, give it to the ALC and LCA every day of your life. Review their Sunday School Material. It's best not to have you as president of my fan club. Don't say things too nice. Say some bad things. Don't ever spill some of this stuff that you know. It's just to be taken to the grave. If you do or if Waldo spills or if you do I'll have to go to Southern Australia and I probably won't have the money to get there.

J.P. Herman and I have been in contact for years at Springfield—it worked beautifully. We got along just fine. It made my life much easier for me up there. There was no way in the world in which these libs could call attention to what I was doing.

G.P. Burn these libs to the ground.

J.P. But I was speaking in handbook language, Glen.[25]

Chet Swanson continued to mistrust Preus in the wake of Preus's post-election repudiations of Otten. He blasted Preus for "your depicting Christian News in a light that would do justice to Messrs. Wolbrecht, Harms, Krieger, etc.," arguing that "even in discussions and debates with liberal pastors, I have gained admission that Christian News presented a more factual, honest and complete narrative than the Lutheran Witness Reporter on given issues and occasions."[26]

For his part, however, Otten kept the faith, even to the point of losing his own supporters. In an August letter to Preus, in which he sticks to his eccentric "we," he assured Preus that they were still solidly in the same "camp":

> P.S. We've lost a number of friends and good supporters because of what we've said since the convention. We've defended you but they have no confidence in the new administration. Some, of course, who have condemned us are malcontents as Marcus Braun mentioned in his speech at Davenport before the Free Conference. One pastor, who visited us, wouldn't even shake our hand after we said that you should be given some time.[27]

A week later he continued to express fidelity even while evincing impatience. "We're asking our readers not to criticize you," he told Preus. "However, one report circulating is somewhat disturbing."[28]

But private assurances to and about Otten and other backers rarely matched Preus's public voice. While he made liberal, clandestine use of *Christian News*, he worked hard to distance himself from Otten publicly. The night before Preus's October repudiation of Otten before the synod's Council of Presidents, Preus put in a conference call to Peglau and Otten. "Herm," he said, "they're going to repudiate you. I don't have the votes to stop it."[29] On October 3, the Council passed the statement unanimously. (It carries Preus's signature, but the minutes reflect that he remained silent during the meeting.)[30] They sent a letter to Otten "asking him to cease and desist from his present activities in accordance with the concerns expressed in the statement of the Council of Presidents, and indicate our pastoral concern also for him."[31] The next day Preus called Otten again: "I'm awfully sorry— and I sincerely apologize for having to do that to you."[32] So did several others. (Some district presidents soon withdrew their signatures. Others stuck to private apologies.[33]) Preus and others later denied having apologized to Otten.[34] In the following weeks, Preus dealt with angry complaints about his repudiation of Otten.[35] Chet Swanson pushed Preus to reverse his decision. Give Otten his "day in court," urged Swanson. "Or, if the day in court is not prudent nor possible, an apology should be issued."[36]

What emerged in the early months of Preus's presidency set the pattern for the decade to follow. As the synod's most powerful conservative, he served as the movement's de facto leader. Yet it became evident that there was no single "movement," only a bloc of like-minded, influential men with a common interest in purging the synod of liberalism. Preus worked hard to sustain a tenuous and often fraudulent and perverse relationship with many conservatives, particularly with Otten, whom he needed for publicity and to mobilize support. (And Otten needed Preus, suggests Fred Danker, to "balance the books" with seminary professors.)[37]

Preus was a pure politician in the sense that unswerving commitment to ideological (and perhaps theological) purity often took a backseat to political interests and long-range pragmatism. "You've got to bide your time, keep your mouth shut, lay your plans, do your work," he stated in a 1981 interview, which remained sealed until 2000, "and then at the right time what you want, there you go."[38] In 1969, Preus was biding his time. Both Otten and Preus looked forward to battle with the moderates, but they differed on strategy. Otten argued for open heresy trials:

> You gotta have, it doesn't sound good, you gotta have a heresy trial. You gotta give the guys a forum to express their view, and then you gotta have the opposition, and then determine what they teach, study the documents, and then you finally decide whether he's teaching in accord with Scripture and the Lutheran Confessions or not. That's how you deal with it.

Preus told Otten that there was simply too much red tape involved with a heresy trial, and that he wanted to get rid of heretics his way.[39] And the

"Preus way," according to Herman Otten, might have involved a more disturbing tactic:

> In fact, one of the things he said, "get some of these pastors, you know, some of them shack up with their confirmands, or something, you get something on them about sex, and tell them scram." I [Otten] says "Bologna." I said, "I don't tolerate sex offenders, but that's not the way to deal with it. You gotta deal with it right out in the open."[40]

Although he initially sustained relationships with Otten and others with private assurances of support, it is clear that at least from the beginning of his first term in office, Jack Preus had no intention of honoring many of his promises. In November 1969, shortly after his repudiation of Otten (and subsequent apology), Preus wrote to a friend, "I think your analysis of <u>Christian News</u> is correct. I believe that in the long run the Council of Presidents will emerge as strongermen [sic] and as more concerned about the true welfare of the church because they have done it."[41] In a two-hour meeting with Martin Mueller on September 4, Preus openly discussed his disdain for Otten. Like Nixon, Preus was obsessed with closing a widening "credibility gap" between the people and their leaders, which he attributed in part to publications like Otten's:

> Direct efforts to counteract publications like <u>Christian News</u> are futile. The best defense against the half-truth, innuendo, guilt by association, character assassination, etc., the stock-in-trade of propaganda organs, is communication of the truth—the what, when, where, how, and especially the WHY.

The only solution, Preus argued, was the development of a "truth squad."[42]

Pressure from the Right

The first months of Preus's presidency were filled with pressure—and Jack Preus did not like to be pressured. "The abuse of people like Herman Otten and in an earlier period the Seminex people," he later remembered, "the plain psychological abuse I have found to be very, very unpleasant. I don't like it. I don't make any secret about it."[43] At times the pressure got to him. He grew weary rapidly of "all the negativism that keeps pouring into my office from all sides every day."[44] "I have gotten kind of discouraged and often times have felt like throwing in the towel," he wrote to one layman in October, "but I guess I will have to stay with it. Things are looking up, and I am beginning to feel as if maybe the good Lord hasn't completely deserted us."[45]

Otten's influence in the LCMS was a beast Preus had fed and now needed to tame. By late 1969, some of Preus's friends were perplexed by a constant stream of "leaks" to Otten from high-placed supporters in the synod. At first, Preus wrote off the leaks as the work of a disgruntled Wolbrecht.[46] But when it became clear that the kind of information being leaked was beyond Wolbrecht's reach, fingers pointed elsewhere. Carl Muhlenbruch, a member of the synod's Board of Directors, expressed concern to Preus that it was the work of a fellow Board member. A letter dated November 5, 1969, suggests that Preus himself may have been the source. Another layman had written Preus to complain, without naming Otten or *Christian News*, that information from the Board of Directors was being leaked to "unauthorized parties." Preus responded, "I do not know who leaked information to <u>Christian News</u>."[47]

Longtime friend Karl Barth commented on Preus's early troubles and long-range vision. Conservatives, Barth stated, felt that Preus owed them something "because they got him elected." But Preus "wasn't the kind of person to give payback." Jack, he observed, was not a purist, which made him less predictable than his opponents on the left and right. Preus would tell Barth, "I'm given to temporary periods of insanity." In coming conventions, Preus would always make sure that there were liberals on the floor committees, Barth recounted, but never enough to determine the outcome. Preus "knew where he was going, knew where the end line was. And he wasn't afraid to go this way sometimes, or that way. . . . Just about the time the conservatives were ready to ditch him, he'd swoop down and slap some liberal." This was his strategy for "outflanking"[48] his more ideologically steadfast rivals. "I can defeat Tietjen easily," Preus told Barth, "because Tietjen is very predictable. You always know what he's going to do. But they don't know what I'm going to do."[49]

Otten was not the only one pressuring Preus from the right. On Labor Day 1969, conservatives, including at least one from each LCMS district, met in Chicago and organized what became known as the "Continuation Committee." Most of its leaders were holdovers from the United Planning Conference (UPC) who were unwilling to trust the movement's fate to Preus. The group included Preus's own brother, Robert. Now that he was running the LCMS, Jack saw no reason to continue organizing politically on the right: his first reaction was to tell Werning to "call it off." Werning refused. The group soon organized a foundation called Balance, Inc. to permanently provide form and funds to the movement.[50] When Balance, Inc. elected Robert its first president, Jack was "livid."[51] Werning's journal idea soon took shape in the form of a periodical, *Affirm*. The Continuation Committee, Lang and Werning would argue later, achieved its purpose in solidifying conservatives for the time being. But it served Jack Preus as well by pacifying "the right-wing conservatives for a couple of years."[52]

Preus's answer to pressure from conservatives was the "Ping-Pong Club." With some regularity, Preus would gather conservatives from across the spectrum for lengthy meetings around a ping-pong table in the basement of his St. Louis home. While it was rarely the same group, old UPC regulars like Werning and Peglau attended faithfully. Otten, sworn to secrecy, attended at least once.[53] New faces included layman Henry Hilst, Concordia professor and rising conservative star Ralph Bohlmann, and Preus confidant and "special assistant" Paul Zimmerman, who was a fellow immigrant from the Norwegian Synod. Preus biographer James Adams says that Zimmerman was a powerful figure by 1972: "Preus was often heard saying 'Zimmerman would never buy that.'"[54] Chet Swanson was also a regular at the meetings, where he gave "reports on the field."[55] Preus served drinks and sandwiches, then sat back and listened—all day long. Bohlmann remembers them as uncomfortable affairs designed to placate critics. "I would sit down there," recollected Bohlmann, "he was chairing, he would always bring me along as a witness. We would listen to these people talk, and basically make demands of him."[56] The Ping-Pong Club was constructed to create the illusion of unity. As long as conservatives had a common goal to purge the seminary, the façade would hold.

Waldo Werning, who had organized and led the insurgency and remained Preus's close adviser, contends that by 1970 he was growing increasingly uncomfortable with Preus's tactics and the "unchurchmanlike" actions of the Council of Presidents. Werning argued that before Preus's election in 1969, conservatives had no choice but to organize an independent and often secretive political party that depended on Otten's *Christian News* as its mouthpiece. Working with Otten was an "emergency" measure, a necessary evil:

> No other alternatives or options appeared since the Synodical system was closed to us, and none of us had any other insights as to what the right course might be under the circumstances. Under God, we did the best we could. As I look at it even today, I can think of no other way that the turnaround could have been accomplished, even though I am very uneasy about using a political organization to do what Biblical procedures should have done, but they were not available to us because the party of the left held us hostage.

But now that Preus held the reins of power in the church, Werning argued privately, it was time to return to "Biblical procedures":

> On a number of occasions both in personal and telephone visits and in letters, I tried from early on to encourage the President, my good friend and ally, to avoid administrative and political tactics as much as possible, but to follow Biblical procedures, to major in theology and to avoid depending too much on procedures.[57]

Preus's ideological infidelity grated on Werning. "He told me a number of times," Werning recalled, "well, we can't win that one. So we're not going to do it." But "delayed justice," Werning believed, "is perverted justice."[58] Where Preus opted for delay and backroom politicking, Werning pushed for action. "The Synod's Constitution and By-Laws," he told Preus, "are sufficient to get the job done."[59] "We must stop private assurances of Synod and District leaders while maintaining public silence. Why must we depend," Werning complained, "upon a political organization instead of active leaders to bring the Synod back to its historic Biblical position?"[60] If Preus continued to rely on what Werning called the "political tactics of the left," Missouri would surely end up like American troops in Vietnam, where "loyal troops are running and bailing out while the Cong is on the attack."[61]

At the same time, Werning continued to participate in the conservative movement's shrouded politics. In late 1970, following a letter from Otten to Preus (with copy to Werning) in which Otten implied that Larry Marquardt and others might spill the beans about Preus's involvement with UPC and Balance, Werning urged restraint and unity. Reminding Otten that these men had committed themselves to "confidential involvement," Werning urged Otten to work for unity in "conservaland."

> There will be peace within the conservative camp when that very small minority who are grieved for real reasons but use wrong methods to make their point become positive and join in a positive fight against the liberal elements within our Synod.[62]

Fred Rutz, who had been bullying LCMS presidents since the 1950s, continued as synod's self-appointed financial watchdog, even though his man was in office. Preus had been complaining privately that the conservative tactic of withholding contributions from synod's budget was continuing under his leadership. "In some churches which have even the worst spending record than ours [sic]," he wrote in November, "contributions are actually on the increase."[63] Preus was right to be concerned. Contributions to the synodical budget from local congregations and districts continued to drop between 1969 and 1970.[64] Rutz, who would soon serve as treasurer of Balance, Inc., answered that Preus had not done anything to merit an alteration in giving patterns. He argued in a letter to Preus in September 1969 that God had actually blessed him for withholding funds from the synod's budget:

1. When you say that Synod has settled down you are living in a fantasy land, a fool's paradise. Its [sic] just a lull before the storm, giving you an opportunity to correct the destructive administration policies of the prior administration;

2. You state withholding of funds accomplishes nothing, you are mistaken. Since I have discontinued contributing to synod and diverted my funds, my income has increased to such an extent that I have increased my contributions 50%;

3. You say that the cooperation you have received has been most grati-
    fying. Well, why should they not cooperate when you have done
    nothing to change their destructive administration policies.[65]

Rutz included a copy of a letter sent to the Springfield seminary indicating
that he would halt his contributions to that institution until its next president
was appointed. And he included a threat to Preus: Do what we elected you
to do, or else. "I hasten to write to you as your recent articles in the Witness Reporter has [sic] caused a furor among those who supported you for
president. If you continue such writings, you could have the distinction of
becoming the first one-term president of the Lutheran Church."[66] In February 1970, when Preus made his choice for president of the Springfield
seminary, Rutz accused him of "coddling the liberals. . . . You will regret this
as it is going to cause you much grief. As you sow so shall you reap."[67]

Preus continued to do just enough to appease conservatives. In early
October, wealthy supporter Roy Guess protested to Preus about William
Wessler, a member of the *Reporter*'s Editorial Commission, who had written an article sympathetic to black author and poet Langston Hughes. The
LCMS, Guess complained, should not be promoting and praising "individuals [like Hughes] who have been identified as Communists."[68] Signi-
fying Missouri conservatism's ties to a broader conservative movement,
Guess attached several articles on Hughes from *The Concerned Presbyterian* and *Methodist Laymen of North Hollywood*. Preus responded first
by playing dumb. "I had no idea that Langston Hughes was involved in
communist activities," he claimed. "I had never even heard of him."[69] But
within the week, Wessler was out of a job. A fuming Martin Mueller tore
into Guess:

> Would Roy Guess like to be judged solely by some of the things he has said
> in cold print? Would he like to be told that a recent letter of his in *Chris-
> tian News* proves he is on the far-out ultra-right fringe using the propagan-
> dist's technique of "divide and conquer"? Men of goodwill and charity who
> became acquainted with Roy Guess along the way will likely say after his
> demise that Roy was a sincere contender for Christian truth as he knew it
> and as he encountered it first as a Baptist, then as a Methodist, then as a
> Presbyterian, and then as a Lutheran.[70]

Charges, Mistrust, and Secrecy

By 1970, the atmosphere of distrust and intrigue was growing even stronger in the Missouri Synod. Moderate Richard Koenig argued that the conservatives who emerged victorious in Denver were men consumed with a "fear of the Blacks, fear of 'liberals,' fear of change."[71] Soon that fear translated into underground action, what Richard John Neuhaus called "manifest institutional paranoia."[72] Paul Zimmerman disagreed, dismissing the talk of "secret groups" as "a bunch of bull." Yes, he argued, political groups did often meet in secret and did gather information from districts, often circumventing district presidents, but it happened on both sides of the ideological divide.[73] Regardless, eavesdropping, tape recording, and spying extended on both sides of the ideological fence, typically followed by indictments. Walter Bouman, professor at the synod's college in River Forest, Illinois, had charges of false doctrine filed against him by Walter Otten following a lecture at a Valparaiso University symposium on creation and evolution. Paul Zimmerman had been one of the conservative participants.[74] Conservatives were not averse to espionage. Through 1971, a secretary at Grace Lutheran Church in River Forest, a stronghold of an emerging moderate organization, funneled private information to Werning, who fed it to Preus.[75] In August 1971, a suspicious F. Dean Lueking, Grace's pastor, threatened to have his staff submit to lie detector tests. His secretary left and never returned.[76] Suspicion ruled the day. At a pastors' conference in the fall of 1969, Preus publicly chided a Lutheran reporter for taping remarks. And during a September 1972 meeting, Preus accused a layman of taping the proceedings. Unable to see the man's hands, Preus interrupted his speech, snapping, "Have you got a tape recorder under there?" The layman, Leslie Kuhlmann, had been clipping his nails under the table.[77]

In early 1970, Herman Otten brought official charges against Martin Marty for his comments cited in *Playboy*.[78] Otten expected Preus to take action where Harms had not, but he encountered the same stone wall. Preus had no real interest in combating Marty. Over Otten's protests, Preus was able to slowly kill the charges by grinding them up in the synodical machinery. Although Otten had been peppering Marty with letters, Preus dealt with Otten's charges the same way the seminary had over a decade before. He enforced the Matthew 18 principle: "The question arose as to whether you had gone through the proper synodical channels on this matter. Neither [English District President] Doctor [Bertwin] Frey nor I knew whether you had ever consulted with Doctor Marty about your charges. You understand that procedurally it is necessary for you first to talk to the person in question and then also to deal directly with his district president." Marty assured Preus in a letter dated June 28, "Nowhere in my scores of books . . . did I attack 'inerrancy.'"[79] Preus responded that he was satisfied, and the issue, for all but Otten, faded away.[80]

On Easter Sunday 1970, Fred Danker, red-haired professor of exegetical theology at Concordia, rendezvoused with seminary president John Tietjen after an urgent phone call. Danker had been eavesdropping on a conversation in Robert Preus's office between Robert and his brother, Jack. (Danker claimed that he "could not help but hear the talk through his window.") In the conversation Danker overheard, the Preus brothers outlined a strategy for Jack's next step, an investigation of the seminary. They had discussed three options: Preus could ask the seminary's Board of Control to investigate, he could ask Martin Scharlemann (now in the conservative camp)[81] to ask the Board of Control to investigate, or Preus could do it himself by assembling a presidential fact-finding commission (headed by his intimate, Zimmerman). Both Preus brothers thought the first two options too risky, because there were too many members of the Board of Control who could not be controlled. The third option was the craftiest. Jack could fulfill his presidential obligations as chief theological officer, while maintaining distance and allowing someone else to do the dirty work.[82]

In January 1970, a "liberal faction" of professors, clergy, and laymen met in St. Louis to protest the growing spirit of factionalism and suspicion in the Missouri Synod.[83] The group had met initially in November after Preus sacked Richard Jungkuntz from his position as executive secretary of the synod's CTCR. The firing, which showcased Preus's knack for duplicity, was "star-chamber dealing all the way."[84] It was the second time Jack Preus had played the powerless advocate and restrained reconciler to Jungkuntz, only to push for his ouster behind closed doors.[85] In response, the assembly of moderates, which included *Witness* editor Omar Stuenkel, Chicago pastor

F. Dean Lueking, and students and faculty from Concordia Seminary, publicly issued a "Call to Openness and Trust," calling for "diversity in unity."[86]
The document, sent to all officials of the synod and circulated to national
media, was a tactical disaster for Missouri moderates. It put in black and
white what conservatives had been claiming all along, that theological liberalism—a rejection of the synod's traditional doctrine of biblical inerrancy and
infallibility—existed in Missouri. For the first time, a public case was being
made against inerrancy and infallibility, even if couched in language that
seemed rather to advocate diversity. "We identify too," the group claimed,
"with the historical confessions of the Lutheran Church understood, as all
statements must be, in the historical setting and terms of their time. . . .
The Gospel that is Christ," they continued, "is not a doctrine which equates
Gospel with Bible." At the core of the document were six principles:

> We specifically hold that differences concerning: (1) the manner of the
> creation of the universe by God, (2) the authorship and literary form of any
> books of the Bible, (3) the definition of the presence of Christ in the Lord's
> Supper, (4) the moral obligation of Christians in individual or corporate
> action, (5) the question of factual error in the Bible, and (6) the role and
> authority of clergy in the church are not to be the basis for inclusion or
> exclusion of people among the true disciples of Jesus Christ or member-
> ship in the Missouri Synod.[87]

The document galvanized conservatives. In March, Otten filed formal
charges against Warren Gritzke, chairman of the group that had published
the "Call to Openness and Trust." In April, he filed more charges, this
time against Bertwin Frey, who was at the time defending both Gritzke
and Marty. While Preus took no action on the formal charges, he did ask
the Committee on Theology and Church Relations (CTCR), which, with
Jungkuntz gone, was now stacked in his favor, to evaluate the "Call to Openness and Trust." The CTCR's reaction was severe: Certain "moderate" elements of "A Call to Openness and Trust" were "in serious disagreement with
the confessional position of the Lutheran Church—Missouri Synod." The
Commission chastised the group for downgrading "the importance of true
Christian doctrine" and for challenging "the synod's historic understanding
of what it means to be a confessional church."[88] Preus himself "exploded in

print," criticizing the document's authors as "troublers of Israel" and inviting them to "leave our fellowship." Stuenkel, who had criticized conservative "doctrinal reviewers" who censored the *Witness,* resigned in protest in May, as did the synod's public information officer, Kenneth Lindsay. Syndicated columnist Lester Kinsolving, branding Preus "Chairman Jao," warned the church that more was coming. "Less than one year after the election of Rev. Jacob A. O. Preus . . . the headquarters of the Missouri Synod looks like a Parisian guillotine basket, circa 1793."[89]

Changes in St. Louis following Stuenkel's resignation were reflected in the *Lutheran Witness.* Missouri's "voice for the poor," as Preus had called it, fell silent in the years after the Denver convention.[90] Like a car out of gas, racial progressivism and social action in the *Witness* rolled forward only by force of inertia until reaching a virtual stop by 1973. More and more, the *Witness* became a bulletin board for official reports and counter-reports as the synod polarized around Preus on the right and the seminary faculty in St. Louis on the left. But Preus had a powerful advantage: the power to control and censor synodical publications.[91] At issue now in the *Witness* wasn't social action, race, poverty, ecumenism, or the Vietnam War, but the theological liberalism of the faculty in St. Louis, many of whom were the loudest voices in the synod on these very issues. Consumed by the hardening split in the church, the *Witness* had little time and even less energy for extrasynodical issues.

Protests from the left against "Chairman Jao" and his "Lutheran Ax" were hardly sufficient to appease Preus's allies on the right, who simply wanted more heads to roll. So loud was the noise from the right over Preus's *inaction* that he and others had to fight to keep conservative churches from bolting. By 1971, several congregations in the Midwest had severed their ties with the Missouri Synod to join the ELS or WELS. One faction left the church to form, in November 1971, the Federation for Authentic Lutheranism (FAL). The FAL movement was spearheaded by Larry Marquardt, a founding member of Balance, Inc. Its inaugural service was attended by Robert Preus.[92]

In August 1970, Werning organized and chaired a "Lutheran Congress" in Chicago's Sheraton Hotel to construct a "Blueprint for Winning the

Confessional Battle."[93] Werning's strategy, as he outlined to Preus and the
Congress, called on Preus to oust what he called the "errorists." "<u>Seek discipline of the errorists</u>," he wrote Preus, "<u>even to their exclusion</u>. . . . Keep
the opposition on the defensive and show them to be disloyal. . . . Don't
give up the church to errorists but ask them to withdraw."[94] The document
Werning's Congress produced, "Evangelical Directions for the Lutheran
Church," heavily emphasized theological rifts in the synod and advocated
a reaffirmation of the "historic Lutheran faith as known from the verbally
inspired and infallible Scriptures as the only authentic, inerrant and completely adequate source and norm of Christian doctrine and life."[95]

But even among the clergy-heavy troop Werning harvested from
the right (only two of the twenty-two authors were laymen), variations of
emphasis revealed the multitude of objections and objectives in Missouri
conservatism. Presbyterian theologian Francis Schaeffer was there to root
out modern liberalism (including rock groups and the drug culture) in theological liberalism's "new humanism."[96] Richard Klann, conservative system-
atics professor at Concordia, took aim at the Mission Affirmations and the
moderate movement's emphasis on "social action," attributing it to "large
quantities of Marxism" that had invaded Lutheran seminaries in America.
Condemning the "offensive actions of some representative individuals at
Denver" and the "harrangues [sic] of unappeasable actionists," Klann
attributed the Lutheran left's drive for "social action" to the most base of
motives—money. "Perhaps a much more likely explanation of their zeal and
offensive behavior lies in their expectation of extracting or extorting from
the Lutheran churches large quantities of cash to be used ostensibly for
their special programs."[97] Most authors, in the wake of the synod's approval
of fellowship with the ALC, took aim at ecumenism. Wilbert Sohns shed
"tears of sorrow" for the decision and called liberals to repentance. And in
a personal note to Lutherans, Francis Schaeffer suggested that denominational loyalties were being superseded by new fraternities, with Christians
increasingly segregated into conservative and liberal theological camps:

> As a Bible-believing Presbyterian I feel very close to you. I feel no separa-
> tion in Christ. I come here and I shake your hand and I speak as though
> I have known you forever. If we got down to certain points of doctrine

we would differ, but the things I have spoken are not rooted in Presbyterianism or Lutheranism; they are rooted in historic Christianity and the scriptural faith. I feel close to you as Bible-believing Lutherans, but I have no closeness to those who are non-Bible-believing Presbyterians. This is where the division lies. In a day like ours, when the world is on fire, let us be careful to keep things in proper order. Let us find ways to show the world that while we do not minimize, and we maintain our distinctives, yet that we who have bowed before God's verbalized, propositional communication—the Bible—are brothers in Christ. This we must do in the face of liberal theology.[98]

Werning and collaborator Erich Kiehl urged participants in their introduction to respect Shaeffer's warning and to recall "the tragic experience of his beloved Presbyterian Church." Lutherans, they warned, "now stand at the same crossroads where his church once stood."[99]

Balance, Inc.: Robert Preus Steps Forward

With the formation of Balance, Inc. in June 1970, it became clear that this was no longer Werning's unit. Nor was it simply the clergy-heavy assemblage of the Chicago Congress. Glen Peglau was a founding member, Fred Rutz was vice president and treasurer, Marcus Braun was among several trustees, Marcus Lang served in a leadership capacity, and Robert Preus became its first president. Balance, Inc. was primarily a political organization headed by an increasingly political theologian. "The key politician [in the synod], I believe," remembered Ralph Bohlmann, "was Robert Preus, not Jack. Already in those days, more than Jack, at least."[100] Nor was Balance exclusively Lutheran. Its founding documents stipulated that any American could be elected to its board.[101] At its first official meeting two weeks later at the O'Hare American in Des Plaines, Illinois, Chet Swanson, O. A. Gebauer, Al Tessmann, and Larry Marquardt joined Balance, Inc.[102]

Robert Preus's first order of business was to raise funds for the organization. A fundraising drive with a goal of raising $100,000 kicked off in June. Robert led a Balance contingent to Otten's Camp Trinity to coordinate efforts and to secure Otten's distribution and donor lists. Many were shocked at what they found. Otten's distribution list was extensive, but his "headquarters" was an undeveloped piece of land miles from nowhere. This was clearly not a man who could summon great sums of money. Still, Robert Preus made use of Otten's mailing list and utilized a conservative world-wide evangelism list.[103] Rutz covered many of the startup costs, and a letter authored by Robert Preus went out to the church.[104] It generated little enthusiasm, producing only $43,000 in contributions, largely by Rutz, Roy Guess, and a handful of big donors.[105]

By October 1970, Balance was preparing to launch *Affirm,* a publication through which conservatives would attempt to return an air of respectability to a movement both molded and contaminated by Otten and *Christian News*. Frederick Danker called *Affirm* "a product of President [Jack] Preus's increasing concern for sanity and the avoidance of extremism," which "aimed to overcome the advantages of notoriety associated with *Christian News*."[106] Balance's great challenge was to hold readers' interest while informing them from a politically and theologically conservative perspective. It was a dilemma Paul Burgdorf had been unable to overcome—and something Otten had mastered. Robert Preus wanted *Affirm* to be short, like "[John] Tietjen's alumni news letter, attractive, brief, perhaps four pages to start with." Like Otten, he saw the political advantages of publishing and wanted it to be ready in time for the 1971 Synodical Convention in Milwaukee. Its contents, he argued,

> should be informative and persuasive, geared toward the concerns of the concerned laymen. It would deal with such concerns as the literature produced by our synod, the theology of our schools and the present investigation of our seminary in St. Louis, the work of the mission board of our synod (and other boards), the entire subject of inter-church relationships (ALC fellowship, our membership in LCUSA, our relationship to LWF, WCC etc. etc.), also matters that relate to present relationships (e.g. woman ordination, possible merger plans of ALC and LCA), the theology of our synod and LCUSA, etc.[107]

Yet it also had to be exciting. He did not want articles that would "bore or 'turn off' the laymen," but simply written articles that would "transcend the type of gossip, name-calling, innuendo style of Koenig's News Letter." "Koenig's paper," he wrote, "is not believed; neither is the *Lutheran Witness* (which had lost 125,000 subscribers)."[108] Achieving both would be a challenge. Al Tessmann wrote cynically to Robert Preus that Missouri laymen needed simplicity. Otten was successful, he suggested, because he was the only one who gave sheep-like laymen the tabloid simplicity they required: "I know for a fact that much effort is going to waste because people do not understand what is being said. This is true in church literature as well as secular publications, and if these publications put out by Balance are going to be meaningful to laymen, they must understand what they are reading."[109]

Left to the task of implementing these difficult aims were editors Walter A. Maier II, Richard Korthals, and E. J. Otto. Maier, who would leave his post in 1973 to become a synod vice president, reasoned that *Affirm* was less proactive than reactive. In the months before Denver there had been "much ballyhoo for establishing fellowship with the ALC." Maier and others wanted to run editorials opposed to fellowship in the *Witness* and *Reporter.* Harms and Wiederaenders refused. Maier asked Harms, "Are you censoring our periodicals?" Harms replied, "Call it what you will, but you're not going to get that in." That moment convinced Maier of the need for a publication like *Affirm.*[110]

As angry as he was at Robert's decision to lead Balance/*Affirm*, Jack was uncharacteristically incautious in his initial dealings with the organization. He worked hand in hand with *Affirm* in 1971, notwithstanding his public denials. In November 1971, Jack Preus gave his stamp of approval by publishing an article, ghost-written by Chet Swanson, in the embryonic periodical.[111] He soon took flak from supporters and detractors alike for using an unofficial publication in his capacity as president.[112] Preus replied that his motives were pure. He was trying to keep the seceding FAL churches in the synod. "As you know, whether we like it or not, there are some individuals in the synod who do not seem to believe what is said in some of our official journals."[113] But privately, the backlash convinced him that he needed to build a public distance from his increasingly assertive brother. "I don't think that I will put anything more in <u>Affirm</u>," he told Swanson in December. "I do not think it's wise for me to make <u>Affirm</u> the way in which I ordinarily communicate with the church."[114] Still, he reserved the right to use Balance/*Affirm* "if the situation requires it."[115]

Preus's Plumber

Richard Nixon had his plumbers and so did Jack Preus. Preus's was Henry Hilst, a part-time farmer and retired plumber from central Illinois intent on dedicating his remaining days to the movement. Hilst was a workhorse, an "absolute iron butt" with a head for "precinct politics."[116] He had a "genius for organization" and soon took over Werning's role as the "numbers guy" of the movement. Hilst had been part of the Balance inner circle at its inception and,[117] at least from 1971, was on the payroll of Balance, Inc.[118] Hilst was not a spiritual man publicly (Paul Zimmerman remembered him as a "moderate, centrist man"[119]), but "he could count." He could "sit on his tail" for endless hours calling supporters, polling delegates, and compiling lists. Hilst's lists were remarkable in detail, pages upon pages containing thousands of names, addresses, and phone numbers, categorized by district. Each man was neatly pigeonholed, "x" for "conservative," "o" for "liberal," "xx" for "vocal conservative" and "co" for "contact man." Bohlmann remembered Hilst as

> a layman from central Illinois, who got an award of some kind from the Board of Regents here, when EJ Otto was chairman, for being such a tireless worker for the Lord. Henry's, I think Henry thought he was serving the Lord, I don't doubt that. But, he did a lot of the legwork, the telephone work in those days, before computers, lining up delegates, money, and just an unassuming, I think a farmer or a small-town businessman, just a very unassuming, down-to-earth, nice, kind of quiet kind of guy. And he'd get on the phone and say, "I'm calling on behalf of Dr. Preus."[120]

Singularly loyal to Preus, for the time being, Henry Hilst became Jack Preus's closest confidant and served as the president's backdoor channel— "the pipeline"[121]—to Otten, Balance, and others.[122] Always cautious, Hilst rarely put anything in print; the phone was his modus operandi.[123] As the gatekeeper to a closet where skeletons were quickly accumulating, it is little wonder that he would become the "power broker of the 1970s."[124] As Werning pulled back from his leadership role in the movement, Jack increasingly exercised covert leadership by coordinating conservative efforts through Henry Hilst.

Prior to the 1971 Synodical Convention in Milwaukee, conservatives wrestled with how best to wield their influence. Some wanted to approach the convention in an even more overtly political manner than they had in 1969 by publishing an official election guide of screened, approved nominees. Werning "pleaded with them not to have election lists." A diluted version was attempted in Milwaukee, where *Affirm* instructed delegates to "vote your conscience." It failed, from the conservative perspective, in several key elections. From that point on, the Preus brothers and Balance committed themselves firmly to distributing voting lists at synodical conventions. By 1975, the *Affirm* list would become "a near-infallible guide to who would be elected."[125]

Through Hilst, and often Otten, Preus used his control of delegate lists to control synodical conventions. The conservative voting "list" for the 1971 convention was compiled largely by Werning, in consultation with Preus.[126] That year Werning was elected to lead the synod's Board for Missions. He quickly pulled out of the political movement, passing his responsibilities on to Hilst. At least for the next three conventions, Jack Preus, working through Hilst, personally controlled the lists and coordinated conservative election efforts. Months before the summer convention, Preus issued an executive order that the names of delegates were not to be made public.[127] Clandestinely, however, Preus had Hilst give the names to Otten, as he did again in 1973.[128] Otten recalls:

> See when Jack was president we were able to get, he saw to it through some other people [Hilst] that we always got the names of the delegates. As long as we were on his side. . . . But in those days, in '73 and all those early conventions, we got the list and that's how, we're not very widely read in Synod, obviously. But by getting to the delegates . . .[129]

Preus's word was not always final, and he did consult his brother, Robert, and others. In 1975, he wanted to water down the list to allow moderates to claim a few, if insignificant, victories. However, against his advice, the conservative machine rammed through all of its nominees. Of some 150 people promoted by the *Affirm* list in 1975, all but one was elected.[130] Preus remarked later, "I told those fellows they should have let twenty or thirty of the other side win."[131]

Few disputed that Preus controlled the lists, but who else was involved is a point of contention. Chet Swanson suggests that Preus confidant Paul Zimmerman was central to compiling the lists.[132] Balance correspondence frequently included Paul Zimmerman, whom Swanson indicated in a letter to Preus and Hilst had full access to local contact lists.[133] Robert Preus called Zimmerman the "Tzar" in Balance correspondence.[134] Zimmerman, who was not an official member of Balance, denies that he played a leadership role, but he did not deny foreknowledge of the lists and acknowledged working "pretty much anonymously" as Preus's assistant.[135] Tom Baker, *Affirm* editor since 1980 and active in Balance (and with Swanson) during the 1970s, tries to provide some insight. Henry Hilst, he insists, kept Preus's inner circle of power brokers "close to the vest." "Only now," claims Baker, "am I finding out who was involved in putting the '*Affirm* list' together." Hilst collected names from district conservatives, "contact men," filtered the list with Preus, then reached a consensus "behind the scenes" with his tiny cabal. Hilst eventually kept the small group connected with a "top level" newsletter called *Promote*. Of Hilst, Baker says that he "never met a guy who was so brilliant politically." That Hilst was so powerful yet hidden impresses Baker still. "Ninety-nine percent of the Synod has never heard of him."[136]

Concordia Seminary: The Noose Tightens

The plan regarding Concordia that Danker overheard the Preus brothers discussing was set in motion in April 1970. The pretext was a letter to Preus from Martin Scharlemann, former liberal icon turned neoconservative who reportedly wanted the job Tietjen was awarded in 1969.[137] Scharlemann lamented the "theological climate" at Concordia and suggested that "a competent committee of inquiry be created to look into the matters that threaten to deface the Lutheran character of the life and instruction going on at Concordia Seminary." Preus could not count on the seminary's Board of Control to target the moderates; an April 20 gathering of the Board affirmed Tietjen's leadership. During the meeting, Preus appeared to hand-deliver an executive order creating a Fact-Finding Committee (FFC) to investigate "alleged departures from our Synod's doctrinal position on the part of individuals serving in various capacities within our church." Chairing the committee was his aide Zimmerman, who was joined by four others, including Karl Barth.[138]

Thus began the central battle Preus's supporters had been clamoring for. From December through March 1971, the FFC held court at synod headquarters, where each of forty-five Concordia faculty members was interrogated for up to two hours on issues ranging from the historicity of biblical narratives to the general principles of inerrancy and infallibility.[139] The interviews were taped by Barth for subsequent evaluation.[140] A challenge to the constitutionality of the committee at the 1971 convention was rejected,[141] and the committee's results were given to Tietjen and the Board of Control.

But in July, the Milwaukee Convention, ironically themed "Sent to Reconcile," did not produce a Preus victory. Preus needed the convention to do two things in order to lay the "constitutional groundwork"[142] for his purge of the seminary: (1) uphold the constitutionality and work of his Fact-Finding Committee and (2) make the synod's doctrinal resolutions binding on its members. Delegates gave Preus the first and rejected the second. Resolution 2-28 directed Preus to monitor the progress of the seminary's Board of Control and report to the church within one year.[143] But Resolution 2-21, Preus's attempt to bind members to synod doctrine, failed. The resolution, as Preus first saw it, read:

> Resolved, That the Synod once again declare its doctrinal resolutions to be of binding force [on "congregations, pastors, teachers, and professors"] until it can be demonstrated to the Synod that they are not in accord with the Word of God.[144]

But moderates muddied the waters by promoting and passing an alternate resolution based on a statement from the Council of Presidents, which referred back to a resolution on doctrine passed by the Denver convention in 1969. The new Resolution 2-21 spoke of "peace and harmony," saw "disunity in the church" as "displeasing to God," and urged those with concerns about "formulation of Scriptural doctrine" to go first to the synod's CTCR.[145] An irritated Preus fumed to the delegates:

Therefore I must say that I express a great deal of regret, as the one who is given the task of supervisor of doctrinal life, at this particular turn of this matter. It will cause us a great deal of difficulty.[146]

Conservatives met unexpected resistance from moderates in Milwaukee, organized now under pastors Bertwin Frey and F. Dean Lueking. To achieve a clear-cut victory, Preus would need a unified conservative movement to control the next convention.

Still, Preus saw the 1971 convention as a tactical victory. He later remembered thinking that Tietjen and the moderates had blown an opportunity:

They died hard. There was a tremendous amount of squawking and so on. Had I been John Tietjen in 1970 and the Synodical president asked for the privilege of investigating that faculty, and that's pretty good language—I didn't really demand it, I simply said I'd like to do it and Tietjen said come on in we're happy to have you. But had I been John Tietjen I would have said this is very nice and it's a fine thing to do, and we have no fears but in view of the fact that it's never been done before, I will suggest to my faculty that they not meet with you or your committee until the convention of 1971 has given its approval. Then I would have gone out to the convention floor and I would have raised holy cain and said this is an intrusion, this is outrageous, this is a question of our integrity and our theological position and I ask the convention to rebuke the president for asking such an unbelievable thing. I think Tietjen might have prevailed because the '71 convention still elected men to his board of Control who were supportive and favorable for him.[147]

Tietjen's failure to do so meant that for the next two years, conservatives and moderates would be consumed by the battle over the seminary. Preus used synod machinery and back-channel alliances to stack the deck against Tietjen and the overwhelming majority of seminary professors (and students) in preparation for the 1973 convention showdown in New Orleans. Preus recognized that in the LCMS presidency he could exercise near-dictatorial powers. In a letter to William Fackler in late 1970, he wrote:

We need to have a separation of powers, such as we have in our federal government. What a terrible thing it would be if President Nixon were also the chief justice of the Supreme Court. Yet that is exactly what we have in the Missouri Synod.[148]

Preus used for publicity not only the *Witness* and *Reporter*, over which he was increasingly exerting his control, but *Christian News* and *Affirm*, with which he coordinated his efforts through Hilst. He also fully utilized the sometimes amorphous power of his office to corner Tietjen and his allies. For his part, Tietjen relied on support from the growing Frey-Lueking organization, the seminary's Board of Control, seminary students, and a sympathetic national media.

Purging Missouri Missions

Waldo Werning, meanwhile, was taking his first steps away from a movement he helped create. Some conservatives believed it a conflict of interest to serve in official synod channels while belonging to an external special interest group. Werning was among them, so after taking leadership of the synod's Board for Missions, he handed over his responsibilities in the movement to Henry Hilst. Already jaded by Preus's penchant for scheming, Werning, the Board member, soon came into open conflict with a president eager to extend his power.

Missions had always been of special interest to Werning, but he was wary of Martin Kretzmann's Mission Affirmations, a conservative punchball since 1965. Until 1971, the Board had been dominated by moderates. With Werning in charge and Preus demanding heads, synod missions experienced rapid and convulsive change. Preus was actively involved but worked tirelessly to maintain the appearance of distance.[149] In late 1972, Martin Kretzmann, Secretary for Planning, Study, and Research, was fired. Its author gone, Werning organized a reexamination of the Affirmations and, unsurprisingly, found them deficient with respect to ecumenical services and cooperative ministry. Like the rest of the church, the Board had polarized; its report to the 1973 convention included a minority report reaffirming tri-Lutheran mission work.[150]

But Preus's heavy-handed tactics took their toll. In early 1974, the Board fired James Mayer, Secretary for Southeast Asia and defender of Kretzmann's Affirmations, as well. In April, William Kohn, Missouri's Executive Secretary for Missions and moderate presidential candidate in 1973, quit, complaining of a "spirit of isolationism and centralization" and Preus's "arbitrary use of power."[151] Later that month, four more from the mission staff quit, intending to found a competing mission society. Soon the entire New Guinea, Indian, and Philippine churches were threatening to leave the fold.[152] By May 1975, sixteen of twenty-three national staff members in LCMS missions had either quit or been fired.[153] Having struggled with Preus "week after week, month after month," Werning puts much of the blame on Preus:

> It was a real offense to me that he always forced us to make a political decision rather than a Biblical one. . . . He would tell me, "now you've got to get rid of Mickey Kretzmann." And "now you've got to get rid of Jim Mayer." And I would say, "hey, you know, I'm supposed to tell our Board majority, you know, vote because Preus said so?" One layman [on the Board for Missions] says, "Well if he wants to run the Mission Board, let himself get elected to it."

Werning, who claims to have rejected Preus's political interference, says, "We stood with principle."[154] Regardless, Preus could not complain about the result. By 1975, Kretzmann, Mayer, and most of the synod's mission staff were gone.[155]

Preus's Statement and the Blue Book

The battlefield in 1972 and 1973 was Preus's "A Statement of Scriptural and Confessional Principles." In February 1972, Preus submitted his statement (he claimed authorship although it was written by Ralph Bohlmann) to the seminary's Board of Control to "assist" the board in evaluating the transcripts of FFC interviews. Moderates saw it rather as a Preus attempt to set a new doctrinal standard for the synod. Preus's statement, wrote Fred Danker, was a brilliant tactical maneuver:

> Preus was about to perform a politically impossible trick in the Missouri Synod. If he was to succeed in controlling the Synod, he would need a document that would define heresy in precise terms. To accomplish this feat he would have to overcome a severe setback suffered by his supporters a little more than a decade earlier.[156]

This was not a new battle. The synod's 1932 convention had adopted then-President Franz Pieper's *Brief Statement of the Doctrinal Position of the Missouri Synod* as an accurate abstract of its doctrinal beliefs; the 1959 San Francisco convention gave it "status next to the Scriptures and the Lutheran Confessions."[157] The *Brief Statement* stated:

> We teach that the Holy Scriptures differ from all other books in the world in that they are the Word of God. They are the Word of God because the holy men of God who wrote the Scriptures wrote only that which the Holy Ghost communicated to them by inspiration. We teach also that the verbal inspiration of the Scriptures is not a so-called "theological deduction," but that it is taught by direct statement of the Scriptures. Since the Holy Scriptures are the Word of God, it goes without saying that they contain no errors or contradictions, but that they are in all their parts and words the infallible truth, also in those parts which treat historical, geographical, and other secular matters.[158]

Pieper's *Brief Statement,* among other issues, elicited a reaction from moderate Missouri Lutherans in the 1940s and remained a center of controversy through the Behnken presidency. The 1962 convention in Cleveland saw resolutions from conservatives who wished to elevate Pieper's *Brief Statement* to the level of the Lutheran Confessions and from moderates who urged the synod "not to expand the confessional basis of our church by the addition of synodically adopted declarations." Delegates there declared the adoption of such statements (specifically one such statement, adopted in 1959) unconstitutional and called for further review of the issue.[159]

Preus's statement was written for a church in crisis in 1971, and as such was a reactionary document. Preus's statement not only affirmed what Lutherans believe in several categories (Christ as Savior and Lord; Law and Gospel; Mission of the Church; Holy Scripture; Original Sin; and Confessional Subscription), but expressly delineated heretical, un-Lutheran belief and action in a way that the Scriptures and the Lutheran Confessions apparently had not done adequately (or at least in a way that could challenge unambiguously the beliefs and statements of specific seminary professors). Each category began with a brief statement of belief followed by a detailed list of rejected views. Preus's statement addressed the liberal predilection for social activism (and the conservative antipathy for the social gospel) by rejecting views that suggest "that an adequate or complete witness to Jesus Christ can be made without proclaiming or verbalizing the Gospel."[160] But the most significant and consequential of rejected views were those outlined in the statement's section on Holy Scripture. Preus and Bohlmann affirmed that Holy Scripture is "inspired," "inerrant," and "infallible," and rejected all implications that "the historicity or facticity of certain Biblical accounts (such as the Flood or the Fall) may be questioned."[161] Preus's statement rejected not only liberal belief but also the instructional methods used to support that belief. In its section "Historical Methods of Biblical Interpretation," the statement rejected views "that methods based on secularistic and naturalistic notions of history . . . may have a valid role in Biblical interpretation."[162] Finally, Preus's statement looked forward to the 1973 New Orleans convention, seeking explicit endorsement from the church. Preus was putting in place procedures to make it easier "to oust pastors and seminary professors not 'in line' with official church doctrine."[163] Winning endorsement of those procedures from the synod would be the key to victory. And controlling the convention would be the key to endorsement.

Preus had Zimmerman secretly edit his "Report" to the Missouri Synod (as charged by Resolution 2-28) and reserved several pages in the September 1972 *Witness* to publicize it. *Witness* editors, still considered untrustworthy by Preus, were not allowed to see the document before it ran.[164] What emerged in the *Witness* was a round condemnation of the seminary faculty: "Within the faculty the doctrine of the Holy Scriptures is subverted to the point where, in effect, a false doctrine is proclaimed regarding them."[165] In his epilogue, Preus warned:

Now we stand at the crossroads. . . . The case now lies before the church. It is evident that the use of the historical-critical method has brought about changes both in our doctrinal stance, our certainty, and our attitudes toward doctrine. And unless things change at our Seminary, this trend will continue.[166]

The excerpt article and full document, a 160-page "Blue Book," were disasters for Tietjen and his moderate backers. And although Preus in print found most of the Concordia faculty guilty of false doctrine, he continued to offer

Tietjen a political solution: Fire a couple of professors and replace them with people "more to the synod's liking."[167]

Struggling for Conservative Unity

The war against Concordia Seminary was the glue that kept conservatives together through 1973, and Preus continued to coordinate the factions skillfully.[168] Preus "flipped his lid" when he found out that Robert would head up Balance, but maintained his control through Henry Hilst.[169] Robert would prove a solid but intermittent ally. Both he and Chet Swanson were firm friends with Herman Otten and worked to keep Balance and Otten conservatives closely linked. Robert Preus and Swanson corresponded in late 1970 and early 1971 about the need to maintain conservative unity. Swanson unmistakably identified with a broader conservative "movement" and told Preus that Balance/*Affirm* must be vigilant in uplifting all conservatives. In April 1970, Swanson wrote a "welcome aboard!" letter to Rev. Bob Jones (of Bob Jones University in South Carolina), generously counting Jones among the ranks of Missouri Lutherans as "some of the most dedicated followers of Christ."[170] Robert, like Swanson, was committed to his friend Herman. An early 1971 list of "suggestions" proposed cooperation, if not full union, with *Christian News*:

> Keep Christian News fully informed. Deserves to be recognized for valiant service. Keep it fully cooperative. Unless a union of the two publications can be effected under a new name and editor (a distinct possibility, maybe before September) its distinctive appeal deserves to be recognized.[171]

For his part, Jack Preus continued to publicly deny his involvement with Balance. He wrote William Fackler in late 1970 that through his brother he would do his best to make certain that "whatever they do will be in keeping with our synodical doctrinal position as well as our polity."[172] But the next spring, Jack received complaints about Balance's drive to raise $100,000. In response, he claimed that "the matter of the $100,000 fund raising campaign came as much of a surprise to me as it did to you" and denied being "in any way, shape, or form" involved with Balance.[173] But Preus had known about the drive and even coordinated the effort with Robert to avoid the appearance of fraternal scheming. In May, Roland Wiederaenders complained to Jack Preus after receiving a fundraising appeal from Balance at his 210 N. Broadway office. Jack then asked Robert to rectify the error and maintain their agreement that solicitations not be made of synodical officials.[174]

Though the war against the seminary provided a shared enemy and focal point for conservatives, Preus's duplicitous ways were frustrating his backers. For all the tactical genius of his actions against the seminary, many conservatives were unsatisfied and pressured him to act more forcefully. Otten wrote him in July 1970: "Please be assured that we are prepared to testify at hearings you may conduct concerning the theology of the St. Louis seminary professors."[175] To Swanson, who had also been anxious for action, Preus pleaded, "With regard to the Seminary, I wish you would just give me time to take care of this matter."[176] In November 1970, Otten asked to meet Preus in St. Louis. When Preus did not respond, Otten reminded Preus of his connection to UPC and Balance. The veiled threat extended to other officials. "Evidently," warned Otten, "a number of other prominent leaders were also involved in the UPC and your election."[177] The threat was not an empty one. In October a supporter wrote Preus to inform him that Peglau was spilling the beans:

> Dr. Glen Peglau really revealed some very unwholesome things to those present. He did it in a most forceful manner. Some things in Synod are even worse than I had suspected. He used names, places and figures. He seemed to be a man who is courageous and determined. I'm certain you know both of these men [including Otten] intimately.[178]

Preus responded by denying the connection with Otten and Peglau. He continued, "Do not believe everything Peglau says. He has a way of twisting the facts in such a way as to make it come out quite far removed from the truth."[179] By 1972, Peglau had had enough of Missouri conservatism. His life was a shambles: he had separated from his wife and was spiraling into alcoholism.[180] He openly broke with Preus, contending that Preus had "double-crossed conservatives" in "welshing" on a number of promises he had made to conservative leaders in 1969 and beyond.[181]

With Peglau gone, Preus found steadfast support and an activist for conservative unity in the person of Chet Swanson. Swanson, an Ohio conservative with big connections and a big wallet, was one of the few men who managed to maintain close relationships with almost all of the conservatives. Swanson's Cincinnati home was a fount of correspondence to St. Louis and New Haven. His productive pen was at once an asset and an annoyance to Preus, whose archived files today contain more material from Swanson than nearly anyone else, Otten included. Swanson was a proponent of Ronald Reagan's 11th commandment, "Don't knock fellow conservatives," a principle he spoke of with great frequency and fervency.[182] Like others in Balance, he saw local organization as the key to domination of the synod. He was a friend to Jack Preus, who visited Swanson's home in Cincinnati several times.[183] Above all, he was a loyal friend to Herman Otten and was able, for a time, to bridge the growing gulf between Otten and Preus.

Swanson was one of the conservative instruments for coordinating efforts between Balance/*Affirm* and *Christian News*. And coordinated they were. "I can assure you," wrote John Baur to Robert Preus in late 1970, "that Rev. Otten will henceforth publish no news about Balance, Inc. unless it has your O.K. Mr. Rutz will be able to second this."[184] Although he complained to Otten about the "cute" techniques conservatives employed, he made certain that Otten received "inner team" correspondence via Hilst by marking letters "cc: Others." (Although composition of the "inner team" changed over time, it included, in 1972, the Preus brothers, Lang, Werning, Hilst, and Tessmann.)[185] Like Otten, Swanson saw Missouri's battle as part of a broader conflict against liberalism and the social gospel.[186] When fractures surfaced, Jack Preus turned to Swanson to keep conservatives in line:

> I appreciate your efforts to be a peacemaker and also I note these efforts from the letters of which you sent me copies. Your letters reveal also the tremendous need for making peace. You emphasize the tremendous degree of agreement that we have among us and yet so much wheel-spinning is going on and so many efforts are wasted on doing what some overzealous brother has done wrong. Thanks for all your [sic] doing and I hope you'll keep it up in the area of getting the conservative wing into a more positive position toward the Synod. They really have no hope outside the Synod of achieving anything, and if they'd work together and quit dividing among themselves, they could do a great deal within the church. As it is, they often bring more embarrassment to themselves than anything else.[187]

Preus added later:

> What can be done to bring the brethren closer together and help them
> act in a more brotherly manner is still difficult. Unless they do this, they
> constantly give encouragement to the opposition and give every reason to
> believe to them [liberals] that if they can just hang on long enough they
> will win the day.[188]

Swanson, like Preus, was politically savvy and quickly grew frustrated by
unyielding conservative ideologues. He particularly wanted Preus to reach
out to Larry Marquardt and the FAL group and keep them from "setting
up conditions for pulling out of the Synod." Exasperated, he wrote, "They
[FAL] constantly divide the efforts we are making at this end to deal with
the most crucial issues facing Synod."[189]

In his correspondence with Swanson, Preus toed the conservative line,
even in the face of Swanson's suspicions. Swanson expressed rare disap-
pointment with Preus in a spring 1971 letter, accusing Preus of chumming
up to the liberals. Preus responded, "I have never tried to make friends with
them [liberals] and have no expectation of doing so."[190]

Organizing the laity was Swanson's pet project. In early 1970, Swanson reviewed a strategy session with Preus: "We agree, therefore, that: 1.
Action at the local level is of primary importance. 2. Action at the local level
should be constructive. 3. Constructive local action must be given support
by Synod officials."[191] While Preus and Hilst focused on controlling synod
machinery by organizing delegates in preparation for the 1973 convention,
Swanson was kept in the dark. He apparently believed Preus's early claims
of innocence with respect to underhanded politicking. "The matter of leaking the names of delegates is," he wrote to Preus, "exactly as you describe
it. Everybody gets them and nobody knows how."[192] Jeffrey Hadden's recent
survey (*Gathering Storm*) convinced Swanson that Missouri's laity were far
more sympathetic to conservatives than moderates; he pushed, in fact, for a
rejection of fellowship with the ALC and reestablishment of ties with Missouri's old synodical partner, WELS.[193] Karl Barth observed that "conservatives can't give speeches; liberals can't count."[194] Swanson agreed that an
undereducated laity had been snowed by slick liberals. He sent a sample of
letters he had received to Preus in early 1971 to demonstrate the views of "a

typical layman who really hasn't studied the issues but is convinced that the liberals are loving and the conservatives are divisive."[195]

But conservatives were not finding a way to reach and involve the mass of Missouri Synod laity. Balance, Inc.'s leadership was growing increasingly frustrated that their efforts to stir up a presumed hornet's nest of lay rage were failing. An irritated Swanson lamented to Lang, "The large majority of our membership are not aware that we have problems. (Some of them believe the conservatives are as much the problem as the libs.)" His frustration extended to conservative elites who focused on manipulating synod machinery. "We'd rather sit on national committees and boards and make demands for action from the top than pursue the arduous task of securing action at the grass roots level [while] we grow impatient with all those who can not and will not 'see the light.'"[196] Balance/*Affirm* was not gaining a following. Robert Preus warned his partners in late 1971 that Balance was in "dire difficulties," not generating sufficient interest.[197] The only money trickling in was "the few hundred dollars of funds being the direct result of personal solicitations on the part of Chet Swanson."[198] In early 1972, after failing to receive adequate financing from a "hard core conservative group" in Missouri, Balance suspended publication of *Affirm* for lack of funds.[199] Robert Preus and Bill Eggers believed in part that the conservative movement's infighting was to blame. After completing a mission to find and tap the source of Otten's funding, Eggers wrote to Robert in May:

> Maybe conservatives are doomed never to understand ekklesia and commonality. Maybe each of us must be specially nurtured in the confusion of conservatism. . . . Maybe we're all too petty to rise to the greatness of losing ourselves in the greatest of all causes. I hope not. But every day it looks more like this is true. That fact is probably one of the worst indictments of the whole conservative movement.[200]

Chet Swanson suggested selling stock in Balance, an idea Robert and others rejected. After borrowing $5,000, Robert Preus hit the big donor circuit to shore up Balance's finances.[201] At an emergency meeting in October, Al Tessmann offered to give $25,000 if Preus could raise $50,000.[202] Robert Preus came close. Walter Dissen, a member of the Concordia Seminary's

Board of Control, donated fifteen shares of his Standard Oil stock to Balance.[203] Waldo Werning informed Preus in November that Roy Guess, "our friend in Casper, Wyoming," would be sending $18,000.[204] Fred Rutz sent funds from his foundation.[205] By the end of 1972, Robert had raised over $55,000—almost all of it from three donors. He excitedly called Jack and Paul Zimmerman, telling them to make certain that Hilst was in "constant contact" with the donors.[206]

Balance/*Affirm* was saved, for now. But populist Swanson was left unsatisfied about the elitist nature of the conservative "movement" he had joined. "If it were not for 20 donors," he wrote to Balance in October (unaware of the still bigger donations to come in November), "we would have only 40% of the income we have at this date."[207]

Swanson's answer was the Doctrinal Concerns Program (DCP). DCP was Swanson's hope for organizing conservative laity under the cover of a doctrinal education program. Its purpose was primarily political, to build a pseudo-official network of conservatives on district levels to circumvent existing synodical channels. Swanson criticized "do-gooder" district presidents in a letter to Robert Preus in November:

> We continue to lose ground (or, at least, make no headway) with the ordinary Synodical channels as they exist in many of the Districts. The ordinary channels have too many "do-gooders" (and apathetic) who don't want to rock the boat. They—in their "neutrality"—merely help the liberal minority control the helm.[208]

So Swanson wanted to go around them. DCP objectives included influencing "the grass roots to contact the 'neutral' District Presidents to back Dr. J. A. O. Preus," generating letters of support for Preus, nominating convention delegates, and submitting overtures to synod conventions.[209] Like other conservatives, Swanson saw his political action group as supportive of the synod, or rather Jack Preus.[210] Ironically (given the "movement's" secretive tactics), he publicly aspired

> to insist on a return to constitutional government in the Synod and to eliminate <u>unethical</u> use of tactics which (often using the public media) cast reflections on motives and which substitute a focus on personalities rather than on issues.[211]

By late 1972, Swanson was increasingly pouring his efforts—and finances—into the DCP, which Lang viewed as a "corollary" to Balance.[212]

Key to DCP's success, Swanson believed, would be an official stamp of approval from Jack Preus. And Swanson pushed hard to get it. By fall 1972, DCP was still floundering. In an October letter to Preus, in which he discussed strategies for getting conservatives to better work together, Swanson complained, "Surprisingly, we don't yet have common goals (well enough spelled out) and our common program (i.e., the lay-pastor program called DCP) is still regarded by many as too much of a 'splinter organization' to win a large following."[213] Preus suggested Swanson make use of a layman named Ed Ziegler, who was willing to volunteer in "the good fight," and Swanson urged Preus to have Hilst "encourage the 'network' to use the materials we send out."[214] In November, modeling his efforts on similar publications in the Presbyterian church, Swanson began pushing for an official "blessings-to-DCP-from-Preus" letter. "Who JAOP responds to," he urged conservatives, "is not the essential but rather it is that the response be made. And it must be made in a fashion that it protects his office . . . and yet is not equivocal or half-hearted."[215] Two days later, in a separate letter to Robert Preus, Swanson revealed that Lang was in favor of the idea, as were Paul Zimmerman and Al Tessmann. "Jack," he pressured the president's brother, "would be well-advised to give DCP that letter we want!"[216]

One week later, Jack Preus complied. Strategically hoping to further distance Jack from Balance/*Affirm*, Lang had wanted him to address the letter to newcomer Ziegler. Preus addressed it instead to Swanson.[217] And it was just what Swanson had asked for, an imprecise but transparent endorsement of the DCP. Despite having condemned Stuenkel, Lueking, and the authors of "A Call to Openness and Trust," Preus wrote of DCP, "I do not know how I could be loyal to the Constitution of the church which I am pledged to uphold if I did not applaud the efforts of those who are attempting to keep our church strong in the faith." He continued:

> At the present time I think it is most proper for groups of people to meet and talk about issues and attempt to see to it that our church remains

faithful to the Word of God, using means that are scriptural and evangelical but nevertheless effective in achieving this end. Thus I see no reason why you should not give help to those who may contact you as to how to proceed.[218]

Even now, secrecy reigned. Swanson told Otten to keep the letter out of *Christian News*, that it was an "open" letter but would be circulated only among conservatives.[219] If the media asked about DCP, Swanson told Phil Giessler to respond that "the status of DCP in LCMS is 'unofficial' but 'recognized' as a legitimate and helpful movement."[220] Finally, in a letter to Hilst, Jack Preus, Zimmerman, and Tessmann, Swanson alluded to DCP's base-building strategy and Hilst's role, suggesting that "Drs. JAOP and PAZ [Zimmerman]" relieve Hilst of all the legwork and "divide the DCP list of contacts and call them to urge them to use . . . the DCP mailings that come from 335 Poage Farm Road [Swanson's Cincinnati home]."[221]

As the synod polarized over the next few years, Jack Preus increasingly made public use of DCP's organization and resources, even while claiming independence from his hard-line backers. In September 1975, he was the featured speaker at a DCP rally in Belleville, Illinois, despite calls from moderates to cancel the appearance before the partisan group. Jim Adams reports that Jack Preus personally assisted a DCP effort in early 1974 to unseat Southern Illinois District President Herman Neunaber:

> On the Sunday before the weekend election, Neunaber emerged from a Lutheran service in Belleville to discover all the cars in the parking lot had conservative flyers on the windshields. Exhibit A of the flyer was a copy of a letter from Preus to Neunaber. Dated the previous Friday, it was a Preus rebuttal of Neunaber's earlier criticism of a Preus report to the church. By Tuesday Neunaber still hadn't received the letter in the mail. He took a witness to confront Preus, who acknowledged that he had released the letter to a layman for distribution. Preus brushed off the episode and expressed a hope their friendship was still intact.[222]

Rumor was, Adams continued, that Preus had personally delivered the letter to Mueller the Saturday evening before its use.[223]

Keeping Otten on the Outside

Of the "inner team," Swanson was the most fiercely loyal to Herman Otten. After Peglau, Swanson was among the first conservatives to pressure Preus to reverse the COP's 1969 repudiation of *Christian News*. Like Otten and Preus, he was somehow able to compartmentalize, criticizing clandestine tactics while practicing them with abandon. "We fight against each other (or face artificial barriers of 'repudiations,' 'secrecy' and 'strategy')," he wrote Otten in 1972, "rather than openly working together."[224] Otten complained publicly as early as 1970 that conservatives should "fight out in the open . . . no behind the scenes meetings, no contact men. I don't think God supports underhanded maneuvering."[225] Yet Jack Preus took Otten to task that same year for printing in *Christian News* "an unsigned and anonymous letter in which vicious attacks are made upon certain people in Synod." Preus, who continued to exploit Otten as a furtive mouthpiece, continued, "I certainly would repudiate any paper which would give space to an anonymous letter, thus allowing an individual who does not dare to put his name to a letter the privilege of attacking other people and thus breaking the Eighth Commandment."[226]

Swanson was at the forefront of the battle to give Otten what he had been denied over a decade earlier—official certification as an LCMS minister. Pressure began on Preus almost immediately following his election to certify Otten. Most conservatives agreed that, for all his faults in print, Otten had been unjustly denied certification in 1958 by a vindictive seminary out to take "revenge" on him.[227] Some wanted to silence him by bringing him, through certification, back into the synod's disciplinary structure.[228] A few, however, saw the value in keeping him in his organizational void, the "perfect position," minister of an LCMS congregation but free from synod control and discipline.[229]

Central to the ongoing debate was the Board of Appeals' 1960 deadlock over Otten's case. Preus had led Otten to believe, prior to 1969, that he would arrange a favorable decision in Otten's case once in control of synod machinery.[230] Shocked by Preus's complicity in the COP repudiation of Otten in 1969, Swanson wrote to Preus, gently reminding him of his private commitments to help Otten:

What you say about "Christian News" is very true. I hope there is some
way that this whole matter can be settled whereby Otten will simply not
[continue] to be looked upon as the arch-villain of the church.

Again, Swanson reiterated, "I certainly want to see that justice is done to
Otten as well as to anyone else who has been wronged."[231] Otten's friends
wanted Preus to rule that the 5-5 vote in November 1960 meant not that
Otten lost his appeal, but rather that he won.[232] At the 1971 convention,
however, Preus again stunned his supporters by killing debate during a committee hearing on the issue. When Paul Burgdorf attempted to speak on
Otten's behalf (Zimmerman was on the committee), Preus closed debate
with a brusque, "He's a blue badger [a reference to the blue badges conservatives wore at the convention]!"[233]

This was Preus functioning again as political pragmatist. Before the
convention, he had confided to Swanson that he wanted the issue resolved,
but not just then. "I certainly do not want to see him suffer any longer than
is necessary," Preus wrote, but "I do not think that now is the time to raise
this matter."[234] Preus did not like the pressure Otten was putting on him.
Following the convention, he complained that Otten had him and Zimmerman "on the spit."[235] Nor did he think it wise to give his enemies ammunition while they still controlled the seminary. A February 1972 letter from
Zimmerman to Preus illustrates the degree to which both men were thinking about political considerations:

February 11, 1972

Dear Jack,

Just a brief note to say that I rather believe that Chet Swanson is right in
saying that it is in the best interest of everyone concerned to settle the
question of what the 5-5 vote in connection with the Herman Otten case
really means. I believe that you can ask for a definite ruling on this that will
legally settle the question once and for all. I don't see how you can lose.
Those who favor Otten will feel that you are being fair. Those who oppose
Otten can hardly object to this that you say it is high time that his cause
for complaint of unfairness be settled definitely so that the matter does
not continue to be something used to irritate the church. I believe you can

take the position of being very neutral about the whole thing and simply indicate that it is in the interest of the church that a matter that has been unsettled for ten years be finally laid to rest.

There are some other possibilities involved here, but I really see nothing that would hurt you, particularly if you make it clear that you are talking about it purely as an administrative matter.

Yours in Christ,

Paul A. Zimmerman[236]

Perhaps Preus resolved, as Swanson had suggested to him, that it was to everyone's advantage to have Otten outside Missouri's discipline structure.[237] In the battle against the seminary, he was still Preus's most valuable asset.

Jack Moves to the Center

Preus consistently tried to paint himself as a centrist, fighting off radicals at either end of the ideological spectrum. Even privately with Swanson, he declared a sneaking "flirtation with the social gospel."[238] Nowhere was this more evident than in his relations with the Missouri Synod's black minority. While Preus was fighting liberal ecumenists at the seminary, he was refusing to move against the synod's fellowship agreement with the ALC as accepted in Denver. Moreover, he was downright encouraging of ecumenical work among Missouri blacks. In early 1970, he encouraged the pan-Lutheran Association of Black Lutheran Churchmen (ABLC) to continue its "important" work. He told DeWitt Robinson that he understood that "difficulties . . . that could arise because of the fact that the Association of Black Lutheran Churchmen includes non-Missouri Synod people." Preus hoped, however, that "the theological differences which may exist among the synods are not troubling the common goals and work which the ABLC has undertaken."[239] Clemonce Sabourin told Preus that he felt "sick unto death" at the spectacle of his "white brethren . . . at each other's throats because of 'doctrinal' differences." Preus answered that he would hold Missouri's blacks to a different standard: "There has never been fear of accepting Negroes into full membership because their theology is suspect . . . orthodox or not."[240]

Preus's only standard for membership in ABLC was that one was black and belonged "to a Lutheran church."[241]

Yet Preus's vision for black membership in the LCMS was not as progressive as he wished it to appear. Preus was committed, he assured his black brethren, to removing "white racism from our midst."[242] Facing pressure from moderate black clergymen threatening to tarnish Missouri's image by bolting the church ("Better hurry though, cause some of us Blacks cannot wait too much longer"[243]), he even feigned concord with black clergyman Albert Pero, who wanted to restrict ABLC membership to black clergymen (excluding white pastors of black or mixed congregations) and promoted reparations for slavery.[244] Here again with Preus, image was everything. In supporting ABLC leadership, his critics noted, Preus promoted segregation in the Missouri Synod while working to avoid "the impression that we favor segregation." "We do want," he wrote Joseph Lavalais, "to let our black brothers know that we give them full responsibility for handling their own affairs."[245] To foster his paternalistic vision, Preus maintained a "special account" to pay expenses for select "black churchmen." Rather than work through traditional synodical channels, Robinson, Pero, and others submitted their expenses directly to Preus, who reimbursed them from his special account.[246] Sabourin warned Preus that his approach was creating "a monstrosity that might plague the church for the next hundred years." Rather than reach out to blacks as brothers, Preus was spending "large sums of money to help support their separate organization," sending the message that "we are willing to tolerate them [blacks], preferably in some unit of their own."[247]

Preus was more the ecumenist than his backers had been led to believe. His 1969 non-renunciation of the convention's call for fellowship with the ALC was typical of President Preus, writes Jim Adams, a "habitual bluster followed by apparent backtracking."[248] In early 1971, Preus announced an ecumenical "crusade" to help America's prisoners of war in North Vietnam, calling on Norman Vincent Peale, Billy Graham, and others to join him in the effort. Within six days he was in the Nixon White House conducting an ecumenical service for the president.[249] More frightening yet for conservatives, Preus soon trekked to Babylon itself—the Vatican—for an audience with the pope. A September 1971 newspaper article, entitled "Dr. Preus Says—SOCIAL MINISTRY AFFIRMATIONS POINT IN RIGHT DIRECTION," included charges that Missouri's FAL émigrés "lie, are not telling the truth, and are guilty of unethical tactics."[250] When Otten objected, Preus refused to respond.[251]

Ecumenism was not a significant theological issue for Preus but rather a political one. In late 1974, Preus arranged full participation in a tri-Lutheran religious service with LCA president Robert Marshall and ALC president (and Jack's cousin) David Preus. Two weeks before the event, he confirmed that he would "be there with bells on." Pressure from conservatives, however, limited his participation to a formal post-service greeting.[252] Years later, Preus reminisced that he wanted fellowship with the ALC only "as a bulwark against merger with the LCA." His greatest concern was not the theological prostitution conservatives heralded, but political influence:

> I don't feel that it was in anybody's interest, either the ALC's or Missouri, that the merger take place. From Missouri's standpoint it puts us in the position of being the little brother. Where there were three churches we could always negotiate and manipulate and maneuver.

But Preus was not alone in his fuzzy approach to ecumenism. Conservatives maintained solid and regular ties to non-Lutherans. And if ever there were an ecumenist, he charged, it was Herman Otten. Otten, he asserted, knocked "every single deviation on unionism" in Christianity, all the while "writing articles and printing stuff by evangelicals which are published without any kind of warning or concern that this party is not even a Lutheran."[253]

Otten's tactics and role as Missouri's self-appointed watchdog, useful come convention, gave Preus fits in the intervening time.[254] In May 1971, a disgruntled churchman went to both Preus and Otten with accusations of adultery against his wife and a Missouri pastor. The churchman went first to Preus, who assured him that "it is not the policy of the Lutheran Church to tolerate adultery among its clergy." For over a week, Preus refused to take his phone calls, pushing responsibility down to Wiederaenders.[255] Unsatisfied, the churchman went to Otten. Otten responded to him and carbon copied Preus a veiled warning. "Please be assured," he wrote the churchman, "that if the officials of The Lutheran Church—Missouri Synod are covering up for an unrepentant adulterer who is responsible for breaking up a home, we will take appropriate action."[256]

Preus's growing celebrity and the perceptible yet dysfunctional relationship between him and other conservatives were drawing attention from the secular media, little of it favorable. Lester Kinsolving regularly took Preus to task, and *Newsweek* editorialized that Preus resembled a "Lutheran Pope."[257] Jim Adams, religion editor for the *St. Louis Post-Dispatch*, began investigating in 1971. He tried to interview Otten, Preus, Werning, and several other conservatives, only to be rebuffed on several fronts. The further he dug, the more conservatives circled their wagons. Otten tried to hide the full extent of his relationship with Preus.[258] Waldo Werning blasted Adams for printing "dirt" and obfuscating the truth.[259]

But when Preus's friends called him to ask for guidance in answering Adams's questions, it was Preus who advised obfuscation. To Herman Preus he advised, "I think that the only thing to do with Jim Adams is simply to say that you have forgotten all of these matters."[260] Even as he refused to answer Adams's questions on the basis of Matthew 18 ("Therefore I do not think it is proper or brotherly to air personal matters in either the religious or the secular press"[261]), he did not hesitate to implicate his adversaries by name. Preus conveyed to Adams that the war in the church had taken on a very personal tone, even engulfing his son at Lutheran High School North in St. Louis. His wife, Delpha, had apparently received "very insulting and humiliating treatment at the hands of two professors, the Reverend James Fackler and the Reverend Arthur Repp Jr., as well as the chairman of the Board, the Reverend Arnold Wangerin, at that time pastor of Concordia Church, Kirkwood [Missouri]."[262]

Preus's dealings with Adams typified conservative mistrust of the "secular media." He wrote to Adams that "it would be far easier to deal with the secular press if one knew that they were truly objective in their reporting."[263] Swanson complained to Adams that the media were biased in referring to Missouri's left as "moderate." Call them "liberals," Swanson urged, because they are liberal "relative to where President Preus stands."[264] William Hecht, onetime member of the Anti-Communist American Security Council and Preus advisor, complained (in refusing to answer Adams's

questions) that Adams had "some type of hang-up or sickness" about prominent people:

> It is as if many people are trying to absolve themselves of any responsibility
> for the moral failures or problems in our society by showing that our great
> leaders had their weaknesses. It is almost a game to pick up the Post in the
> morning or the Star in the afternoon to see who is going to be next: Nixon,
> Hoover, and LBJ have been blasted to the point that writers seem to be
> always looking for someone new like JFK, Bobby Kennedy, Truman, Ike
> and no telling who else![265]

When word reached Preus that Adams was preparing to publish his book in
1976, Preus issued a threat to Clayton Carlson, Publisher at Harper & Row:
"If you proceed to publish any book about me you will be doing so at your
own peril."[266]

Seminex

For all the infighting, conservatives in 1973 were still united against one
rival: moderate-dominated Concordia Seminary. As the headstrong captain
of Concordia, John Tietjen became the personification of the moderate
camp and Public Enemy Number One for conservatives. The noose tighten-
ing, moderates in 1972 hastily organized, using secular media and their own
resources to get their message out to the church. The Frey-Lueking organization provided a political base for moderates, but the seminary was where
the action was. In June, Tietjen warned Missouri through the *New York
Times* that Concordia's future academic viability depended on an LCMS
rejection of Preus's grab for power.[267] That same month, the American Association of Theological Schools (AATS), the seminary's source for accreditation, placed Concordia on suspended status due to restrictions on academic
freedom. In May, Preus called on faculty members to respond individually
to his statement. All refused and instead worked furiously on a collective
response. In late June, the moderate-dominated Board of Control issued
its report to Preus, finding no false doctrine at Concordia. Privately, George
Loose, chairman of the board, complained that power politics as much as
theology was driving the debate:

A well-organized minority has used political methods to gain control of key boards and committees of Synod. Their greatest success was in defeating Dr. Oliver Harms and electing Dr. Preus president of Synod at Denver. Dr. Preus has continued to centralize power by getting rid of people who did not agree with him (e.g., Jungkuntz, Wolbrecht) and appointing his own men to key positions. Such "political" maneuvering in the church is obnoxious to some of us.[268]

If the growing controversy was absorbing the passions of Missouri clergy, its laity seemed to be tuning out. In July, Preus had his staff compile an analysis of the correspondence he had received since issuing Preus's statement. Only 19 percent of the letters Preus received were from lay members of the church. The report did its best to put a positive spin on the fact that 79 percent of responses were negative, informing Preus that most of the respondents were Concordia Seminary graduates, and almost half of those had graduated after 1960. The tone of the evaluation also suggested that liberals were not the only elitists in the church: the report argued that most of the lay responses had been ghost-written by pastors, indicating that most were too theologically or legally complex for the simple mind of a layman.[269]

Both sides wrote to the clergy as the battle intensified in September. Early in the month, Preus finally issued his massive report, known simply as the "Blue Book," to the synod. It argued that while the seminary faculty did accept "many" of the church's teachings, he had "grave concern" over the use of the historical-critical method. His case reasoned, in part, as Otten might in *Christian News:* that while the faculty did profess "a doctrinal stance in harmony with the Scriptures and the Lutheran Confessions," they were at fault because they were "reluctant to condemn deviating positions."[270] Preus then directed the Board of Control to ensure that faculty members be prohibited from using "any method of interpretation which casts doubt on the divine authority of the Scriptures" or deviating "in any other way" from "the doctrinal position of the Synod." "The world and the church," he continued, "do not need more questions or more debates. We need answers."[271] The faculty responded, in a report spearheaded by Tietjen known as the "Brown Book," by calling Preus's report "garbage." "Fact Finding or Fault

Finding?" it questioned, branding the Blue Book "unrealiable," a distortion, "un-Scriptural," and "un-Lutheran." Its findings, Tietjen argued, were pre-judged and put "the worst construction on everything."[272]

Conservatives coordinated their efforts in advance of the 1973 con-vention. "The War Is On," blared *Christian News* in March. "The liberal professors at Concordia Seminary . . . have no business remaining in the LCMS," wrote Otten, who urged Preus to remove Tietjen and take "deci-sive action" against the rest.[273] Other conservatives, in spite of their criti-cism of the moderate camp's use of the secular media, reached out to the newspapers. Chet Swanson, anticipating the climactic convention, boasted that the LCMS would become "the first great denomination to turn back the inroads of humanism."[274] Meanwhile, Swanson and Paul Zimmerman urged Ben Kaufman, religion editor at the *Cincinnati Enquirer*, to see the moderates for what they were—liberals. Kaufman responded that Missouri "liberals" sounded "pretty orthodox" to him, and Swanson agreed but, rela-tive to "where President Preus stands," Swanson wrote, they are liberal.[275] In November, Preus had the CTCR, now solidly in his camp, rule on "A Statement." They approved, finding that it was "in accord with the Holy Scriptures and the Lutheran Confessions."[276]

Early in 1973, Preus saw to it that Otten, through Hilst, was again given names of all the delegates to the coming convention.[277] Otten, ever the work-horse, had been assembling a massive and expensive 850-page *Christian Handbook on Vital Issues* to be distributed to the thousand-plus delegates. The *Handbook*, a compilation of articles and documents published in *Chris-tian News* over the course of its ten-year life, was divided into nearly thirty topical sections including "Music and the Arts," "Communism," "Church and State," "Abortion," "The Bible," "Freemasonry," and "Concordia Semi-nary, St. Louis." It was the quintessential resource for Missouri conserva-tism, one Otten and Preus hoped would have an impact at the convention.

In January 1973, the seminary's Board of Control, under mandate from the 1971 convention and Preus to reexamine the doctrine of Concordia's pro-fessors, "commended" all forty-four faculty members following two months of interrogation.[278] Furthermore, the Board—not yet under Preus's con-trol—elaborated that not one faculty member needed to be "corrected."[279]

Herman Scherer, Missouri District President and a dissenting member of the Board, complained that the decision was based less on theology than on personal hostility toward Preus: "The majority on the Board of Control at that time simply voted in favor of those professors because they were anti-Preus."[280] Preus, in an April "Brother to Brother" newsletter, warned that he would now take the issue to convention.[281] His machine fully mobilized, he now made plans to bring the endgame.

The synod's 1973 convention in New Orleans, dubbed the "Confrontation Convention" by the *Witness*, showcased the contrasting personalities of its lead celebrities, Jack Preus and John Tietjen. Preus's political savvy and genius for tactics paid huge dividends in New Orleans, where he played his opponents with virtuoso dexterity. John Tietjen, conversely, shared much in common with Preus's conservative backers. He was a proud ideologue, steeped in Lutheran tradition and, quite possibly, anticipating a Luther-at-Worms moment. That made him predictable, and predictability made for bad politics. Months before the convention, Preus's friend Art Beck, a Minnesota pastor, wrote at Preus's behest to Tietjen with an offer to secretly mediate a deal. Preus bet Beck ten dollars that Tietjen would never respond. Tietjen never did. "You see now clearly why I was willing to bet you," Preus wrote to Beck. "The man [Tietjen] recognizes no human authority. This has been the problem all the time."[282]

Tietjen and the moderates entered New Orleans with the deck stacked against them. Preus had used his power as synodical president to stack the convention's floor committees—the committees that decided what would come before the convention. Here Preus made no bones about his intention to control the convention, jamming the most powerful committees (Theology and Church Relations, Seminary Issues, Constitutional Matters) with his cronies while feigning even-handedness by ceding less controversial matters (such as Committee 11, Special and Sundry Matters) to moderates.[283] Preus later recalled with pride his control over the convention committees:

> [There were] some committees that I stamped like mad. Committee three at New Orleans [Seminary Issues] came up with all those things—and that was an absolute 100% conservative committee. But at the same convention when it came to social ministry questions [Committee 9], I had one

floor committee that dealt with racial questions that I think had something like 8 blacks, one Indian, and one anglo. And the minority elements said, "Hooray!"[284]

Moderates initially placed their hopes on the candidacy of Oswald Hoffmann, popular speaker of the *Lutheran Hour*, the synod's radio program. Hoffmann refused to stand for election against Preus, however, under a new bylaw adopted at the 1971 convention requiring candidates to give prior consent not only to be nominated but to serve if elected. Hoffmann saw this bylaw as a clear violation of the church's long-standing view of the divine call, by which a minister should not consider a call until he had received it.[285] Ellis Nieting, Preus's chair of the Constitutional Matters committee, cemented the matter by ramming through a resolution reaffirming the controversial bylaw.[286] The Frey-Lueking organization scrambled to find a backup candidate and quickly settled on William Kohn, who was easily defeated by Preus on the first ballot.[287]

A week of furious politicking followed. The conservatives, having distributed their election guide, proceeded to push through nearly all of their candidates—143 of the 147 they endorsed.[288] One by one their candidates were elected to synodical offices, boards, and college boards of control—and most by the same thin majority of about 55 percent. Edwin Weber, Otten's pick for the presidency in 1969, was elected vice-president, as were Harry Krieger and Walter Maier Jr.[289] The key result was published midway through the convention. Preus's candidates, including Balance hand E. J. Otto (who had recently published an *Affirm* article entitled "Close the Sem"[290]) and Preus relative Alfred Briel, were elected to Concordia Seminary's Board of Control.[291] George Loose, the Board's former chair now planning to return home to Florida, was contacted by a neighbor who had heard from Preus. "George Loose is coming down to your district," said Preus. "I'm going to get that bastard."[292] But Preus was victorious. He now controlled the Board with a 6-5 majority. The faculty's fate was nearly sealed.

Preus, in firm control of the convention, now flexed his muscle in one last attempt at a negotiated solution. Six weeks earlier, meeting with conservatives in Oklahoma, Preus told his backers, "Tietjen must go," a call he echoed and repeated to the synod's Council of Presidents.[293] In New

Orleans, meeting privately with Tietjen, Preus offered a deal: Resign from the presidency of Concordia within twenty-four hours, and I'll push through a resolution praising your "God-pleasing and selfless churchmanship."[294] Again Tietjen rejected political compromise.

The convention rolled to a boil in its tenth day, Tuesday, July 10. Preus was lining all his ducks in a row. That morning, the convention approved a resolution that made synodical statements "binding upon all its members."[295] Even more contentious was Resolution 3-01, to adopt Preus's statement as a "formal and comprehensive statement" of the synod's doctrine. Preus initially had to suppress a charge from the right. Conservatives wanted to make "A Statement" a synodical litmus test for all confirmed members of the LCMS. Karl Barth, chair of the Committee on Theology and Church Relations, asked delegates to leave the resolution as it was. After fending off several maneuvers from the Frey-Lueking organization, a vote was taken. The resolution passed, as had the others, with 55 percent of the vote. All hell now broke loose. Herman Neunaber, having survived in office despite a Preus-led effort to defeat him in southern Illinois, led a chorus line of moderate delegates to the podium, where they deluged the synod secretary with paper to officially register their objections, all the while singing the first stanza of "The Church's One Foundation." The day ended with a surreal devotion by Paul Streufert, obviously unprepared for what had just happened, who compared the "happy day which these workers now experience" to the "happy day which we still anticipate."[296]

After a day-long breather, delegates met again to deal more directly with Tietjen and the seminary faculty. A lengthy resolution, 3-09, was drafted to officially declare Concordia's faculty majority guilty of false doctrine and turn them over to the Preus-dominated Board of Control for discipline.[297] The resolution passed with a 56 percent majority. That evening, with time running out for the convention, the conservatives brought to the floor Resolution 3-12, a move to officially censure and fire John Tietjen from his position at the seminary. Debate was furious. With insufficient time to deal with the glut of amendments and procedural roadblocks, the conservatives substituted an amendment simply stating that Tietjen should be dealt with according to procedures now firmly in place. Tietjen was furious. He had been publicly maligned as a defender of "doctrinal aberrations" and accused of intimidating Board members and demeaning faculty members and Preus himself.[298] Now he was denied an opportunity to defend himself. After passage of the substitute resolution, Tietjen took to the microphone. Eleven years earlier, Martin Scharlemann, himself a target for conservative doctrinaires, survived a scare by apologizing to convention delegates. Now John Tietjen instead demanded that delegates give him an apology:

> I believe I have been grievously wronged by the convention. . . . Even though I have been wronged, I forgive you. I forgive you because I think you really do not know what you are doing. I think in time you will recognize what you are doing and will grieve over this day. But more important, I forgive you because of the suffering and death of our Lord Jesus Christ and because his blood takes away all our wrongs.[299]

Tietjen was easy prey for Jack Preus. Refusing to be humbled or even to accept a backroom compromise, he instead forgave sinful delegates as Jesus had forgiven those who had crucified him.[300] Preus later recounted that Tietjen could have easily won had he not been so predictable, such an ideologue, although it was also "very hard to know what Tietjen believed because he always identified with any aberration that anybody taught at that seminary." His first tactical error had been in even allowing Preus to investigate the seminary in 1970. He should have refused to allow professors to be interviewed. He could have offered "one or two" professors as sacrificial lambs.[301] He should have "bought time and forestalled [Preus]." He could have won each battle, believed Preus. Instead, "each one dug his grave deeper than the last." Preus commented:

> Tietjen was a very arrogant man and very stubborn. I never in my life heard him ever say that he was sorry. And I very early in the game concluded that it was this quick temperedness that was going to destroy him. And he couldn't back up. . . . I think Tietjen's underlying mistake was that he neither knew or understood or basically cared for what the Missouri Synod brought. He came from out East, he had lived in a very limited part of the church, and he simply did not have the picture of the Missouri Synod which I had. I never lived over 100 miles west of the Mississippi River and I think I understand the Missouri Synod as well as I understand my own mother.

Had Tietjen apologized, as Scharlemann had, Preus believed "he would have won the day even of the New Orleans delegates and I would have walked out the back end of that convention hall a beaten man."[302]

Notably absent at New Orleans were the numerous liberal social resolutions that had been so prevalent at conventions through 1969. Two resolutions were approved—one to combat racism, the other to work for women's rights.[303] But many more were ignored, including bids to reach out to Jews, intensify ministry to minorities, encourage more equitable minority representation in the synodical administration, eliminate racism in the church, and improve ministry to women and to promote equality.[304] Perhaps they were passed over because of the all-consuming nature of the theological controversy. More likely, their exclusion reflected a new direction the church was taking and would continue to take in the future now that the synod's main proponents of social action were being driven from the church.

The New Orleans convention was a strategic victory for Jack Preus and the conservative movement. The synod had officially adopted his "Statement," crafted and directed specifically in opposition to the faculty majority, as church doctrine. It made church doctrine binding on all church members. It gave Preus control over all key synodical boards, including the seminary's Board of Control. It condemned the faculty majority as heretics. And it turned over Tietjen to Preus and his Board of Control for discipline. Yet the victory was far from complete. It was no easy task dismissing respected and tenured faculty members, who would remain, even without Tietjen, a dominant majority at Concordia. Moreover, Preus was anxious to avert a painful and costly split in the church, and reached out again in compromise. But again the Luther Syndrome took effect, this time among the moderates, and quickly brought decisiveness to a war whose outcome was anything but inevitable.

By late 1973, the new Board of Control was geared up to take action against Tietjen and the faculty. The Board was now chaired by Preus ally E. J. Otto, a man even some conservatives found "rude," "autocratic," and "myopic."[305] In December, the Board voted to forcibly retire seven faculty members over the age of sixty-five, including Otten's old nemeses, Arthur Repp and Arthur Carl Piepkorn. Both vowed to fight the decision.[306] That same month, Tietjen was offered a final deal—accept a "call" to a parish and save the synod from destruction. In January he threw the deal back in Preus's face by announcing it to the church and condemning the continuing "immoral" political maneuvering and collusion among the conservatives.[307] The Board then hit back by cutting nineteen courses they deemed questionable from the curriculum. And on January 20, Tietjen was suspended. Martin Scharlemann was now in charge of the seminary.

This final chapter in the short life of Tietjen's Concordia was marked by an almost messianic and certainly desperate religious fervor. In mid-December 1973, Arthur Carl Piepkorn died after entering a barbershop bordering the seminary. Tietjen christened him the moderate camp's first martyr. One friend, wrote Tietjen, suspected that Piepkorn had died "of a broken heart." Reflecting on Piepkorn's December 17 funeral at the Concordia chapel, Tietjen wrote:

> Even more important was the profound subliminal impact [of Piepkorn's death]. I was clearly the pastor of a grieving spiritual community. In a coffin laid out in state in the CS chapel people could see the ultimate price that might have to be paid for confessional integrity.[308]

Herman Otten was unable to resist a final swipe at Piepkorn. Seeing the conflict from no less messianic a perspective than Tietjen, Otten reported, "God in his grace and wisdom took one of the principal actors in the [liberal camp] to Himself in heaven."[309] In January students voted to boycott classes after the announcement that Repp would be retired.[310] On January 22, the faculty majority told Preus that they too would boycott classes if Tietjen was suspended. Preus ordered them to return to work, and they refused. Scharlemann, intent on crushing the "rebellion," was ready by mid-February, with the Board's approval, to have the majority fired. They were given until February 19 to return to work.

February 19 was a day long on imagery and imagination but short on impact, the consummation of a long and rough journey begun at Denver. The fate of much of the faculty majority had already been decided. But they were determined to produce one final show in an effort to awaken an apathetic majority they were certain existed in Missouri. That morning, most of the students and faculty of Concordia Seminary gathered in the campus

quadrangle. Surrounded by Tudor Gothic buildings and onlooking reporters and photographers, students planted white wooden crosses in the cold
ground for each faculty and staff member, and one each for themselves.
Leaving the quadrangle, they boarded up the entrance to the seminary with
two large frames marked "EXILED" and began a staged march out of the
campus that would soon lead to formal separation from the LCMS. When
the reporters left, they turned around, walked back to campus, and had
lunch. It would take a little while longer to pack up their things.

4

Genie on the Loose:
1974–1981

In the years following the walkout at Concordia Seminary, the façade of conservative unity began to fracture. 1974 and 1975 were mopping-up years for conservatives, who continued to cement their hold on the synod by cowing or expelling the last pockets of moderate resistance. Moderates, for their part, formed a separate and formal association in the synod on the carcass of a defeated Frey-Lueking organization, and quickly moved to separate from the synod. When they did in 1976, the conservative movement degenerated into internecine warfare, driving many stalwart but sickened founders from its ranks while perfecting the techniques that had made them so dominant a force in the church. Less tolerant of Preus's political nature and desperately in need something to crusade against, they ultimately turned on him—and he on them.

After the Battle

Moderates licked their wounds after New Orleans and made plans to reorganize. In July, Tietjen supporters published a "Declaration of Protest and Confession." One month later they met, eight hundred strong, in Chicago to inaugurate Evangelical Lutherans in Mission (ELIM), an organization headed by Tietjen and Lueking that would exist in Missouri in a state of dissent. Former seminary faculty, meanwhile, organized a competing institution that soon became known only as Seminex (Concordia Seminary-in-Exile) and continued to graduate young men for the Missouri Synod ministry. ELIM, at its National Assembly, made a series of "demands" of delegates at the upcoming 1975 Anaheim convention: Rescind the several resolutions passed at Milwaukee and New Orleans that contributed to synod controversy; recognize Seminex-certified graduates as pastors; recognize as a synod that "acceptance of the Scriptures and the historic Lutheran confessional writings" constitutes "sufficient criterion for membership and ministry in the Synod": and apologize to "brothers and sisters unjustly wronged" in the controversy. ELIM had Tietjen's fingerprints all over it, the Luther Syndrome its core value. Tietjen was photographed for *Missouri in Perspective* at the assembly in 1974 standing before a massive poster extolling the words "Here We Stand."[1]

Preus swiftly dispatched his minions. The Committee on Theology and Church Relations (CTCR) met and ruled in an "Opinion on Dissenting Groups" that organizations like ELIM subverted the synod's constitution and the "majority" will must be respected.[2] Now fully in control of the *Witness,* Preus publicly condemned ELIM in September and October, saying, "Synod has spoken and we ought to listen." ELIM was "a rebellion not only against our Synod and its recent convention, but, more importantly, against God's holy, inspired, and inerrant Word."[3] More likely, Preus was motivated by the increasingly painful financial pinch generated by the controversy. Between 1965 and 1975, contributions to St. Louis from the districts for the synodical budget had been cut nearly in half. The most precipitous decline took place between 1973 and 1976, when contributions fell by over 30 percent.[4] Missouri Lutherans were still giving to their churches in record numbers. They just did not trust Preus with their offerings. Conservatives blamed the moderates. "ELIM," Otten warned Preus in a 1974 letter, "is draining the Synod's finances."[5]

Having conquered Concordia Seminary, Preus now set out to control the districts. The last significant battle of Missouri's civil war was fought over the authority of congregations and districts to ordain ministers. Seminex held its first commencement in 1974, and eight of the synod's sympathetic districts ordained its graduates. The synod's Commission on Constitutional Matters (CCM) soon ruled that congregations ordaining Seminex graduates would forfeit their membership in the synod; Seminex grads must first be interviewed and certified by the faculty of Concordia Seminary.[6] In June issues of the *Witness,* Preus urged congregations to reject the rebels, stating that it would be better to do without a minister than to have one from Seminex.[7]

Conservatives brought the issue to the 1975 convention in Anaheim. Preus issued his report to the delegates by challenging dissidents to leave the synod. "No church body can long support two theologies which are in conflict," he wrote. "If there are those who are doctrinally at such odds with the church that they cannot live at peace with their church," he continued, "it would seem that wisdom would dictate that they try to find a church home in which they could live with greater happiness."[8] To force the issue, conservatives approved Resolution 5-02A, which gave Preus the authority to fire rebellious district presidents. The resolution passed, as was becoming standard practice in the LCMS, with just over 55 percent of the vote.[9] A similar majority at the convention then censured ELIM as a schismatic movement. Moderates, their motion to include Balance, Inc. and *Affirm* in the censure resolution defeated, voiced their protests by singing "I Walk in Danger All the Way," forcing the chairman to declare a recess.[10] Finally, with a 56 percent majority, conservatives voted to close Concordia Senior College in Fort Wayne, Indiana, widely regarded as a feeder school for Seminex, and to disperse its faculty.[11]

The war sputtered to an end in 1976.[12] Preus, awakening with new powers the day after Anaheim, fired four district presidents who refused to bow to his authority. Later that year, Tietjen led what he hoped would be a massive exodus from the Missouri Synod into the newly formed Association of Evangelical Lutheran Churches (AELC). Moderates, who could count on a solid 45 percent of delegates at recent conventions, predicted that almost half of Missouri's 2.7 million members and six thousand congregations would follow. They were shocked by the tepid response. By year's end the AELC could count no more than one hundred thousand members and two hundred fifty congregations.[13]

Once again, elitism had returned to haunt moderates. Tietjen, who thought twelve hundred congregations would join him, blamed moderate pastors. "Pastors who wanted to join could not bring their congregations along because they had neither properly informed them about the events in the Missouri Synod nor adequately prepared them for the formation of a new church."[14] Frederick Danker, in his eulogy to Missouri, acknowledged that this was a battle of elites that left a laity largely alienated and disillusioned:

> Erroneously we thought that as the pastor goes, so goes the congregation. In the early stages of the war we thought primarily in terms of reaching the ministers. This was a basic error in judgment; Preus knew better. He knew that the primary allegiance of the members of the congregations would be to the Synod, not to the ministers. The ministers were intermediaries of authority, but the Synod was the bed-rock of authority, especially in the ethnic Midwest, and he as the President would be the court of final appeal. By addressing the fears and anxieties of the articulate people far to the right, he was able also to pick up those in the mainstream. Most of the pastors could be counted on not to 'disturb' their people, for most of them [laity] were of sound mind and viewed the 'taking of sides' as a posture of imbalance.[15]

Karl Barth chalked up the AELC's failure to draw a following to an elitist incapacity to relate to mainstream Lutherans. Moderates, he argued, "simply no longer knew where the church was, and figured that they represented [it]."[16] But Barth's conservatives were no less elitist, no more capable of drawing a sizable grass-roots following. *Affirm* and *Christian News* were aimed at synodical elites and consistently struggled to stay afloat in a sea of lay disinterest. And conservatism's two offshoots, Federation for Authentic Lutheranism (FAL, 1971–1975) and Lutheran Churches of the Reformation (LCR), could assemble no less insignificant an exodus from a synod they found too liberal.[17] "You'd better look behind you to see who is following," Barth had warned FAL in 1971.[18] More likely, pastors themselves simply had too much to lose by leaving the LCMS. The synod had grown large and wealthy since World War II, and ministers now had significant medical and retirement benefits tied up in its machinery. It would have been a great deal to sacrifice.

The Movement Fractures

The conservative camp was splintering and polarizing. Larry Marquardt left with a handful of churches to form FAL in 1971. Glen Peglau, who had been so instrumental in seeing to it that Preus was chosen over Ed Weber as the conservative candidate in 1969, broke with conservatives in 1972, claiming that Preus had "double-crossed conservatives" by defaulting on promises made to conservatives before his election in Denver.[19] Ozzie Gebauer faded away after New Orleans. Gebauer, remembers Chet Swanson, relied on "openness" and may have been frustrated by the movement's political stealthiness.[20] Tom Baker remembers that Gebauer had brought him into Balance to combat the growing power of Henry Hilst, who was keeping everything close—some thought too close—to his chest. The move backfired, and although Baker remained, Gebauer left after a falling out with Hilst.[21]

Jack Preus, anxious to keep moderates from stampeding en masse out of the synod, followed his own path, alienating his benefactors. Friend Paul Zimmerman, head of Preus's "Fact-Finding Committee" and "special assistant" to Preus in St. Louis, became president of the synod's college in River Forest, Illinois, over the objections of the faculty committee. Moderates called the move a "political payoff."[22] Still, Preus publicly moderated, to the chagrin of conservatives. Under enormous pressure to close the synod's "liberal" colleges, Preus instead reached out to district presidents in college towns and "won back some areas." Furthermore, in his 1981 interview, Preus revealed that he had wanted fellowship with the ALC to continue, in spite of pressure from conservatives to sever ties. Preus blamed cousin David Preus, ALC president, for souring a relationship that he had hoped to maintain.[23] Finally, Preus's slow-motion assault on rebellious district presidents aggravated conservatives. Fred Rutz, perennial thorn in the side of LCMS presidents, demanded that Preus move firmly and quickly to dismiss the eight who dared defy his authority. Preus told Rutz that it was time to move to the political center:

> I am moving away from extremists on one hand, who wish to tear congregations out of the Synod, and also those on the other hand who demand instant removal of the district presidents even before the various steps can be carried out.[24]

Three months later, Rutz, too, broke with Preus and issued a threat:

> In just five short months you moved from Middle to the extreme left. . . .
> Your consistent political maneuvering in appointing "political hacks" to
> various committees hoping to placate your adversaries . . . From all reports
> you have come to the end of your line.[25]

Finally, in mid-1978, Preus received a summons to appear in court. Fred
Rutz was suing Preus for financial mismanagement of the synod.[26]

Chet Swanson was ecstatic over the victory at "BONO" (Battle of New
Orleans)," by which conservatives were "turning back the tide of liberalism
that has engulfed other denominations and has sent rivulets of doctrinal
pollution into the mainstream of Missouri."[27] Swanson had worked hard
in advance of New Orleans to distribute "CROSSROADS," a "Faith Forward—First Concerns" type petition he hoped would overwhelm moderate
opposition. The petition included a letter from Walter Maier II to "every
pastor in the Synod," and was signed by the Who's Who of Missouri conservatism, from Robert Preus to Paul Zimmerman.[28] No one knows for certain
exactly how many signatures were collected. Swanson claimed, by February
1973, to have 75,000 signatures;[29] that number somehow jumped in three
months to over 274,000.[30] Even Swanson chum Otten, however, dismissed
those numbers as highly inflated. Swanson, Otten claimed, included the
membership lists of entire congregations when just a handful of members
may have signed his petition.[31]

Meanwhile, Swanson wrestled in vain to maintain conservative unity.
To his eleventh commandment ("Thou Shalt Not Air Your Differences with
Fellow Conservatives Publicly"), he added a twelfth in 1975: "Thou Shalt
Take Up Your Personal Differences with Fellow Conservatives Privately."[32]
Swanson identified three dominant conservative factions in 1975, and himself as one of the only men to bridge all three. The increasingly "tenuous
nature of the coordination and cooperation" among them was, he worried,
"a weakness and a potential concern." The first of them, Balance, Inc., was
purely conservative and received support from "all individuals and groups
who appreciate the work conducted by and through [it]," including those
who were not members of the LCMS. The second faction was the Continuation Committee, a small group of no more than 150 original members

that was working to maintain "contacts" in each LCMS district. The third faction he identified as the "Doctrinal Concerns Program Network" (DCP), a pseudo-official organization supported by Preus that "would use normal Synodical channels." Swanson, perhaps presumptuously, included Otten and *Christian News* in this faction, as the DCP's newsletter, the *DCP TRUM-PET,* operated "within the confines of CHRISTIAN NEWS."[33]

But Swanson's relationship with Otten was killing his friendly relations with Jack Preus. Swanson had consistently urged the conservative inner circle to coordinate efforts with Otten. In January 1973, he noted that Otten was receiving praise for the "timely topics," "improved tone," and "increased impact" of *Christian News*, whose author was finally responding to pressure to clean up the paper by making use of "guest editorials" from other conservatives. While pushing conservatives to support *Christian News* ("But let's not just receive benefits <u>from</u> CN. Let's also help CN"), he warned conservatives to state the rules of Otten's use of their materials up-front, given Otten's tendency to throw even personal correspondence into his paper.[34] Jack Preus did coordinate with Otten but continued to denounce him publicly, a pragmatic duplicity for which Swanson would not stand. In November, Swanson slammed Preus in a handwritten letter for public statements that were dividing conservatives and the LCMS:

> "I told you so" are not words I like to use. But:
>
> 1. I told you that you should NOT label the Chicago [ELIM] attendees as rebellious. I even offered to help (you and Huth) prepare a pastoral letter that would carefully differentiate between <u>dissent</u> (which some who attended the "moderate" meeting in Chicago were practicing) and <u>disobedience</u> (which some others at that meeting were practicing).
>
> 2. I've told you a dozen times to stop taking public swipes at CN in a way that would indicate you regard that publication as "right wing" or "extreme." If we must differ with each other, for heavens sake let's be specific! Not labels, but issues!!!

Swanson noted that John Baur, who was advocating a split in the LCMS, had also suffered a falling-out with Preus. He warned Preus not to take on Baur:

But I would not THINK of labeling him [Baur] with an extreme label. I
would not do so because:

A. It is an unfair label and
B. It would help divide rather than unify our needed conservative
    forces.[35]

Swanson was still embarrassed by a late 1972 meeting in Cleveland that
some conservatives refused to attend because Swanson was "an Otten man."
"We fight against each other (or face artificial barriers of 'repudiations', 'secrecy'
and 'strategy')," he complained, "rather than openly working together."[36]

Swanson was nearly fed up with Preus by 1976. Like other conservatives, he wanted Preus to quickly fire the rebellious eight district presidents.
He complained to Jim Adams in February that "discipline . . . does not seem
to be a popular trend. So we wince but do not whimper to see justice once
more delayed and anarchy served again." Swanson was slowly working his
way out of a shrinking "inner team," sinking more of his time and money into
DCP. "I probably spend more money," he told Adams, "than any single individual in the movement."[37] Waldo Werning, in a letter to the team on the eve
of the synod's 1977 convention in Dallas, was concerned about Swanson's
independent drift. "Proper handling of Chet Swanson might be encouraged
at the same time to let Chet know that we expect him to remain on the team
of all of us rather than going out on his own."[38] Karl Barth, concerned that
Swanson was getting "off the track a bit" by moving away from Preus, also
tried to corral Swanson. Swanson replied that Barth and Preus were using
theological language to disguise political objectives. Barth responded:

> Chet, you're like a guy who wants to fly the airplane. And when the pilot
> tries to show you everything, you say, "don't confuse me with all these gad-
> gets here." If you want to get into the battle, don't hide under the excuse
> that we are using theological terms.[39]

Barth never heard from Swanson again.

Werning, meanwhile, continued to flirt with a movement no longer his
own. Like other conservatives, he alternately repudiated and ingratiated
himself to Herman Otten. After New Orleans, Werning rebuked Otten for
his fondness for libel:

The slanderous and libelous innuendo by the Rev. Earl Zimmerman of Kansas in the recent Christian News, which Zimmerman ties up with being sick, and a tool of the devil, has resulted in a letter by me to Zimmerman asking him for an immediate and complete apology and retractions without conditions and limitations. I trust that you will receive a letter from him to be printed in the very next issue of Christian News. I would think that your editorial policy would include not printing such irresponsible letters which contain slanderous innuendo against somebody else, when you have been provided no proof that this individual has dealt with the brother whom he condemns in such an unChristian manner. I trust that you will adopt a policy which refuses to print any letters by men who do not have the courage to deal first with the people whom they charge with certain things unless they are willing to provide proof for same.[40]

Yet Werning continued to feed Otten information and ghost-write articles for *Christian News*. One such article promoted Robert Preus for the board of Lutheran Bible Translators (LBT), an auxiliary organization: "Electing conservatives who have experience in LBT will strengthen this organization."[41] And Werning, funneling information to Otten from *Affirm*, did not hesitate to practice, through Otten, the very policy he condemned. In an undated, post-1973 letter to Otten, Werning told Otten to print allegations while hiding the source:

Herman: Enclosed is a statement of Rev. Horstman: DO NOT USE OR QUOTE FROM IT OR LET ANYONE KNOW AFFIRM SHARED IT WITH YOU. You might write R. W. Meyer + tell him Rev. Horstman has been sharing his complaints with others + that is how you heard about it. Write Meyer that Horstman has been known to say that he was robbed of being delegate to Milwaukee + when that was settled with Neunaber who admitted that he had gone over the head of the Circuit visitor + appointed a delegate without consulting the visitor. Horstman was the alternate delegate who was bypassed. (Neunaber had no right picking an alternate from the Denver convention which was ridiculous.) Say nothing about the N.O. [New Orleans] delegates since you are not challenged on that.[42]

Werning's relationship with Jack Preus had soured from the day he took his place on the Board for Missions. Werning's refusal to serve as a Preus automaton on the Board led Preus to consider ousting Werning. In 1975 at its Anaheim convention, Karl Barth told Werning that Preus was out to have him removed.[43] The relationship grew more strained as Preus embarrassed Werning in a 1975 flare-up with the synod's Hong Kong mission. Delegates in Anaheim had reaffirmed Martin Kretzmann's Mission Affirmations and, in an effort to repair the mass exodus from LCMS missions in the wake of Werning's election, instructed the Board to "refrain from involving themselves in the supervision and counseling of missionaries and sister churches which is properly the function of the mission staff."[44] Werning was accused of crossing that line by encouraging a conservative faction under Rev. Martin Chang to establish a competing church body in Hong Kong.[45] The accusation was false, Werning contends, but appeared nonetheless in a 1975 issue of ELIM's *Missouri in Perspective*. Preus, looking to avoid scandal, made Werning write a carefully crafted apology. "Jack all the way," remembers Werning. Years later, Werning recalls, one of the accusers repented to him and asked for his forgiveness.[46]

Werning was, by 1977, either uncomfortable with the tactics of the conservative movement or concerned with the perception they were creating. Preparing for the 1977 convention, Werning pleaded with his colleagues to abandon the publication of *Affirm*'s straightforward election list. Some conservatives, and most moderates, complained that the lists had the effect of disparaging the names of those not on the list, a decidedly unchristian practice. Werning believed that momentum was so strong against the use of lists that it threatened to finally destroy the conservative movement. Opposed to Werning were Balance chiefs E. J. Otto, Bill Eggers, and Robert Preus. To avoid a conservative split, Werning fashioned a compromise. Rather than distribute an *Affirm* list of approved candidates, simply give delegates premarked copies of their official election guides. Hilst told Werning that the compromise met with his approval. Werning believed that the use of marked books could be spun as a less insulting way to promote candidates:

> The way I read the situation is that there is such gross fear on the part of the ones who insist on a published list [Otto, Robert Preus, and Eggers] that they feel we will take a shellacking by simply using marked books, and the fear also causes them to misunderstand reasoned arguments that marking books is simply a witness one to another, while a published list is a gross embarrassment to those that are not selected and is a red flag

to others in a way that arouses anger and violent reaction. . . . Furthermore, I am convinced that it will leave a very bad taste in the mouth of all
middle-of-the-roaders and many responsible conservatives who happen to
disagree rather strongly with such tactics in 1977.[47]

Herman Otten's contradictory campaign to synthesize Missouri Lutheranism and political conservatism further alienated him from Preus. From one
side of his mouth, Otten denounced what he saw as a vestige of Missouri
liberalism, the church speaking out on issues not purely theological. In a
series of lectures in early 1972, he called "mixing church and state" a "pitfall
of conservatives." "It is generally recognized," he argued, "that theological
liberals have attempted to get the church involved in political, economic,
and social issues where it has no business. Unfortunately some conservatives
are similarly attempting to get the Church to speak out on matters where
it should remain silent."[48] The synod, at its 1971 convention, had approved
a series of "Social Ministry Affirmations" that pledged the synod to combat
racism, poverty, and injustice, and to promote universal health care in the
United States.[49] Preus supported the measure, calling it "significant, good,
and pointing in the right direction,"[50] identifying "the ongoing problem of
combating racism in our own nation and church."[51] But Otten was worried
by Preus's cozy relationship with what he considered to be black radicals like
Will Herzfeld and Albert Pero, a connection he exposed in an early 1975
issue of *Christian News*. Herzfeld replied to Otten by calling him a racist,
asking him to "get off my back!!!" and demanding, "You peddle your sickness among those who need you."[52]

From the other corner of his mouth, Otten exhorted Christians to be
active, political conservatives. His selective opposition to mixing religion and
politics quickly fizzled when no longer applied to a liberal agenda of racial
equality, tolerance, and justice. At a lecture outside Milwaukee in early
1973, he touted C. F. W. Walther's book, *Communism and Socialism,* and
boldly stated that it is the Christian's duty to oppose communism, defend
the right of private property, and staunchly support the free enterprise system.[53] Ralph Moellering soon reprimanded Otten for a "narrow bigotry"
that "undermines and discredits the cause of authentic conservatism. Your
pseudo-orthodoxy is all too apparent." Moellering continued that Otten's

writings fused the entire "ecclesiastical-socio-political spectrum" and demonstrated "a preference, if not an affinity, for the religio-political synthesis
which undergirds the 'Nixon-Graham silent majority.'"[54] Otten's myopic
conservatism did identify with Nixon, Graham, and his parochial brethren,
but also equated his views with God's will. That doomed him to isolation.

Preus's scheming and Otten's aggressive tone doomed their relation-
ship as well. Otten's case had been caught up since Milwaukee in synod's
Byzantine bureaucracy. Preus and his allies had tied up Otten's case since.
Paul Zimmerman, who had originally urged Preus to settle the matter, cut
Otten off in 1971.[55] The New Orleans convention, calling "this continued
denial of Rev. Otten's entry" into the pastoral ministry a "long-standing
unresolved injustice," had referred the matter to Preus for resolution, and
Preus shoved it back to the delegates in 1975.[56] The Anaheim convention
pushed it back to Otten, advising him to reapply to the newly conservative Concordia Seminary.[57] Otten, with Baur, Paul Burgdorf, and his son,
Larry Burgdorf, then met with Ralph Bohlmann, who told Otten to take
his case back to the Board of Appeals, where the whole mess had begun.
But Otten's belligerence undermined his case. One week after Christmas
1974, Otten wrote Preus, livid at reports from an informant that synod's
recent "elaborate" Christmas party included drinking, dancing, and former moderate employees. "You are supposed to have been present," he
chastised Preus.[58] Otten followed up later that year, again informed by
his moles of Preus's shenanigans. The *Minneapolis Star* had reported that
Preus called Otten "irresponsible," a charge Preus now admitted.[59] Cut
off by Preus after Anaheim, Otten told him what others were saying about
him: "Jack wants others to do his 'dirty' work for him so that he can come
up smelling like a rose."[60]

What likely most frustrated Preus and finally destroyed the movement
was his big brother, Robert. Jack had been angered by Robert's decision to
join Balance, Inc. after Denver, and was just as frustrated in 1974, when he
accepted a call to take Jack's old seat as president of the Springfield seminary (the seminary moved to Fort Wayne, Indiana, after the 1975 convention's decision to disband the Senior College).[61] Robert spent much of his
time at the Balance helm performing political gymnastics, sounding the

same false note that echoed from his brother's office in St. Louis: Balance was not political, and there was no relationship between it and Jack Preus. He claimed that *Affirm's* editorial policy was independent of Balance, even though he served as president of Balance and on *Affirm's* editorial committee.[62] He and Marcus Lang denied that Balance predated Jack's 1969 election—technically true (it was not incorporated until 1970), but a deliberate misrepresentation of its relationship to the UPC and Continuation Committee.[63] Finally, he denied that Balance was a political organization, insisting instead that it was merely there to support and publish *Affirm*.[64] This despite Robert's knowledge that only half of Balance's 1972 funds had gone to *Affirm*, and half of that went to Henry Hilst, who was organizing for Jack, and to other conservative groups.[65] Balance under Robert Preus was very political and, over the objections of some conservatives, even embracing of non-LCMS members.[66]

The brothers' relationship turned sour after 1974. Jack, who had opened letters to Robert with "Dear Big," now signed off with a cold and formal, "Sincerely, J. A. O. Preus."[67] The two had different approaches to the synod. Karl Barth commented, "I don't think Robert would have been able to do what Jack did [as synodical president]." Jack took his time with moderates he wanted to get rid of, while Robert's instinct "was to fire [them]." The disconnect made it very easy for Jack to seem irresolute and Robert impractical.[68] Robert's cozy relationship with Herman Otten also put Jack at arm's distance. From at least 1959, Robert Preus and Otten enjoyed a very close friendship. Robert was one of Otten's informants at Concordia before the walkout and continued the relationship even after assuming the presidency at Fort Wayne.[69] He ghost-authored articles for *Christian News*.[70] And he actively coordinated the efforts of *Affirm* and *Christian News*.[71] Unlike Jack, Robert consistently supported Otten. But like Jack, he was careful to conceal that relationship. If typewritten, letters to Otten were official in nature. Handwritten and undated notes of a more personal or political nature would be paper-clipped to official correspondence. His big brother's comparatively close relationship with Otten frustrated Jack to no end. Otten joked with Robert in 1976, "This week Jack tried to find out who feeds us data, but I kept him hanging on his fishing expedition."[72]

Robert refused for six years to heed Jack's call to extricate himself from Balance. Not until 1980 did he resign from the *Affirm* board. But after assuming the presidency at Springfield/Fort Wayne, Robert became more drawn in, even using the seminary as a headquarters for Balance.[73] Waldo Werning later served as the seminary's Development Director. Soon, Robert Preus was holding regular and weekly Continuation Committee conference calls out of his office.[74] By 1977, his office was an increasing source of power in the synod, uniting many conservatives alienated by his brother. To Jack's dismay, Robert did not heed his (and Werning's) call to distribute marked books in lieu of lists at the 1977 convention. The *Affirm* list went out, conservatives again dominated, and Jack was again elected. Jack was now in the uncomfortable position of being beholden to his brother.

Blackmail

The thickest docket in Jack Preus's 1977 Herman Otten file is the one labeled "Blackmail." Otten, sporadically critical of Preus in *Christian News* through 1977, still preserved the public veneer of unity. But behind the scenes, he was fed up. Otten asked Preus in a March 17, 1977, letter, "We have just received a report which comes from some of your closest friends and supporters that you are supposed to have said that you are going to 'annihilate' Fred Rutz and Chet Swanson. Did you say this and are you out to silence these men?"[75] Preus refused to take Otten's calls. In a phone call later that day, Otten told Preus's vice president, Robert Sauer, that "we are all fed up with his double talk. His closest friends say he lies to them." Otten told Sauer to remind Preus about "The Peglau information." Confused, Sauer asked for clarification. Otten told Sauer that Preus would know what he meant.[76] Two days later, a lengthy letter Preus labeled "Blackmail" arrived on his desk. In it, Otten threatened to make public the long record of Preus duplicity:

> You seem quite disturbed when you called and I told you that you could never be caught like Nixon was caught. Others have told you the same thing. You asked rather heatedly whether I was calling you a liar. What else can both your friends and opponents conclude when you say one thing to

one group one place in the nation and then say about exactly the opposite to another group elsewhere. You asked me to give you some documentation. I won't depend upon what others have told me about your double-talking but merely cite a few things you told Glen and me five years ago during our series of conference calls. You can check the accuracy of the quotes with Glen.

Rutz and Baur were also fed up, Otten told Preus. He continued that the synod would be better served if an "honest consistent conservative like Barth, Maier, Zimmerman, Merkens, Weber, etc." was to run, and gave Preus a small sampling of incriminating quotes transcribed from phone conversations.[77] "Just recently," he told Preus, "you said that you wrote to Rev. Richard Neuhaus that you were sitting in the smallest room in your house with his paper before you and that in a few moments you would have it behind you. I have this statement and many others far more damaging on tape." Otten continued, "I won't take time to compile statements you made elsewhere which completely contradict what you said during our conference calls. You have repeatedly denied that you ever told me that you were sorry for repudiating *Christian News*." He concluded by threatening, "Please don't make it necessary for us to continue the series on the Preus record."[78]

The pressure worked. Within the month, Preus had again caved to coercion from the right. Otten made it known to Preus that he might support the candidacy of Walter Maier II at the synod's 1977 convention. Soon afterward, Preus advisor William Hecht reached out to Otten to stave off a last-minute move toward Maier. "I am as strongly committed to the authority of Scripture and the need for pure doctrine in the Church as you or any of the other conservative pastors," he wrote. "Human beings do err and make mistakes," and Jack Preus is only human. "Jack has been naïve on some occasions but then Peter, James and John could certainly sympathize with him." Even Elijah hid in a cave, after all. He concluded:

> Herman, if Jack Preus is re-elected I can absolutely assure you that he will make more mistakes but then so would Walter Maier, Ed Weber, Robert Preus, Ralph Bohlmann or anyone else who may be elected. . . . Let us rejoice in the accomplishments that have been made under the Preus administration.[79]

Then, in April, Preus agreed to support a CTCR statement that urged the synod to back out of its 1969 fellowship agreement with the ALC and enter instead a state of "protesting fellowship." He then endorsed another conservative position, asking the synod not to accept a new hymnal jointly developed by the LCMS, ALC, and others until all of its contents could be reviewed by the CTCR and synod's seminary faculties. In response, Otten gave Preus his official, if unenthusiastic, support, predicting in print that he would be a shoo-in for reelection in Dallas.[80]

Preus was reelected in Dallas. The *Affirm* list had gone out to delegates, and Preus's name again topped the slate. But conservatives gave him a scare, pushing his election through to a second ballot. Fifteen percent of them, led by an uncompromising Swanson, cast their lots with Walter Maier.[81] Fred Rutz bragged to Otten, "May be [*sic*] they are finding out that they are not so secure as they thought they were."[82] Ed Weber, Maier, Texan Guido Merkens, and Sauer won election as synod vice presidents. On day five of the convention, ballots were distributed to delegates for remaining officers and boards. At this point, Otten's sister, Marie Meyer, who was on the Committee for Convention Nominations, rose to give a tearful and impassioned plea to delegates to reject the *Affirm* list and instead rely on God's guidance.[83]

Dallas ended the chimera of public and even private unity among conservatives. Richard Korthals, conservative professor at the synod's college in River Forest and co-editor of *Affirm*, was the next to leave the movement. Writing to Preus the Monday evening the *Affirm* list was distributed, he lamented:

> I would also like to personally apologize for what took place today—namely the distribution of the preferred list by AFFIRM. It was done without my knowledge or consent, and I consider it a serious breach of faith. Assurance had been given to many people that this would not happen, and it was only under these conditions that I went along with the initial limited mail distributions.
>
> Today has been a literal hell for me. I believe I finally have empathy with you in your feelings toward the hard-nosed right. I was always sympathetic and felt I understood why you acted in some ways—now I know. I worked on AFFIRM because I felt I could be a moderating influence—that

now appears impossible. As a result I have resigned from Balance, and have severed all relations with its endeavors.[84]

Preus thanked Korthals and agreed, "I'm sick and tired of a small group of people sailing under the flag of *Affirm*, putting out these lists. . . . The whole thing is a lot of phoney baloney, and I'm glad you did it."[85]

Marie Meyer also wrote to Preus, soon after the convention, apologizing for the tone of her speech, praying that it had not set back woman's suffrage in the LCMS.[86] Preus responded that she had nothing to apologize for: "You were elected as a woman, and everybody knew it, and that is nothing to apologize for."[87] He later wrote her a more personal note, empathizing that he knew what it was like to have such a jerk for a brother.[88]

Brother Robert was less charitable to Mrs. Meyer. Winfred Schroeder, a pastor in Vancouver, Washington, wrote to Robert Preus, noting, "Even Pres. Jack applauded" Marie Meyer's "emotional, almost tearful, appeal." Robert responded by condemning Meyer's speech as "not inspired, in my opinion, by sound judgment and certainly not on motives of fair play or Christian charity."[89] He also defended Balance, telling Schroeder that the *Affirm* list was not at all "unethical," and that he would not apologize for having distributed it and having benefited from it.[90]

Jack struggled privately to convince supporters that he was the aggrieved centrist distinct from his right-wing brother. To one he assured:

> I asked the Affirm brethren not to publish the list. I certainly did not ask them to put my name on the List. I feel very strongly about this matter because I feel that it puts particularly the defeated candidate in a very awkward position. He was willing to let his name be used and offered to serve his church and then even before the delegates have a chance to vote he is blackballed. I feel this is extremely unfair and I told this to the Affirm people. The only good thing that I can see in this is that it proves that I am not a pope. My admonition is not listened to in that quarter either.[91]

Another complained to Preus that although he was a supporter and conservative who worked "in a spirit of loyalty" to Jack, the *Affirm* people treated him poorly. "Not only were we completely ignored nomination-wise," he complained, "but I was refused entry at the Affirm headquarters."[92] Preus chided Robert, "I think you ought to see the problems we run into with our own conservatives. This is a man who has broken his neck on behalf of Synod out in the California area."[93]

Yet here again, Jack Preus showcased his flair for mendacity. In September, Marcus Lang wrote to Preus with a detailed "STATISTICAL ANALYSIS OF DALLAS ELECTIONS RE 'AFFIRM' LIST." In it he bragged that the *Affirm* list was a smashing success, critical to the victory of nearly half the 126 conservatives elected. *Affirm's* greatest flaw was not that it distributed the list, but that between 75 and 150 conservative delegates "did not have the pre-convention 'Affirm' list with them."[94] Preus, who had in other circles condemned the list, here reproached Lang that it had not been effective enough. "If a concerted effort of a small group of people, which began only at the time of the convention, can overturn the *Affirm* list in the case of a well known and highly respected man like Gene Fincke," he worried, "the same kind of activities on behalf of more people could overturn the whole *Affirm* list." Preus bewailed what he believed to be critical losses at the treasurer level and on the synod's Board for Higher Education:

> In the case of the treasurer, we know that some people really went to work, including some people who had previously been supportive of *Affirm*. In the case of Elmer Moeller, we have no way of knowing why he was elected. These are questions I would like to see looked into also.[95]

Otten and Preus: Open War

After the Dallas convention, conservatism's internecine conflict finally exploded into public view. The release of Jim Adams's *Preus of Missouri* in 1977 stirred the synod, nowhere more, however, than in New Haven, Missouri. Preus's double-dealing was now in the public domain, and Otten gleefully broadcast quotes of Preus in Adams such as his vow to "put Otten out of business."[96] Preus, anxious to preempt Otten, released selected portions of their "blackmail" correspondence. He also came out swinging at former allies at *Affirm,* including Swanson and board chair (and *Affirm* editor) E. J. Otto, denouncing both the magazine and Swanson's DCP. Preus, beneficiary of the same, asked, "Is the Synod to be run with threats, intimidation and cronyism?" Swanson fired back that Preus's comments were "an affront to a lot of hard-working, orthodox Missourians that deserve far better treatment than they are receiving."[97] For fear of damaging the movement, Otten still did not release the goods on Preus, suggesting only that he was "two faced."[98] But he still pushed, as always, in print, Preus to retire:

> Something has happened to the LCMS president. He needs our sympathy and prayers. Right now it appears that it would be best both for him and the LCMS to declare he will not seek re-election. This is exactly what we told him in the letter he is using as evidence for his charge that C.N. is guilty of "blackmail."[99]

The mudslinging went both ways. Preus first threatened to reveal what many already knew by then, that Otten and his informants secretly tape recorded conversations. Otten responded that Preus was only offended by the tactic when he was its victim:

> While you have severely faulted us for using tape recordings, we fail to see what else we can do to support a report in which a person denies saying something which we reported he said. . . . We then published a statement from a tape recording made at a speech which you gave in Lisle, Illinois where you said exactly what we had reported.[100]

Preus wrote in December that he had more dirt on Otten: a Preus informant told him that Otten had applied for a call in a West German church body.[101] Using a favorite Otten approach, he asked, "Is this true?"[102] Finally, in a move that caused Otten considerable hardship, Preus pulled synod support from William Beck's *An American Translation* (AAT) of the Bible. "Bible Beck," an eccentric Otten enthusiast who worked in a freezing office to keep his mind alert, translating the Bible with fingerless gloves and without socks, had his New Testament translation published by synod's CPH in 1963.[103] Preus now claimed it doctrinally deficient and pulled his support. Otten felt the pinch, having just paid the bill for 50,000 copies of AAT he now had to sell.[104]

Preus was not afraid to fight Otten on his home turf—in the mud. In April 1979, Otten wrote to Preus and Victor Constien, head of Parish Services, to command action against an allegedly immoral pastor working for

Constien at synod headquarters. Otten had sent this pastor a questionnaire demanding to know if the rumors were true that "he had an unscriptural divorce and had not repented of the sin." When the man refused to answer, Otten took the rumors to Preus. This man, Otten told Preus, "is supposed to have 'lusted' after the woman to whom he is now married before he ever got his divorce."[105] The reply from Preus and Constien rivaled Otten's own dirty tactics. Carl Hoffmeyer, Otten's old SOC ally, had fallen on hard times in recent years and was facing accusations of child molestation. Otten was considering serving as Hoffmeyer's court-appointed supervisor.[106] Somehow word had gotten to Preus, as reflected in Constien's reply:

> I have received your letter regarding _____. I understand your con-
> cern. I can think of parallel situations. It's been reliably reported that you
> offered to have the Rev. Carl Hoffmeyer come to New Haven to stay with
> you so that you could minister to him. Can you tell me the current status
> of this matter?[107]

The Preus-Otten war was felt elsewhere: The tried and true formula of covert cooperation with Otten was affecting even Waldo Werning's relationship with Preus. Werning, who in 1978 was still sending Otten articles and information for *Christian News*, was reprimanded by Preus when someone exposed the Werning-Otten connection. Werning, anxious to maintain Preus's trust, reached out to Otten:

> Dear Herman, This may seem a bit odd to you but our synodical presi-
> dent had gotten the false rumor that I wrote some of the campaign articles
> or editorials in the <u>Christian News</u>' 1977 presidential campaign. He will
> believe me only if I write you a letter with a carbon to him, and that is the
> purpose of this letter. I am sure that you will recall that I tried to discour-
> age you from a hard-hitting campaign, adding to the voices of Reverend
> Walter Hoffmann and Henry Hilst. . . .[108]

Yet again, Herman Otten was losing friends fast and was increasingly hurt by the rapid defection of his superficial allies.[109]

The Otten-Preus relationship was consuming both men by 1979. In January, Preus composed a massive, nineteen-page letter to Otten. Preus cut right to the heart of Otten's pain, his clear and unmet expectation that Jack Preus, a man he had helped put into office, would see to it that justice was

finally served—that he would be certified as an LCMS minister. Preus, who
had wielded power so successfully during his tenure as president, claimed to
Otten that he just did not have the power. He told Otten that three conventions, 1962, 1965, and 1971, had ruled Otten's case closed. He took heated
issue with Otten's claim that he had worked to keep Otten out of the ministry of the LCMS, and called Otten an "unrepentant liar." "You are dishonest,
you are evading the facts. There is only one person who is keeping Herman
Otten out of the ministry and that is Herman Otten. All of which reminds
me," Preus continued, "that you are taking on a herculean task in sitting in
judgment on virtually every political movement and trend not only within
Christendom but within international politics, pagan religions, and many
other areas." Preus closed by suggesting that Otten take an extended vacation, leave his congregation in the hands of a "competent man," and stop
making "Are you still beating your wife?" accusations.[110]

One of Otten's few consistent friends, Kurt Marquart, took up his case
privately with Preus. Writing to both sister Marie and Jack Preus, Marquart
wrote in March:

> Perhaps no one else in our church except President Preus himself and
> Martin Scharlemann at the time of the 'exile' has suffered the massive and
> sustained vitriol and vituperation which has been Herman's lot for years.

The key to a "pacification" of relations between synod and *Christian News,*
wrote Marquart, was "the regularization of Herman's clergy status."[111] But
Preus responded to Marquart that Otten was "beyond redemption":

> I don't see how it is going to be humanly possible for either the Colloquy
> Board or the faculty to certify him until there is a massive and sincere act
> of repentance and a retraction of all of the unkind and unloving statements
> he has made. . . . I know that you supported the Herman Otten of 1957.
> I probably would have done the same, and certainly was sympathetic to
> him back in those early days. But we're dealing with the Herman Otten of
> 1979, who has become bitter and vindictive.

Preus concluded by holding out an olive branch he was sure Marquart
would pass on to Otten. "The regularization of his clergy status, it seems to
me, is absolutely contingent upon shutting down *Christian News* and having

a condition to his clergy status that it shall not be revived or contributed to by him." Otten's choice was "very simple," wrote the man who had just told Otten he was powerless to resolve the crisis. "It's either *Christian News* or non-inclusion in the clergy roster of the Synod."[112]

Otten again applied to the seminary for certification. This time, Preus openly killed the application, telling Otten that "we do not want an unrepentant liar for a pastor."[113] Aiding Preus was W. T. Janzow, eager for payback after resigning from the presidency of the synod's college in Seward, Nebraska, in 1977, after Otten published "A Call to Investigate Concordia, Seward" in *Christian News*.[114] Again Preus issued Otten an ultimatum: *Christian News* or certification. "The obvious answer is that you put out a final edition of Christian News in which you humbly ask the forgiveness of all that you have injured, either intentionally or unintentionally, and then go out of business." That, said Preus, would virtually assure certification. However, he concluded, "I am still not certain that you wish to be certified for the ministry."[115]

Even now the fires of personal animus could not trump the primacy of politics for both men. As another convention approached in the summer of 1979, they were careful still to keep their private rage from damaging the movement. Preus, speaking to synodical denunciations of *Affirm, Christian News*, and ELIM, argued that they were not all bad, at least when they suited his purposes: "It also perhaps could be cogently argued that occasionally at least some of these journals make a genuine contribution to the cause of the church at large and The Lutheran Church—Missouri Synod."[116] Otten, on the eve of the 1979 St. Louis convention, pulled back from his threat to publish a "special issue" denouncing Preus.[117] Their personal differences were a "relatively minor issue" when compared to the threat of liberalism: "Whether or not Herman Otten gets into the ministry of the Lutheran Church—Missouri Synod or can prove he is innocent of all your serious charges is really not all that important."[118]

Preus vs. Preus

By the end of the 1979 convention, Jack Preus was at war with the movement that had brought him to and kept him in power. He consistently defended his role in the intrigues of Balance and *Christian News* before 1977 as an emergency measure, but wanted them to disappear now that he dominated the church. So he attacked both in the press. E. A. Weise, chairman of California's DCP program, reminded him that the synod in 1975 had specifically excluded *Affirm*/DCP from a resolution that denounced outside groups as "divisive."[119] Preus responded by thanking Weise for a job well done in a district that "was drifting to the left very rapidly." But now Preus wanted the genie back in the bottle: "I don't think that the Synod needs as much help from some of the free-lance organizations as it once did."[120]

He brought the same message to *Affirm* fire-eater E. J. Otto. *Affirm*, again hurting for money and unable to generate any widespread appeal, was begging for support (while "looking forward to the day when publications such as *Affirm* are no longer necessary").[121] Jack Preus's power over *Affirm* was that two of its remaining editors after 1978, Otto and brother Robert, were certified pastors, subject to his discipline as synodical president. This was his chance to kill off Balance. Preus warned Otto that continuing "character assassination" would allow him to discipline its editors under the synod's statement of ethics. "I do not oppose politicking," he told Otto. Nor did he mind election lists that kept him in power. What did bother Preus was that someone other than himself was serving "as a nominating committee."[122]

Other Balance members and supporters reacted strongly to Preus's denunciations. Martin Scharlemann, under pressure from Otto, joined the editorial staff in 1979 and immediately took fire from Preus.[123] Preus defended himself from charges of duplicity to Walter Otto. "If anybody in the Synod has played politics it is AFFIRM, with their preferred election lists."[124] Preus also acknowledged and defended his reliance on situational ethics. Friend Walter Forster told him that "any member of Synod [should] express his dismay at your apparent abandonment of them [conservatives]."[125] Preus repied that he was simply following Forster's advice to be "kind of the center in the storm." "Where I think the problem with some of these groups," he told Forster, "is they do not realize that the Synod has changed enormously since back in 1969 and requires different tactics and different approaches. I'm sure you are an astute enough political scientist to recognize that fact."[126]

William Eggers, one of three remaining editors of *Affirm* in 1978, demanded an apology from Preus. Eggers, with Preus from the beginning, wasted little time reminding Jack that, like Otten, he had plenty of dirt to throw:

> Dear Jack: Yesterday I had an opportunity to read your scathing letter to E.J. During the middle sixties, when you were one of us promoting the effort at the O'Hare American Inn meetings to try to turn Missouri around, your attitude toward conservatives was considerably different than it presently is. In case you have forgotten, I would like to remind you that the politicking you deplore now was the politicking that put you into office.[127]

But the problem with dirt throwers is that they tend to get dirty. Eggers was soon booted from Balance after divorcing his wife, and lingered on in the movement briefly, occasionally writing articles for Otten under a pen name.[128]

Last to leave *Affirm* was big brother, Robert Preus. Under tremendous pressure from Jack to leave Balance while serving as a synodical officer, Robert relented in September 1979 after Jack demanded it of the seminary's Board of Control. In a letter to Bill Eggers, Robert explained that he was resigning "against my will":

> In response to the Board of Control action I tender you my resignation from <u>Affirm</u>'s editorial group. I want to assure you that I do this against my will and only because I owe our fine Board of Control my cooperation. Neither I nor the Board were persuaded by any of the president's arguments, which I think were unfair to me. Especially unfair was his argument which states that the issue is one of "ethics and morality," as though I acted unethically by not resigning at his request (my promise had the word "order") when before I had promised to do so. I told him in my office that by his public attack against <u>Affirm</u> and its editors (including me) all over the Synod in 1978 he lost any right he might have had to "ask" me to leave the editorial group of <u>Affirm</u> or expect my acquiescence.[129]

Though he left officially, he continued to actively lead the movement from Fort Wayne.[130] As always, there was one more battle yet to fight.

Retirement and Vengeance

"I knew Jack," remembers Waldo Werning. "Boy, you cross him," and you're his enemy for life. Jack Preus believed he had been double-crossed at Dallas. Not by the liberals, not by *Affirm*, not by Otten. But by Walter Maier. Maier, like several others, allowed his name to sit on the first ballot against Preus. What angered Preus was that Maier left it there for the second ballot. Months later, in a conversation with Werning after the Kansas City Lutheran Laymen's League convention, Preus asked, "What will you do with a vice president who stabbed you in the back?" Werning knew what Jack meant. Preus would have been elected on the second ballot regardless of the opposition. Walter Maier insulted him by not removing his name. "Jack," said Werning, "had been crossed."[131]

In February 1980, Chet Swanson organized a national DCP conference to unify conservatives around their presidential candidate for the 1981 convention. DCP, purportedly concerned only with doctrine, included in its agenda a discussion entitled "Need for Cooperation of Conservative Individuals and Groups: Rundown on the Conservative Conglomerate or Coalition." It was a contentious meeting, where representatives bickered over whom to support at the next convention. Their initial survey indicated a very slight preference for Preus. But they were divided. Three weeks later, the results of a national "Preliminary (Non-Binding) Preference Ballot" reversed that result. Walter Maier won.[132]

Soon afterward, conservatives sent a formal message to Jack Preus. Their messengers were laymen Henry Hilst and Hyman Firehammer. Hilst, whom Jack still trusted "implicitly,"[133] told Preus that he was finished. "Don't run," was the message. "We're going to fight you."[134] Coming from Hilst, Preus realized that this battle he could not win. The movement, remembers Waldo Werning, was still "that powerful."[135] So the embattled president Preus finally gave in and agreed to step down.

But if Preus was going down, he was going to take Maier with him. In October, he took the unprecedented step of using synod publicity in a vicious attack against his likely successor. In an article published in the October *Witness* and subsequently mailed to all LCMS congregations, Preus warned the church that Maier, an elected vice president of the synod and faculty member at Robert's Fort Wayne seminary, was dangerous. Again, he used theological language to obscure political motives. "The contents of this letter," he told the pastors, "have nothing to do with my decision not to run for re-election, and it would have been necessary to write exactly the same letter had I been a candidate, although it would have been interpreted as a political action." As doctrinal chief, he told them, it was his duty to inform them of Maier's faulty theology of "objective justification." Robert Preus himself, Jack jabbed, had written that it was the president's duty to see to it that "heretics and false teachers or confused theologians do not run for office or attain to office in the Missouri Synod." He continued by implying that Maier was "the creature or possession of [a] faction or clique," careful to name Herman Otten, "the same man who attempted to blackmail me into not running in 1977." If Walter Maier is successful, he concluded, "we can expect endless demands for payoffs and rewards for <u>Christian News</u> for succeeding in electing the candidate."[136] Few knew that so well as Jack Preus.

A humiliated Walter Maier told the synod's Board of Directors that Preus's letter had "impugned my theological integrity and might serve to undermine my career as a teacher in the church."[137] Although Swanson and Otten continued to support him,[138] Maier's opportunity to serve as synodical president disappeared. In a confused, last-ditch effort at consensus, conservatives united in 1981 behind Ralph Bohlmann, one of the "Faithful Five" to remain at Concordia back in 1974. Jack Preus, eager to leave his stamp, lobbied hard for Bohlmann. Herman Otten approached Karl Barth on day one and said, "Hey, I hear there's a deal being made. You get the 'Big 4' [district presidents from Michigan, Wisconsin, and Illinois] to vote for Ralph [Bohlmann] for president, and they'll get you in as president of the seminary."[139] Barth later confirmed as much to Bohlmann, telling him that he did get "in there through politics, too."[140] The effort worked. Bohlmann was elected on the fourth ballot. More important for Jack Preus, Maier was eliminated on the third.[141]

Conclusion

Monday, July 6, 1981, the day after Ralph Bohlmann was elected president of the Lutheran Church—Missouri Synod, Bohlmann's wife had a confrontation with Robert Sauer's behind the convention hall stage. Sauer's wife was angry and offended and let Mrs. Bohlmann know it. Soon Bohlmann and Sauer joined the fracas, and the source of the pain was exposed. Sauer explained that Jack Preus had promised him the presidency, leading him to believe that he was the choice of the invincible conservative machine. With Sauer's resentment palpable and his name still atop the list of candidates for first vice president, Bohlmann wondered, "If you're elected, how will we work together?" They agreed to try.[1] Sauer left his name on the ballot and was elected.[2]

Once again Jack Preus had told a friend and supporter only what he wanted to hear. Truth was, Preus had decided weeks beforehand to begrudgingly support Bohlmann. In an interview with August Suelflow on June 18, two weeks before the convention, Preus made it clear that although none of the candidates were as capable as he, Bohlmann would get the nod. At the age of sixty-five, Gerhardt Hyatt, President of Concordia College in St. Paul, Minnesota, was too old and he lacked diplomatic skill.[3] Walter Maier II was not qualified "intellectually or temperamentally." "I worry specifically about him," Preus said, "because lacking those qualities he will be surrounded by people, some of whom are villains, some of whom are stupid, who will push him from pillar to post and put him into a position where he will make many, many bad decisions." Robert Sauer, who had been promised privately

Preus's support, was "less than as imaginative, and creative, and invisionary as I think he should be." Bohlmann, although he had "difficulty making decisions," was "the best candidate for the presidency."[4]

"Preus's way of destroying things," said Jim Adams in a 1977 interview, "is part of his whole history."[5] Jim Adams chose Jack Preus as the subject of his book because he believed Jack Preus responsible for the destructiveness that enveloped the LCMS in the 1970s. That destructiveness, however, transcended the idiosyncrasies of politician Preus. Jack Preus gained and lost allies because of his pragmatism. Herman Otten, conversely, gained and lost allies because of his I-am-right-at-all-costs posture. Both entered a new decade in 1981 considerably less influential and more unpopular than they had been in 1969. The church they left behind was divided, dwindling, and more discouraged than it had been at any time since its beginning in 1839, when founding bishop Martin Stephan was excommunicated for sexual misconduct and embezzlement.

But the precedents of pragmatism, secrecy, and means-to-ends rationalization Preus and Otten developed and fostered lived on. Within a few years, the LCMS was again engulfed in conflict, sparked this time by a bizarre episode that exposed Robert Preus's duplicity to Ralph Bohlmann, who was LCMS president at the time. In early 1984, Preus sat down in his Fort Wayne office to dictate a letter to Bohlmann. He gave instructions into his dictaphone that the letter be mailed to President Ralph Bohlmann at synod headquarters in St. Louis and began the letter with "Dear Ralph," before pausing the dictaphone. He returned to the task later, but he apparently forgot having started the letter to Bohlmann, and continued instead with a letter to Herman Otten in which he enclosed an article for Otten to publish in *Christian News* attacking some of his critics at the seminary as "very disturbed people."[6] Preus's secretary missed the error and addressed the "Dear Herman" letter to Bohlmann. Preus signed it and it went to Bohlmann. With a smoking gun in hand, which was rare for him, Bohlmann soon moved to have the Fort Wayne Board of Regents remove Robert Preus from the presidency, in part for his secret relationship with *Christian News*. (Robert Preus's defense was, "Your predecessor [Jack Preus] did the same many times in respect to the Christian News. I do not see anything disturbing about this.")[7] The conflict between Preus and Bohlmann would dominate LCMS politics for much of the next decade, for many of the same reasons, and including many of the same players.

The fortunes and foibles of the conservative movement in the LCMS may speak to the nature of conservatism itself. The conservative movement was, in its own way, an ecumenical movement. It was a movement of the lowest common denominator, driven by men who frequently differed on a whole range of issues including church polity, the status of clergy, styles of worship, and, in the unusual case of Walter Maier, "objective justification." Men who would not dare share Holy Communion with liberals would freely commune with each other in spite of the strong divisions that kept them, to Chet Swanson's vexation, from true unification. Men felt free to pray with Herman Otten, include him in meetings, and coordinate strategies with him even while shunning him publicly, content for him to remain excluded from their denomination. Otten himself was the most ecumenical of all, bringing Missouri's case to the conservative world and political conservatism to the LCMS.

For Missouri conservatism to thrive, it needed an enemy. Before the Harms era, the enemy had often been everyone who was not of the Missouri Synod. But by the 1960s it included synod moderates and Harms himself. With moderates defeated and exiled, conservatives had the synod in their hands, but they still needed heretics to hunt and a church to purify, the only rationale for their organized existence. So they turned on one another. Soon Bohlmann, one of the "Faithful" or "Fearless Five" and author of "A Statement," became the target, a beneficiary of the movement in 1981 and its victim in 1989.[8] For twenty years following, the church consumed itself with charges and counter-charges, sometimes about liberals but often conservative against conservative.

This was not a movement of laypeople; in fact, its greatest effect was to drive laypeople from the synod. For this hybrid political and theological conservatism to succeed here where it had failed elsewhere, a clergy-heavy polity was necessary, which is precisely what the LCMS offered. Jack Preus's triumphalistic confidants Paul Zimmerman and Karl Barth insist that it was the "lay people, under God" who were responsible for the "miraculous work the Holy Spirit achieved" in the 1970s.[9] As this study demonstrates, however, through Balance, Inc.'s inability to draw lay support to the conservative movement's delegate- and convention-focused strategy, the movement's Pyrrhic victory had little to do with lay support.

No Apologies

The enthusiasm for heresy hunting hasn't ended. Twenty-five years after the walkout, Daniel Preus, Robert's son and recently deposed first vice president of the LCMS, urged his synod to continue the hunt. Inciting conservatives to action, he warned that Missouri still has not learned "the lessons history teaches" and "we need to be very careful that in our attempts to be reasonable and to display a civilized tolerance and to permit a certain level of freedom of expression, we do not also fail in our calling to warn God's flock against false teachings and practices which would harm the church and betray our Lord." There are still heretics to hound, among them "hundreds of seminary graduates who had been taught and trained by eventual Seminex professors" who stayed in the LCMS.[10] Preus told this author in a July 2000 interview that his first act, were he elected to the synodical presidency, would be to fire at least one district president.[11] The hunt must go on.

Waldo Werning was out by the late 1980s. On the losing side of a battle with a machine now controlled by Robert Preus, Werning wrote to Otten to lament what a movement he helped found had become:

At this time, the conservative movement is in shambles and as a movement practically bankrupt. Don't wring your hands and say that now the liberals and Ralph will beat us, as many of the political conservatives are saying, as that is only proof that we have taken things into our own hands and put God on the sidelines. I have not changed one bit, but both the liberals and conservatives generally have settled into organizational politics as the method of operating the church. The Bible is something they preach about, teach, and use for devotions, but it does not provide the practical day-by-day method of operations. . . . It must be recognized that journalism and the printed page is an important emergency tool in the midst of the liberal-conservative controversy, but even then it cannot supplant

Matthew 18. The conservative movement never understood this, and so replaced Matthew 18 with Christian News and Affirm. The propaganda pipeline took the place of Biblical procedures.[12]

Yet even in 1990, while breaking off his relationship with Otten, Werning justified the means to Missouri's conservative end. "Don't apologize for anything we did," he concluded. "Apologize for what it became."[13]

In 1992, in the midst of a nasty internecine battle with Robert Preus at the Fort Wayne seminary, Werning published *Making the Missouri Synod Functional Again*. His intent was to establish that, by the 1980s, a political "party of the right" had emerged under the leadership of Robert Preus at the Fort Wayne seminary, one similar in structure, purpose, and tactics to the "party of the left" that functioned under Tietjen's leadership before the schism. His book stands as a revealing window into the right from one of the few "functionaries" willing to talk. Werning recalls, "I was one of the last loyal party members to bail out of the Robert Preus boat—in fact, I was kicked out." And in his estimation, he alone remained constant in principles and purpose during his decades of political activism: "I was a hero to these people twenty years ago, but now a bum. I have not changed, but they have."[14]

To make his case, Werning traces the development of a movement he helped found and, through 1969, led in reaction to a "party of the left" organized around an "academic mafia" and liberal administration that had hijacked and held hostage the synod.[15] Desperate times required desperate measures, says Werning. He did not like having to depend on a political machine allied with Herman Otten, but saw "no other alternatives or options," given the left's control of synod machinery.[16] For Werning, as Marquart and others, the ends—a Preus victory and a seminary reclaimed—justified desperate means.

But the means Werning and others employed to achieve those ends haven't gone away. Conservatives of Werning's era left in their wake a synod, and a conservative movement, that degenerates again and again into politicized internal strife. Werning, who generously shared opinions and information for this study, will likely disagree with its conclusions. Like many others, he unrepentantly ignores the visible lines linking his reactionary movement—one that included Robert Preus, Otten, and elements of the Fort Wayne seminary faculty and staff—and concedes little culpability for a movement that admittedly employed unethical tactics. Save a few trivial criticisms of Jack Preus, Werning, in *Making the Missouri Synod Functional Again*, glosses over the 1970s, the pubescent decade of a beast that soon turned on him with full force in the 1980s. Werning's is a study in incongruity. The man partly responsible for organizing the synod's first great political party writes in the same breath, "I believed at the time [1970], as I believe now, that what is required in the Synod is not the organization of political parties of any kind." Werning's book illustrates the dynamic of contrariety that characterizes the church and, principally, its conservatives.[17] Acknowledging a genie on the loose, they blink at the open bottle in their own hands.

Jack Preus himself lamented what his movement and his church had become by 1981. The movement, he forlornly acknowledged, had "had enough" of him: "Everybody is very preoccupied with the new candidates. I think it shows they're like kids with a new toy—you throw the old rag doll in the corner." Now critical of cronyism, he complained that the convention's nominating committee was stacked with "five men" who were "avowed, active, open, aggressive members of various district DCP groups." He also noted without implicating himself that the synod had become fully and openly politicized. Pat Wolbrecht's speech that was critical of politicking at the Denver convention in 1969, he remembered, was "considered quite inappropriate because it came across as a totally political speech." Things were different in 1981. "Today," Preus noted, "nobody would think of saying such a thing. Everybody has their election committees and their brochures and their newspaper support and all that kind of thing."[18]

From Growth to Decline

In 1992, after nearly twenty years of denial, the Missouri Synod changed a long-standing category in its *Statistical Yearbook* from "Two Decades of Missouri Synod Growth" to "Two Decades of Change." I tell my students that in history there are rarely coincidences: it is no coincidence that a church that had grown almost continuously since its inception in the mid-nineteenth century began, at the height of the conflict in the 1970s, to hemorrhage membership. For insiders, the statistics were heartrending. In 1972, membership in the Missouri Synod peaked at nearly 2.9 million members.[19] Since then the church has lost over five hundred thousand members.[20]

Moreover, the dramatic exodus from Missouri defied religious trends in America during the same period, when biblically conservative churches largely flourished. The Southern Baptist Convention added nearly six million members between 1960 and 2000.[21] Moreover, Missouri Lutherans trusted their synodical bureaucracy with less and less. In 1970, over 12 percent of their contributions went to the synod; by 1980, they had fallen to 6 percent.[22] Missouri's clerical oligarchy had alienated the laity and atomized the church. Finally, fewer men were entering the ministry: 251 in 1972, just 177 in 1992.[23] By these measures, a once-thriving church poised for growth had become an also-ran, struggling for existence and relevance even as it continued the fight to define itself.

✿   ✿   ✿

In my last face-to-face interview with Herman Otten in July 2000, I asked him if he had any regrets—words he had said, positions he had taken, tactics he had used. None, he confidently replied. After a few moments of silence, he said, yes, there was one regret. Herman Otten, from a family with a long and proud history of clerical service, could claim not a single pastor among his own children. Perhaps, he reminisced, the years of crusading, conflict, and controversy had soured his own children to the prospect of professional church work. I could not help but wonder if he recognized that his children were not the only ones he and his movement might have estranged.

Abbreviations

ABLC	Association of Black Lutheran Churchmen
AELC	Association of Evangelical Lutheran Churches
ALC	American Lutheran Church
CCM	Commission on Constitutional Matters
CHI	Concordia Historical Institute, St. Louis, Missouri
CN	*Christian News*
COP	Council of Presidents (LCMS district presidents)
CTCR	Committee on Theology and Church Relations
DCP	Doctrinal Concerns Program
ELCA	Evangelical Lutheran Church in America
ELIM	Evangelical Lutherans in Mission
ELS	Evangelical Lutheran Synod ("Little Norwegian Synod")
EOR	Executive Office Records, Concordia Historical Institute, St. Louis, Missouri
FF-FC	"Faith Forward—First Concerns"
FCC	Federal Council of Churches (predecessor to NCC)
FAL	Federation for Authentic Lutheranism
FFC	Fact-Finding Committee
ICCC	International Council of Christian Churches
JAOP	Unprocessed files of J. A. O. Preus, Concordia Historical Institute, St. Louis, Missouri
LBT	Lutheran Bible Translators
LCA	Lutheran Church in America

LC-USA	Lutheran Council of the United States of America
LCMS	Lutheran Church—Missouri Synod ("Missouri Synod")
LCR	Lutheran Churches of the Reformation
LHRAA	Lutheran Human Relations Association of America
LLL	Lutheran Laymen's League
LN	*Lutheran News*
LW	*Lutheran Witness*
LW-R	*Lutheran Witness–Reporter*
NAACP	National Association for the Advancement of Colored People
NAE	National Association of Evangelicals
NCC	National Council of the Churches of Christ in the United States of America
NLSRA	National Lutheran Soul Relations Association
RP	Files of Robert Preus, Concordia Historical Institute, St. Louis, Missouri
Seminex	Concordia Seminary-in-Exile
SOC	State of the Church Conference
ULC	United Lutheran Church, predecessor to the LCA
UPC	United Planning Conference
WCC	World Council of Churches
WELS	Wisconsin Evangelical Lutheran Synod ("Wisconsin Synod")

Notes

Preface

1. Tom Heinen, "Presidential Race Finds a Forum in Churches: Professors Frame Election Using Lutheran Ideals," *Milwaukee Journal Sentinel*, September 19, 2004, A1.

2. James Burkee and Jeff Walz, "Survey of 5,000 ELCA and LCMS Laity and Clergy, 2005–2009," publication forthcoming.

Introduction

1. Matthew 18:15-18 (NIV): "If your brother sins against you, go and show him his fault, just between the two of you. If he listens to you, you have won your brother over. But if he will not listen, take one or two others along, so that 'every matter may be established by the testimony of two or three witnesses.' If he refuses to listen to them, tell it to the church; and if he refuses to listen even to the church, treat him as you would a pagan or a tax collector."

2. Examples taken from "Summary of Interview with Professor Edward H. Schroeder," Meeting of Board of Control, December 18, 1972. 25a–26a. JAOP.

3. "Seminex" was the nickname given Concordia Seminary-in-Exile (later Christ Seminary Seminex), founded in 1974 by former faculty, staff, and students of Concordia Seminary.

4. Mary Todd, "'Not in God's Lifetime': The Question of the Ordination of Women in the Lutheran Church–Missouri Synod" (Ph.D. diss., University of Illinois at Chicago, 1996); Todd, *Authority Vested: A Story of Identity and Change in the Lutheran Church—Missouri Synod* (Grand Rapids: Eerdmans, 2000).

5. James E. Adams, *Preus of Missouri and the Great Lutheran Civil War* (New York: Harper & Row, 1977).

6. Frederick W. Danker, *No Room in the Brotherhood: The Preus-Otten Purge of Missouri* (St. Louis: Clayton, 1977).

7. Richard Koenig, "What's Behind the Showdown in the LCMS? Conservative Reaction: 1965–1969," *Lutheran Forum* 7 (1973): 21.

188   Notes to Introduction

8. James Davison Hunter, *Culture Wars: The Struggle to Define America* (New York: Basic Books, 1991).

9. John H. Tietjen, *Memoirs in Exile: Confessional Hope and Institutional Conflict* (Minneapolis: Fortress Press, 1990). Tietjen begins his "Context for Conflict" in 1969. Danker, in *No Room in the Brotherhood,* provides minimal background before launching his account with the election of Preus. Adams, *Preus of Missouri.* A notable exception is Waldo J. Werning, *Making the Missouri Synod Functional Again* (Fort Wayne: Biblical Renewal Publications, 1992).

10. Martin E. Marty, *The New Shape of American Religion* (New York: Harper & Row, 1959), 1.

11. "Whither the Conservatives?" *Affirm* 9 (October 1981): 1.

12. By the end of the 1960s, even some former liberals—"neoconservatives"—were saying as much. See Samuel P. Huntington, *Political Order in Changing Societies* (New Haven: Yale University Press, 1968); Irving Kristol, *Neo-Conservatism: The Autobiography of an Idea, Selected Essays 1949–1995* (New York: Free, 1995).

13. "God is a god of order." Cited in Bryan V. Hillis, *Can Two Walk Together Unless They Be Agreed? American Religious Schisms in the 1970s* (Brooklyn: Carlson, 1991), 85–86. Preus continued, "We want to be fair in our treatment of all our officials, yet at the same time we must be firm. No church can run on organizational anarchy."

14. Todd, *Authority Vested,* 6.

15. Constitution of the Lutheran Church—Missouri Synod, Article 2. Teachers and other church workers can be considered "clergy" but are unrepresented within the synodical power structure, considered neither clergy nor laity at conventions, attending only in "advisory" capacities.

16. Jeffrey K. Hadden, *The Gathering Storm in the Churches: The Widening Gap Between Clergy and Laymen* (New York: Doubleday, 1969). Table 16 (p. 49) demonstrates that Missouri clergy and laity shared similar beliefs with respect to biblical interpretation. (Ninety-two percent of LCMS laity answered "completely true" to "Jesus was born of a virgin." Ninety percent of LCMS ministers answered "definitely agree" to "I believe that the virgin birth of Jesus was a biological miracle.") The greater gap in "Literal Interpretation of Scripture" was between younger LCMS clergy (72 percent of clergy under age 35 agreed with "I believe in a literal or nearly literal interpretation of the Bible," table 17 [p. 51]) and older clergy (79 percent of clergy ages 45–54 and 84 percent of clergy over 55). Lawrence Kersten, *The Lutheran Ethic: The Impact of Religion on Laymen and Clergy* (Detroit: Wayne State University Press, 1970), supports Hadden's conclusions. Table 9-4 (p. 209), ranks clergymen on a Religious Beliefs Index. Thirty-one percent of LCMS clergy under age 30 ranked "liberal" on the index. None over age 61, and only 11 percent of those ages 31–40, ranked "liberal." Kersten also reveals that LCMS laity were actually less likely to view the Bible literally than the synod's clergy. Table 2-1 (p. 34). Sixty-two percent of LCMS laity agreed that "the Bible is God's word and all it says is true," while 74 percent of clergy agreed.

17. Several anonymous contributors referred to themselves, positioned against Otten, as "centrists" or even "moderates."

18. "Whither the Conservatives?" 1.

19. *Exodus from Concordia: A Report on the 1974 Walkout by the Board of Control, Concordia Seminary, St. Louis, Missouri* (St. Louis: Concordia College, 1977), 106.

20. The huge Executive Office Records (EOR) files on Otten testify to his significance. Harms and Preus both maintained large files on Otten, complete with photocopies and full issues of *Christian News*, underlined and personally annotated. See EOR, f.1787, Herman Otten, 1968–1969.

21. Adams, *Preus of Missouri*, 172. The "professional opinion survey" Adams references was completed in early 1970. In it, only 43 percent of LCMS pastors "strongly agreed" with the statement "Concordia St. Louis is true to sound Lutheran principles," while 75 percent surveyed "strongly agreed" that the Springfield seminary was theologically sound.

22. Anonymous, 2002. Reference to Luther's stand before Emperor Charles V at the Diet of Worms (1521) where Luther, risking a death sentence and asked to recant, exclaimed, "*Hie steh' ich, ich kann nicht anders, Gott helff mir. Amen*" ("Here I stand. I can do no other. God help me. Amen").

23. Anti-Defamation League (ADL) to James Burkee, June 21, 2001. See also the ADL's website: http://www.adl.org/learn/ext%5Fus/friends.asp (accessed September 27, 2010).

24. 1918—current. Formerly known as the Norwegian Synod of the American Evangelical Lutheran Church (1918–1957). Also known as "Little Norwegian" Synod after it split from the Norwegian Synod.

25. Lutheran Church—Missouri Synod, *Proceedings of the Sixty-First Regular Convention of the Lutheran Church—Missouri Synod* (St. Louis: Concordia, 2001), 159. Resolution 6-05A, "To Encourage Participation in President Bush's Faith-Based and Community Initiatives." Amended title read, "To Encourage *Cautious* Participation in President Bush's Faith-Based and Community Initiatives." http://www.lcms.org/convention/ (accessed September 27, 2010).

26. http://www.wels.net/news-events/forward-in-christ/june-1986/lutheran-church-missouri -synod. WELS argues that the Missouri Synod inadequately enforces its own rules. One significant point of departure is Missouri's acceptance of woman suffrage, which WELS rejects. LCMS, *Proceedings of the Church* (2001), 142; http://www.lcms.org/pages/rpage.asp?NavID=15817 (press release, C-06-52, July 20, 2001). Missouri's 2001 convention overwhelmingly stated that "we cannot consider them [the ELCA] to be an orthodox Lutheran church body." Resolution 3-21A. http://www.wfn.org/2001/08/msg00129.html (ELCA press release 01-CWA68-JI, August 14, 2001). Raymond Hartwig, secretary of the LCMS, said as much to delegates at the ELCA's August 2001 convention. "He [Hartwig] also elaborated on an LCMS convention resolution that," as he said, "affirmed the judgment of our late President Barry that we cannot consider you, the ELCA, to be 'an orthodox Lutheran church body,' given the fact that you have entered into altar and pulpit fellowship—that is 'full communion'—with Reformed church bodies, the Episcopal Church and the Moravian Church." (All accessed October 11, 2010.)

27. LCMS, *Proceedings of the Church* (2001), 22. Rule 15 was amended to include, "The use of sound producing and electronic wire or wireless communication devices, including voice and data, shall not be permitted in the voting delegate section of the convention."

28. Synodical president, Rev. Dr. Robert T. Kuhn, to convention, July 15, 2001. Detail from press release C-01-04: "Noisy voices advocating their agendas among us tend to drown out the faithful, quiet voices of those in our Synod," Kuhn told the delegates, "people like you from our Synod's grassroots who love our Lord and His Word." Kuhn did not identify the "noisy voices," but earlier in his address he had made allusion to two separate groups known as "Jesus First" and "Daystar," which had been critical of the Barry administration and had urged certain

convention actions and supported specific nominees for synod offices. "Brothers and sisters in Christ, it truly hurts me that in our Synod in the past several years, there have arisen groups that claim to put Jesus first, or that they are trying to shine like stars, when it is obvious they are attempting to advance an old liberal theology and practice, an agenda that has haunted this church body since the days of Seminex and even before," Kuhn said. (The reference was to a controversy over Scripture some thirty years ago that centered on the then-faculty of Concordia Seminary, St. Louis.)

29. Adams, *Preus of Missouri*, 25. Adams calls Jack Preus "a hero who can do no wrong to the editors of *Christianity Today*, the leading journal of evangelical Protestants."

30. Jack Preus referred to the Missouri Synod as a "mainline" denomination in an address to the 1973 Synodical Convention in New Orleans. LCMS, *Proceedings of the Fiftieth Regular Convention of the Lutheran Church—Missouri Synod, New Orleans, Louisiana, July 6–13, 1973* (St. Louis: Concordia, 1974), 19.

31. Tietjen, *Memoirs in Exile*, 326ff. Also, "Lutheran Roots in America," http://www.elca.org/Who%20We%20Are/History/Lutheran%20Roots%20in%20America.aspx#newplayer. "In 1977 the LCMS decision to place fellowship with ALC 'in protest' along with the AELC's 'Call to Lutheran Union' nudged the three church bodies, ALC, LCA and AELC, toward merger."

32. Leo P. Ribuffo, "God and Contemporary Politics," *Journal of American History* (March 1993): 1515–33.

33. See Alan Brinkley, *Voices of Protest: Huey Long, Father Coughlin, and the Great Depression* (New York: Vintage Books, 1983); Leo P. Ribuffo, *The Old Christian Right: The Protestant Far Right from the Great Depression to the Cold War* (Philadelphia: Temple University Press, 1983).

34. Will Herberg, *Protestant—Catholic—Jew: An Essay in American Religious Sociology* (Garden City, N.Y.: Anchor/Doubleday, 1960), 87. Herberg argues that the three dominant expressions of American religion were conflated as "equally legitimate" forms of faith in America. Robert Wuthnow, *The Restructuring of American Religion: Society and Faith Since World War II* (Princeton: Princeton University Press, 1988), 71–99. Jerome L. Himmelstein, "The New Right," in Robert C. Liebman and Robert Wuthnow, *The New Christian Right: Mobilization and Legitimation* (New York: Aldine, 1983), 18. Himmelstein writes, "The cornerstone of this emerging conservatism was the conviction that the United States and Western civilization were threatened by a growing tide of what was termed statism, collectivism, or rationalism—the trend toward centralization of power in the state and the use of that power to reorganize and plan social life in a systematic, self-conscious way." Communism and liberalism were similar expressions of that trend.

35. Ribuffo, "God and Contemporary Politics," 1520.

36. Liebman and Wuthnow, *New Christian Right*.

37. Ribuffo, "God and Contemporary Politics," 1520.

38. Chet Swanson for Balance, Inc., "Ideas for Position Statements or Information Statements." A "how to" guide in dealing with media liberals. Sound bytes such as "Conservatives can be intellectual," or "Academic freedom has its limits." Swanson notes, "Liberals can agree to disagree, and therefore the umbrella can cover any theological position. Conservatives are therefore at a disadvantage." JAOP, Supp. II, Box 35.

39. Daniel Patrick Moynihan wrote of ideology in 1993, "Beware of certainty where none exists. . . . Ideological certainty easily degenerates into insistence upon ignorance." http://www.

highbeam.com/doc/1G1-69845682.html. Cited in "Filling Pat Moynihan's Shoes," *The Economist*, January 6, 2001 (accessed October 4, 2010).

40. Richard John Neuhaus, *America Against Itself: Moral Vision and the Public Order* (Notre Dame: University of Notre Dame Press, 1992), 56. Neuhaus complains that as "the Movement" changed during the 1960s, it became less and less acceptable to defy ideological "positioning." He wrote, "In the early 1960s, I declared that I hoped always to be religiously orthodox, culturally conservative, politically liberal, and economically pragmatic. That 'quadrilateral' still seems to make a good deal of sense. The main change over the years has been in what people mean by politically liberal." Neuhaus also believed King personified "the Movement," and that he was not moving toward socialism or Marxism: "I believe Dr. King had no serious complaint about democratic capitalism, if only it could be more democratic by including the poor in its opportunities." Ibid., 56.

41. In 1877, when a group of English-speaking Lutherans professing doctrinal conformity with Missouri asked to join the synod, they were rejected and told to form their own, independent synod. H. P. Eckhardt, *The English District* (n.p.: English District of the Lutheran Church—Missouri Synod, 1946), 47. Cited in Wayne William Wilke, "Changing Understanding of the Church-State Relationship: The Lutheran Church—Missouri Synod, 1914–1969" (Ph.D. diss., University of Michigan, 1990), 22. The English Synod did eventually join the Missouri Synod, in 1911, as its English District.

42. "Whither the Conservatives?" 1. *Affirm* 5:1 noted in 1981, "Today, above all, we must not let the political victories of the Moral Majority blind us to the dangers which beset their kind of conservatism and ours."

43. "Actually, the terms 'liberal' and 'conservative' were for a long time not so mutually exclusive, and their application, without some proviso, to members of the Missouri Synod prior to the Seventies merely contributes to historical confusion." Danker, *No Room in the Brotherhood*, 353.

44. Richard John Neuhaus, interview with author, October 13, 2000. In a late 1960s strategy meeting, Neuhaus argued against the use of "moderate," which he believed many Missourians would equate with "liberal." He urged instead the use of "Orthodox."

Chapter One

1. Stormer quotes J. Edgar Hoover, who warned that the Communist Party works by "encouraging churchmen to endorse, support and even participate in communist-front groups, communist-sponsored petitions; *to neutralize clerical opposition to* communism." In John A. Stormer, *None Dare Call It Treason* (Florissant, Mo.: Liberty Bell, 1964), 133.

2. *The New American*, February 26, 1990. *CN* Archives.

3. Robert Wuthnow, *The Restructuring of American Religion: Society and Faith Since World War II* (Princeton: Princeton University Press, 1988), 113–14.

4. Louis Hartz, *The Liberal Tradition in America: An Interpretation of Political Thought Since the Revolution* (New York: Harcourt, Brace & Jovanovich, 1955).

5. Lionel Trilling, *The Liberal Imagination: Essays on Literature and Society* (Garden City, N.Y.: Doubleday, 1953).

6. Quoted in Jonah Goldberg, "Who's Yelling 'Stop!' Now?" *National Review Online*, May 2, 2000, http://www.nationalreview.com/comment/comment050200a.html (accessed September 27, 2010).

7. Sydney E. Ahlstrom, *A Religious History of the American People* (New Haven: Yale University Press, 1972), 920.

8. Ibid., 956–58.

9. Wuthnow, *Restructuring*, 179.

10. Richard Donald LaBore. "Traditions and Transitions: A Study of the Leadership of the Lutheran Church—Missouri Synod During a Decade of Theological Change, 1960–1969" (Ph.D. diss., St. Louis University, 1980), 17.

11. Michael Beschloss, interview by Jim Lehrer, "Barry Goldwater," *NewsHour with Jim Lehrer*, PBS, May 29, 1998. For Hypertext, http://www.pbs.org/newshour/bb/remember/1998/goldwater_5-29.html (accessed September 27, 2010).

12. John Strietelmeier, *The Cresset*, April 1971, 27, Strietelmeier, on the faculty at Valparaiso University, claimed in 1971 that there already had been a liberal takeover of LCMS, one reversed in 1969: "For something like 25 years prior to 1969, the Lutheran Church—Missouri Synod was controlled by a coalition of Liberals and Moderates. . . . These years of Liberal ascendancy ended suddenly and decisively at the Synodical Convention in Denver in the summer of 1969. . . . Having come to power, the Conservative party did what the Liberals had done a generation before. They consolidated their power and began to divide the spoils." In Kurt E. Marquart, *Anatomy of an Explosion: A Theological Analysis of the Missouri Synod Conflict* (Fort Wayne: Concordia Seminary Press, 1977), 86.

13. Lawrence Kersten, *The Lutheran Ethic: The Impact of Religion on Laymen and Clergy* (Detroit: Wayne State University Press, 1970), 58. In 1964, 68 percent of LCMS laity voted for Johnson, 31 percent for Goldwater. Forty-seven percent of LCMS clergy voted for Goldwater, 52 percent for Johnson. (Johnson won 61 percent of the national popular vote in 1964, Goldwater 38 percent.)

14. Ibid. LCMS laity were significantly more liberal theologically than their clergy. Kersten's survey demonstrates that even in 1969, nearly half of LCMS laity believed women should be allowed to become ordained ministers (47 percent), while only 8 percent of clergy agreed. At the same time, the laity were less socially liberal, decidedly more parochial, than their clergy: Seventy-six percent believed it was "the primary responsibility of the local congregation" to "serve the needs of its membership before serving the needs of those outside the church" (versus 47 percent of clergy).

15. Richard Koenig, "What's Behind the Showdown in the LCMS? Missouri Turns Moderate: 1938–65," *Lutheran Forum*, February 1973, 19–20.

16. Larry Burgdorf, interview with author, July 9, 2000.

17. "We therefore deplore," they wrote, "the tendency to apply this non-Biblical term [unionism] to any and every contact between Christians of different denominations." They proceeded to state that fellowship "is possible without complete agreement in details of doctrine and practice which have never been considered divisive in the Lutheran Church." Portions from sections 9 and 11 of "A Statement," in Frederick W. Danker, *No Room in the Brotherhood: The Preus-Otten Purge of Missouri* (St. Louis: Clayton, 1977), 21–24.

18. Mary Todd, *Authority Vested: A Story of Identity and Change in the Lutheran Church —Missouri Synod* (Grand Rapids: Eerdmans, 2000), 132.

19. *Speaking the Truth in Love—Essays Related to A Statement* (Chicago: Willow, n.d.), 7–9; "A Statement," in Carl S. Meyer, ed., *Moving Frontiers: Readings in the History of the Lutheran Church—Missouri Synod* (St. Louis: Concordia, 1964), 422–24.

20. James Adams relays Behnken's lack of knowledge or interest in academia: "As late as 1960, he revealed his ignorance that one got a Ph.D. *in* something. Behnken had been taking it literally. A Ph.D. was a master of philosophy, a well-educated man." James E. Adams, *Preus of Missouri and the Great Lutheran Civil War* (New York: Harper & Row, 1977), 109.

21. LCMS, *Proceedings of the Fortieth Regular Convention of the Lutheran Church—Missouri Synod* (St. Louis: Concordia, 1948), 15–16; "A Statement," *Moving Frontiers*, 424. The 1947 Missouri Synod convention passed a resolution that "the President [alone] continue to submit to pastors and congregations material for the Scriptural study of the question at issue."

22. Wayne William Wilke, "Changing Understanding of the Church-State Relationship: The Lutheran Church—Missouri Synod, 1914–1969" (Ph.D. diss., University of Michigan, 1990), 271.

23. Population increased 27 percent while government grew by an astonishing 362 percent between 1940 and 1960. United States population in 1940 was 131.6 million, 179.3 million in 1960. Source: United States Department of Commerce, United States Census Bureau. Total government expenditures adjusted for inflation (1996 dollars) were $980.7 billion in 1940, $2,376.7 billion in 1960. Source: United States Department of Commerce, Bureau of Economic Analysis.

24. LCMS communicant membership increased 45 percent between 1940 and 1960. Missouri Lutherans gave $15.5 million in 1940, $150 million in 1960. LCMS, *1960 Statistical Yearbook of the Lutheran Church—Missouri Synod* (St. Louis: Concordia, 1961), 280–81.

25. John W. Behnken, *This I Recall* (St. Louis: Concordia, 1964), 84–85. Church leaders organized a "Faith Forward" campaign in 1963 to "educate" church members to greater "stewardship" and add $10 million to the synod's annual budget.

26. LCMS, *1961 Statistical Yearbook of the Lutheran Church—Missouri Synod* (St. Louis: Concordia, 1962), 279–87. Remitted for synod's budget: 1951: $4,334,911, or $3.62 per communicant. 1961: $17,825,414, or $10.93.

27. Behnken, *This I Recall*, 85. In retrospect, Behnken hinted concern over an increasing predilection in Missouri for deficit spending.

28. The synod's organizing convention in 1847 had resolved that "Synod is only an advisory body in regard to the self-government [*Selbstregierung*] of the individual congregations. Accodingly, no resolution of the former, if it imposes [*auferlegt*] something upon the individual congregations as a Synodical resolution, is of binding force for the latter. Such a Synodical resolution can have binding force only when the individual congregation has voluntarily [*freiwillig*] accepted it and itself has ratified it [*bestaetigt*] by a formal resolution of the congregation." *Convention Proceedings 1847*, 6. In August R. Suelflow, ed., *Heritage in Motion: Readings in the History of the Lutheran Church—Missouri Synod, 1962–1995* (St. Louis: Concordia, 1998), 173. For background on the advent of congregationalism in the early period of the LCMS (1810–1847), see Walter O. Forster, *Zion on the Mississippi: The Settlement of the Saxon Lutherans in Missouri, 1839–1841* (St. Louis: Concordia, 1953), and Carl S. Mundinger, *Government in the Missouri Synod: The Genesis of Decentralized Government in the Missouri Synod* (St. Louis: Concordia, 1947). See also chapter 2, "Defining Decade, 1831–1841: The Formative Years," in Todd, *Authority Vested*. Todd agrees with Forster and Mundinger that Missouri Lutherans reached

consensus in the wake of the Stephanite crisis on congregationalism, but posits that they failed to address the issue of clerical authority—an oversight largely responsible for twentieth-century battles over the roles of women in the synod.

29. Synod clarified, "A sovereign congregation which has voluntarily joined Synod will also voluntarily abide by the regulations of Synod," although it did restrict the synod from binding "conscience." LCMS, *Proceedings of Convention* (1953), 762, in Meyer, *Moving Frontiers*, 398–99.

30. LCMS, *Proceedings of Convention* (1956), 397, in Meyer, *Moving Frontiers*, 401.

31. LCMS, *Proceedings of the Forty-Fourth Regular Convention of the Lutheran Church—Missouri Synod* (St. Louis: Concordia, 1950), "Reports and Memorials," 411–37; Suelflow, *Heritage in Motion*, 152–57.

32. Richard John Neuhaus, interview with author, October 13, 2000.

33. Adams, *Preus of Missouri*, 108.

34. Church construction in America soared from $26 million in 1945 to over $1 billion in 1960 (not accounting for inflation). In Ahlstrom, *A Religious History*, 953.

35. Martin E. Marty, *The New Shape of American Religion* (New York: Harper & Row, 1959), 35. Will Herberg calls the "American way of life" its civil religion, "the characteristic American religion, undergirding life and overarching American society despite indubitable differences of religion, section, culture, and class." Will Herberg, *Protestant—Catholic—Jew: An Essay in American Religious Sociology* (Garden City, N.Y.: Anchor/Doubleday, 1960), 77. President Dwight D. Eisenhower stated that American government "makes no sense unless it is founded on a deeply-felt religious faith—and I don't care what it is." In Ahlstrom, *A Religious History*, 954.

36. Wuthnow, *Restructuring*, 88–96.

37. Forty-eight percent of Lutherans in a survey conducted between 1969 and 1971 answered "agree" to the statement "A merger of all Lutheran groups in the United States into one organization is desirable." Twenty-three percent answered "disagree." Moreover, 52 percent disagreed with the statement "Unity among Christians can come only after complete doctrinal agreement." Thirty-four percent agreed. Specifically, 62 percent of Missouri Synod Lutherans did endorse the desirability of unity among Lutherans. From Merton P. Strommen et al., *A Study of Generations: Report of a Two-Year Study of 5,000 Lutherans between the Ages of 15–65, Their Beliefs, Values, Attitudes, Behavior* (Minneapolis: Augsburg Publishing House), 109–10. For the widening gap between social attitudes among clergy and laity in the Missouri Synod, see Jeffrey K. Hadden, *The Gathering Storm in the Churches: The Widening Gap Between Clergy and Laymen* (New York: Doubleday, 1969).

38. Kurt Marquart finds the relentless pressure of the ecumenical movement in the years following World War II at the heart of this shift. "Denial of the old doctrine of inspiration and inerrancy came to be tolerated in the Missouri Synod [as earlier, he points out, in the ALC and ULC] largely because Lutheran union received top priority." Marquart, *Anatomy of an Explosion*, 13.

39. Pieper's *Brief Statement of the Doctrinal Position of the Missouri Synod* (St. Louis: Concordia, 1932) declared that the Holy Scriptures "are throughout *infallible truth*," without error or contradiction.

40. Cognizant of the controversial nature of their position, the faculty proceeded cautiously. In 1957, Art Simon, editor of the student quarterly *The Seminarian*, approved an article written by Bill Jacobsen that challenged the *Brief Statement*, arguing that post-Luther orthodoxy had strayed from Luther and grounded biblical authority in a verbally inerrant Scripture rather than (for Luther) the saving work of Christ. When it was submitted for faculty review, the faculty committee rejected it and suggested less controversial revisions, which were incorporated before publication. Art Simon, telephone interview with author, August 9, 2001.

41. Cited in Todd, *Authority Vested*, 178.

42. Norman Habel, "Form and Meaning of the Fall Narrative," 22ff. Cited in H. P. Eckhardt, *Exodus from Concordia: A Report on the 1974 Walkout by the Board of Control, Concordia Seminary, St. Louis, Missouri* (St. Louis: Concordia College, 1977), 7.

43. Arthur Carl Piepkorn, "What Does 'Inerrancy' Mean?" *Concordia Theological Monthly* 36 (September 1965): 578.

44. The LCMS gave official sanction to integrating the church only in 1956.

45. "Under the editorial review of the faculty of the St. Louis Seminary," *Lutheran Witness* represented the "official doctrinal position of the Missouri Synod." "*Lutheran Witness*, 1882–1957: Synod's Official Organ," *LW* 76 (April 9, 1957): 20.

46. Andrew Schulze, "Segregation—in Public Schools . . . in the Church," *LW* 73 (July 20, 1954): 10. As time progressed, news of Schulze and of the LHRAA would appear in the *Witness* with increasing frequency. For example, see "Human Relations," *LW* 74 (August 30, 1955): 13.

47. "A Plea for Patience," *LW* 73 (September 28, 1954): 8. These represented a remarkable shift. Only four years earlier, the editorial staff of the *Christian Witness* still defended the church's segregationist practices, affirming that the Lutheran preference was to establish separate black churches—exceptions only when "no separate church for [the Negro] is possible." In "Race Relations Issue Must Be Faced," *LW* 69 (August 22, 1950): 265.

48. "Problems of Integration," *LW* 75 (May 8, 1956): 8. See also Rueben C. Baerwald, "What Can the Church Do About Integration?" *LW* 78 (May 19, 1959): 6.

49. Danker, *No Room in the Brotherhood*, 34.

50. Richard John Neuhaus, interview with author, October 13, 2000.

51. Students went to Chicago for the "urban plunge" as part of a course at Concordia. They visited poorer neighborhoods in Chicago, met with black radicals, visited Jesse Jackson's "Operation Breadbasket" (now PUSH), and visited a southside church where the black street gang Black P Stone Nation "hung out." Marvin Huggins, e-mail to author, July 8, 2002.

52. Schulze linked the decision to church mission work, suggesting that the decision was "a mighty boon for Missionaries in foreign fields." Andrew Schulze, "Synod's Witness on the Race Issue," *LW* 75 (December 4, 1956): 15.

53. William Drews, "The Church in a Changing Community, Part 2: What About the Downtown Church?" *LW* 75 (March 27, 1956): 5, 11.

54. William Drews, "The Church in a Changing Community, Part 3: What About the Church in the Older Residential Areas?" *LW* 75 (April 24, 1956): 5, 10.

55. Otten says that he was actually pleased with the "new spirit" on campus, that he considered it a "healthy corrective for the dead orthodoxy and scholastic dogmatism which I had come to associate with our Synod's past, and which I regarded as a danger to a vital Christian faith." EOR, APPENDIX C: A Declaration of Facts. Herman Otten, December 4, 1958, RP, f.129.

56. Adams, *Preus of Missouri*, 130.

57. Marie Meyer, interviews with author, 2001–2002.

58. Ibid.; Paul Behling, telephone interviews with author, July–August 2001. Herman Otten writes that Oma Tibke continued, "I have one Heiland, and that is Jesus Christ." In "Pastors and Politics," *CN*, June 11, 2007, 8.

59. Marie Meyer interviews.

60. Paul Behling interviews. Behling suggests that his father might have been most shocked by the value of the payment; a bottle of whiskey was then worth five dollars.

61. Ibid. Herman Otten confirms that his father, although initially supporting Roosevelt as a member of the America First Committee, later opposed him. "Pastors and Politics," 8.

62. Hereafter referred to as "interns."

63. Herman Otten, interviews with author; Art Simon interview; Marie Meyer interviews; John Damm interview; and Walter Bouman, interview with author, August 8, 2001.

64. Marie Meyer interviews; Art Simon interview. Simon was unsurprised by Herman's sympathy to socialism, which he believed flowed from German tradition.

65. Walter Bouman interview.

66. Walter Bouman, e-mail to author, August 1, 2001.

67. Kathryn Weidmann, interviews with author, 2001–2002; Marie Meyer interviews; Herman Otten interviews.

68. Kathryn Weidmann interviews.

69. Marie Meyer interviews. Herman Sr. was angry only because (1) Walter had gotten caught, and (2) he wasted money by not getting the bottle deposit.

70. The LCMS owned and operated several preparatory schools across the country, most existing today as the ten-school Concordia University system. The prep schools began as high schools, later adding freshman and sophomore college education. Many graduates would transition to Concordia Senior College in Fort Wayne, Indiana (now Concordia Theological Seminary), where they would complete junior and senior years of college before enrolling at the seminary in St. Louis. (Married students would often enroll at the seminary in Springfield, Illinois.)

71. Walter Bouman interview.

72. Herman Otten interviews.

73. Walter Bouman interview.

74. Walter Bouman interview. Bouman was vicar at the time, and present in Trinklein's office. Otten did not initially remember the incident and did not dismiss Bouman's account (Herman Otten interviews). In 2007, however, he disputed Bouman's account. "Pastors and Politics," 8.

75. Many seminarians, Otten included, recognized that "Marquart's got the brains and Otten's got the mouth." Herman Otten interviews. Richard John Neuhaus interview. Paul Behling interviews: "Marquart could argue in Latin with Piepkorn, and could quote chapter and verse in the Confessions."

76. Herman Otten interviews.

77. E. Merrill Root, *Collectivism on the Campus: The Battle for the Mind in American Colleges* (New York: Devin-Adair Company, 1955), 363, 337.

78. Bernard M. Loomer, quoted in Root, *Collectivism*, 357.

79. Ibid., 361. "Only an apology for telling the truth and an abandonment of his principles would make it possible for him to graduate from the Theological School."

80. EOR, APPENDIX C: A Declaration of Facts. Herman Otten, December 4, 1958, RP, f.129.

81. Ibid.; Herman Otten interviews; EOR, 1944–1981, Box 48, f. 777, Herman Otten, through 1978.

82. Missouri's polity gives authority to the seminary's faculties to certify that graduates are fit to serve as pastors in the church.

83. *CN*, June 14, 1999, 35.

84. Art Simon interview. The student debates were first organized by Walter Bouman in 1954 as an outgrowth of the student body's Lyceum program, which he [Bouman] chaired. Walter Bouman interview.

85. Art Simon interview.

86. EOR, APPENDIX C: A Declaration of Facts. Herman Otten, December 4, 1958. RP, f.129.

87. The group was comprised of Paul Dorn, David Scaer, Robert Stockman, George Lobien, Robert Cordes, Richard Beitz, Kurt Marquart, and Herman Otten. The accused included Paul Heyne, Duane Mehl, Arlis Ehlen, William A. Olsen, Art Simon, and three others. RP, M-0016, Herman Otten: Case File, vols. 1–2, f.129. Personal animosities may have factored into Otten's decision to file formal charges. Walter Bouman suggests that Otten was often a target of ridicule by moderate students. Each Friday afternoon, students gathered to purchase books at the student-run auction, where books were auctioned off with a humorous commentary. The wittier and more comic the commentary—about the authors and the buyers—the better. "Herman would buy these cheap, conservative books, and would become the butt of the auctioneer's comments when he would bid. People would laugh at him." Bouman even personally teased Otten when, one day, Otten came to purchase books Bouman thought useless and was preparing to discard. Walter Bouman interview.

88. Herman Otten interviews.

89. Ibid. Art Simon recalls that Scharlemann wrote him a note after the controversy stating, "If you are ever challenged I want it known that I consider you to be of sound theological conviction." Art Simon interview.

90. Walter Bouman interview. Lewis Spitz Sr., not Lewis Spitz Jr. (Stanford scholar).

91. Ronald W. Stelzer, *Salt, Light, and Signs of the Times: The Life and Times of Alfred M. (Rip) Rehwinkel* (New Haven, Mo.: Lutheran News, 1993), 128.

92. Ibid., 129. Otten, himself in doubt of the veracity of the Holocaust, said of Rehwinkel: "He knew the power, what was controlling our country." Herman Otten interviews.

93. Walter Bouman interview; Herman Otten interviews.

94. Stelzer, *Salt, Light, and Signs of the Times*, 261.

95. Walter Bouman interview. Bouman recalls that Mueller made all students purchase a copy of his summary of Pieper's *Dogmatics,* and would tell students what to underline in his book.

96. Herman Otten interviews.

97. Ibid.

98. Paul Behling interviews.

99. Herman Otten interviews. Jim Adams writes, "Behnken had been no match for the professors when he tried to deal frontally, and at times antagonistically, with them." Adams, *Preus of Missouri,* 124–25.

100. Herman Otten interviews. Otten recalls a meeting with David Scaer to discuss strategy. "The problem with you," Scaer told Otten, "is that you're like redcoats, standing out there in the open, being shot at. I'm like the minutemen, standing behind trees, shooting at the enemy." Scaer's strategy was to get an advanced degree, ascend to the seminary, and work from a position of power. "And that's just what he did," remembers Otten.

101. EOR, APPENDIX C: A Declaration of Facts. Herman Otten, December 4, 1958. RP, f.129.

102. Herman Otten interviews.

103. Ibid. Danker, in *No Room in the Brotherhood*, suggests what Scharlemann also did—that private conversations were recorded by students: "Even private dialogues between a professor and student were no longer considered private, for a student previously coached might have an interview with a professor while a student outside his door took notes" (37).

104. Herman Otten interviews.

105. Behling interviews.

106. Kurt Marquart, telephone interview with author, July 2001.

107. Herman Otten to Repp, March 4, 1958, RP, M-0016, Herman Otten: Case File, vols. 1–2, f.129.

108. EOR, APPENDIX C: A Declaration of Facts. Herman Otten, December 4, 1958, RP, f.129.

109. Herman Otten interviews.

110. Rehwinkel and Merkens were not voting members of the committee. Herman Otten interviews.

111. Ibid.

112. Herman Otten "To the Faculty of Concordia Seminary, Saint Louis, Missouri," May 20, 1958, RP, M-0016, Herman Otten: Case File, vols. 1–2, f.129.

113. Martin Scharlemann to Herman Otten, "This I expect," May 28, 1958, ibid.

114. L. C. Wuerffel to Herman Otten, November 10, 1958, ibid.

115. "Appendix A: McCarthyism—The Fight for America," December 4, 1958, ibid. Otten cites Joseph McCarthy himself (*McCarthyism—The Fight for America* [New York: Devin-Adair, 1952]) in arguing that McCarthy fell from grace by allowing the focus of the debate to become a battle between Republicans and Democrats rather than one between Americans and communists.

116. Herman Otten interviews; RP, M-0016, Herman Otten: Case File, vols. 1–2, f.129.

117. Herman Otten to John Behnken, August 15, 1959. Otten continues to quote from Merrill Root's *Collectivism on the Campus* in constructing his conspiracy case. EOR, 1944–1981, Box 48, f.1779, Herman Otten, through 1978.

118. John Behnken to Herman Otten, January 12, 1960, ibid.

119. EOR, 1944–1981, Box 48, f.1779, Herman Otten, through 1978.

120. John Behnken to Herman Otten, February 8, 1961, ibid.

121. EOR, 1944–1981, Box 48, f.1779, Herman Otten, through 1978.

122. Ralph Moellering would later take issue with Otten's use of Rehwinkel as an "ally." He wrote, "What must finally be affirmed is that it is a falsification (a serious error), especially in view of the total record of the man, to allow Alfred Rehwinkel to be claimed as a comrade and an ally by Mr. Otten and his ilk." Any claims that Rehwinkel supported Otten were, according

to him, "totally false." *CN*, March 1, 1993, quoted in Stelzer, *Salt, Light, and Signs of the Times*, 349. Rehwinkel, says Moellering, was simply defending Otten's right to be certified—a stance that gave him "an undeserved reputation as a militant Fundamentalist." Stelzer, *Salt, Light, and Signs of the Times*, 354.

123. Herman Otten, "What I Cannot Concede," RP, M-0016, Herman Otten: Case File, vols. 1–2, f.129.

124. LaBore, "Traditions and Transitions," 40, 44.

125. Jeffrey Hadden in LaBore, "Traditions and Transitions," 44.

126. In the 1980s, Jack Preus would compile a massive file on Rutz including a black folder that contained many of Rutz's threats. Outlined in yellow were sentences showing that he was always a problem for synodical presidents and, since 1956, had been threatening lawsuits for financial mismanagement. JAOP, Fred Rutz.

127. LCMS, *Proceedings of the Forty-Fourth Regular Convention of the Lutheran Church—Missouri Synod* (St. Louis: Concordia, 1959), 249.

128. Herman Otten interviews.

129. LaBore, "Traditions and Transitions," 277.

130. John Baur to Arnold Grumm, March 31, 1959, EOR, Synodical Survey Commission; JAOP. It does appear that Grumm could take no more of Baur and Rutz by spring 1959, and not only had stopped inviting them to meetings but no longer informed them of commission actions, despite the fact that Baur and Rutz were voting members.

131. John Baur file, JAOP, December 1958.

132. Synodical Survey Commission report in *LW*, Ralph Bohlmann Files, Preus Miscellaneous Files, Box 24.

133. Arnold Grumm to John Baur, May 1, 1960, EOR, Synodical Survey Commission.

134. Arnold Grumm to John Baur, May 7, 1959, ibid.

135. "An Analysis of Two Minority Reports Addressed to the Convention of 1959 by Two Members of the Synodical Survey Commission," EOR, Synodical Survey Commission. Synodical spending had grown 174.1 percent while membership had grown by 28.8 percent.

136. In 1959, North and South American, foreign, and black missions received 6.1 percent less than in 1952. Ibid.

137. Ibid.

138. Koenig, "What's Behind the Showdown in the LCMS? Conservative Reaction," 20.

139. Marquart, *Anatomy of an Explosion*, 95.

140. Larry Burgdorf interview. When asked about the fragmentation of the State of the Church Conference, Burgdorf replied: "In any kind of protest movement, you almost inevitably encounter the dissidents and malcontents that will gravitate toward a protest movement for whatever reasons that they have which may or may not be confluent with the nature and thrust of that movement."

141. Adams, *Preus of Missouri*, 128.

142. The help Marie Meyer lent her big brother in 1961 almost ruined her engagement: her fiancé's family was frequently the subject of Herman's attacks. Marie Meyer interviews.

143. Marquart, *Anatomy of an Explosion*, 94. Meyer's "evaluation" was sent to all pastors and teachers in the LCMS.

144. Herman Otten interviews.

145. Ibid. Otten and Hoffmeyer produced two publications: *The Faithful Word* and *Books of Documentation*.

146. Marie Meyer interviews.

147. *CN* Archives, State of the Church Conference (SOC), 7/1.

148. Adams, *Preus of Missouri*, 128; Herman Otten interviews.

149. *CN* Archives, SOC.

150. An agreement had been reached beforehand between Behnken and seminary president Fuerbringer to keep Scharlemann on the faculty. Scharlemann did not retract the content of his essay. John H. Tietjen, *Memoirs in Exile: Confessional Hope and Institutional Conflict* (Minneapolis: Fortress Press, 1990), 14. Danker, *No Room in the Brotherhood*, 30.

151. Herman Otten interviews.

152. George Loose, interview with author, July 17, 2002; Herman Otten interviews. Otten does not recall the specifics of the confrontation, but does remember a scuffle: "He [Loose] roughed me up pretty good."

153. Herman Otten interviews.

154. Larry Burgdorf interview.

155. As early as January 1962, the SOC was promising a new paper. "New Journal Pledges More Controversy on Doctrine," *St. Louis Lutheran* (January 20, 1962): "To be published by SOC, listed as price of $4.00." Also in *CN* Archives, SOC.

156. Herman Otten interviews. One such supporter was Walter Lang, executive director of the Bible-Science Association, an organization that promoted creationism. Lang invited Otten to speak and provided him with the Institute's mailing list.

157. Habel, *Exodus from Concordia*, 5.

158. Larry Burgdorf interview.

159. One friend wrote Herman on the eve of the election, "If we are a nation of slaves, LBJ will be elected—if otherwise, Goldwater will be elected." November 3, 1964, letter to Herman Otten, *CN* Archives, SOC.

160. "None of Them," editorial in *CN*, March 22, 1971; Herman Otten, ed., *A Christian Handbook on Vital Issues: Christian News 1963–1973* (New Haven, Mo.: Leader, 1973).

161. Bryan V. Hillis, *Can Two Walk Together Unless They Be Agreed? American Religious Schisms in the 1970s* (Booklyn: Carlson, 1991), 51; Marquart, *Anatomy of an Explosion*, 92; Habel, *Exodus from Concordia*, 8–9.

162. Herman Otten interviews.

163. Martin E. Marty, letter to author, July 30, 2002.

164. Ibid.

165. Adams, *Preus of Missouri*, 117–20; Hillis, *Can Two Walk Together*, 167; Herman Otten interviews.

166. Adams, *Preus of Missouri*, 117, 168.

167. Herman Otten interviews.

168. Adams, *Preus of Missouri*, 119.

169. Waldo Werning, interviews with author, 2000–2002. Preus later recounted this story to Werning.

170. Rutz's commitment in 1964–1965 alone was $5,500.00. JAOP, Fred Rutz.

171. Koenig, "Conservative Reaction," 20.

172. Frederick Neuhaus to John Behnken, March 3, 1962. John Behnken to Frederick Neuhaus, March 7, 1962, JAOP.

173. Fred Rutz to Oliver Harms, ibid.

174. Walter Bouman e-mail.

175. Kurt Marquart interview; Herman Otten interviews. "Pastors and Politics," 8.

176. Elmer. A. Kettner, "Is the Church Retarding INTEGRATION?" *LW* 79 (January 12, 1960): 1, 6–8.

177. "Intercultural Outreach," *LW* 81 (July 10, 1962): 12.

178. "Color Crisis, Part 1: The Problems Are Opportunities," *LW* 82 (September 3, 1963): 3–10.

179. "Please Cancel," *LW* 80 (November 14, 1961): 3.

180. Kettner, "Is the Church Retarding INTEGRATION?" 6–7.

181. "Letters," *LW* 79 (February 9, 1960): 22, 28.

182. "Notes and Quotes: Brother-in-Law," *LW* 80 (December 12, 1961): 23.

183. Frederic E. Schumann, "Interracial Marriage," *LW* 81 (February 20, 1962): 5–7.

184. Passage taken from Martin E. Marty, *Church Unity and Church Mission* (Grand Rapids: Eerdmans, 1964). "The context," says Marty, "was to say that both the prophetic and evangelical message of Christianity are always going to be inside structures, all of which are finite and limited and short-sighted (certainly every aspect of the ecumenical movement is at least as much so in its structures as denominations are!). It ought to be pretty obvious that if something conspiratorial and literally subversive was to be entertained, the LAST thing a 'plotter' would do would [be to] put it in a public book that he hopes all kinds of people will read." Martin E. Marty, e-mail to author, February 25, 2002.

185. Marquart, *Anatomy of an Explosion*, 86. Also cited frequently in *CN*.

186. Adams, *Preus of Missouri*, 112.

187. J. A. O. Preus, interview by August Suelflow, June 18, 1981, CHI Oral History Collection, 1976–1995, M-0014, f.4.

188. Harms told Preus that he was being appointed "so he wouldn't have that seminary to worry about." Ibid.

189. Wilke, "Changing Understanding," 278.

190. "Effective Christian Social Action," *LW* 82 (May 14, 1963): 22–23.

191. "Personal and Congregational Responsibility," *LW* 82 (May 14, 1963): 238.

192. "Color Crisis, Part 1," 3–10.

193. "Lutheran Human Relations Association Urges Against Discrimination," *LW* 82 (August 6, 1963): 18. One professor mentioned in the article was Richard Caemmerer, a key figure in the Seminex controversy.

194. Richard J. Neuhaus, "Letters: Racial Demonstrations," *LW* 82 (September 17, 1963): 21.

195. "News in Photos," *LW* 82 (October 1, 1963): 17.

196. "Whether Lutherans should take part in 'freedom marches' and sit-ins," *LW* 83 (February 18, 1964): 4–5.

197. "Civil Rights: Human Dignity," *LW* 83 (April 14, 1964): 4.

198. "Law of the Land," *LW* 83 (July 7, 1964): 4.

199. "Rioting," *LW* 83 (September 15, 1964): 6. See also "Waves of Violence," and "Love, Truth, and Justice," *LW* 86 (September 1967): 3–5.

200. Eugene W. Wiegman, "Campaign Issues," *LW* 83 (October 27, 1964): 10–11.

201. "New Trends in Mission: What Effect Are the Mission Affirmations Having?" *LW* 86 (May 1967): 13–14.

202. Wilke, "Changing Understanding," 294. The resolution allowed for work only in "areas of Christian service," still too porous a boundary for conservatives.

203. Hillis, *Can Two Walk Together*, 49.

204. Wilke, "Changing Understanding," 238, 278. In 1962, the convention had fielded just six positive resolutions on social issues.

205. Hillis, *Can Two Walk Together*, 49.

206. Ibid., 49–50, 166; LCMS, *Proceedings* (1966), 478–80. Conservative thoughts on the 1965 affirmations are in a paper, "The Mission of the Christian Church in the World: A Review of the 1965 'Mission Affirmations,'" in LCMS, *Proceedings of Convention* (1976), 471ff. Hillis finally cites F. Dean Lueking in *Mission in the Making: The Missionary Enterprise Among Missouri Synod Lutherans, 1846–1963* (St. Louis: Concordia, 1964), who calls those in favor of affirmations "evangelical confessionalists" who have a "strong sense of continuity with the past and present community of the Church Universal." He juxtaposes themselves with "scholastic confessionalists," who use seventeenth-century confessions to separate themselves from the church universal. Lueking: "Those who refused to drop conflicting views on any of the wide range of doctrines considered essential by the scholastic confessionalists were relegated to the invisible church." Hillis says that both groups (conservative and moderate) had been in the LCMS since its inception.

207. Neuhaus interview.

208. LCMS, *Proceedings* (1965), 7.

209. Hillis, *Can Two Walk Together*, 49.

210. Handwritten note to Roland Wiederaenders from T. H. Hartman, editor of *Lutheran Correspondent* (AAL), at bottom of letter from Carl Hoffmeyer to Hartman: "RCW—'Rev' Otten is a self-appointed 'pastor' at New Haven Missouri. Not a grad. of Mo. Synod Seminary or any other seminary. He is not recognized as a pastor in Mo. Synod. Rev. C. Hoffmeyer is apparently one of Otten's henchmen. Otten and associates have proved themselves to be a reprehensible and unauthentic group and, in my opinion, are to be ignored." December 17, 1965. EOR, f.1786, Herman Otten, 1966–1967.

211. Neuhaus interview.

212. "Taking Casualties Casually," *LW* 85 (May 1966): 21.

213. Ralph Moellering, "I Stand Opposed," *LW* 85 (June 1966): 18–19. R. Moellering was the Luthean campus pastor at the University of California–Berkeley.

214. Habel, *Exodus from Concordia*, 13. That so many new faculty members had attended Concordia Bronxville was an implicit sign to the Board of Control of the seminary's liberal bent. However, Herman Otten, his brother, Walter, David Scaer, and Kurt Marquart were also students at Bronxville.

215. "The Christian and Social Responsibility," *Concordia Theological Monthly* 37 (1966): 713.

216. Norman Habel, http://www.harpercollinsreligious.com.au/authors/profiles/norman_habel.html (accessed September 27, 2010).

217. Ralph Bohlmann, interview with author, August 10, 2001.

218. Bohlmann interview in "A Warrior of God, a Man of Peace: The Life and Times of Jacob Preus," video recording (St. Louis: Lutheran Church—Missouri Synod, 1995).

219. Bohlmann in "Warrior of God."

220. Piepkorn, "What Does 'Inerrancy' Mean?" 591.

221. *LW-Reporter: Great Lakes Edition*, May 8, 1966, 1. Conservative theologian J. W. Montgomery took issue with the decision: "Whenever we reach the point of affirming on the one hand that the Bible is infallible or inerrant and admitting on the other hand to internal contradictions or factual inaccuracies within it, we not only make a farce of language, promoting ambiguity, confusion, and perhaps even deception in the church; more reprehensible than even these things, we in fact deny the plenary inspiration and authority of Scripture, regardless of the theological formulae we may insist on retaining. . . . I must—if only on the basis of common sense—protest the idea that 'error can't affect inerrancy.' This is like saying that the presence of corners can't affect a circle." *LW-Reporter: Great Lakes Edition*, May 22, 1966, 7. In John W. Montgomery, *Ecumenicity, Evangelicals, and Rome* (Grand Rapids: Zondervan, 1969), 89.

222. Habel, *Exodus from Concordia*, 9–10.

223. Hillis, *Can Two Walk Together*, 168.

224. Adams, *Preus of Missouri*, 125.

225. John W. Behnken, *This I Recall* (St. Louis: Concordia, 1964), 195.

226. Waldo Werning interviews. In Werning's words, Harms said, "Don't tell anyone you met with me, or the liberals will want to meet with me too."

227. Werning interviews.

228. Herman Otten to Oliver Harms, March 3, 1963, EOR, Box 48, f.1782, Herman Otten.

229. Roland Wiederaenders to Oliver Harms, March 13, 1963, ibid.

230. Ibid.

231. Marquart, *Anatomy of an Explosion*, 97. LCMS Public Relations Department news release, January 24, 1974.

232. Herman Otten to Oliver Harms, September 18, 1963; Oliver Harms to Herman Otten, September 22, 1963, EOR, Box 48, f.1782, Herman Otten.

233. John Behnken, "The Case of Mr. Herman Otten," EOR, Box 48, f.1784, Herman Otten.

234. Oliver Harms to Herman Otten, December 16, 1963, EOR, Box 48, f.1782, Herman Otten.

235. Carl Eberhard to Oliver Harms, Oliver Harms to Carl Eberhard, December 1963, EOR, Box 48, f.1784, Herman Otten.

236. "Lutheran News," *LW* 83 (April 14, 1964).

Chapter Two

1. Ronald W. Stelzer, *Salt, Light, and Signs of the Times: The Life and Times of Alfred M. (Rip) Rehwinkel* (New Haven, Mo.: Lutheran News, 1993), 229, 234–35.

2. Walter Otten, "Declare the 'New Morality' to Be Anti-Christian," *CN*, July 3, 1967; Herman Otten, ed., *A Christian Handbook on Vital Issues: Christian News 1963–1973* (New Haven, Mo.: Leader, 1973), 123. Otten cites Marty from an interview with *Playboy* in June 1967. In "The Playboy Panel: Religion and the New Morality," Marty is quoted: "I can picture what might be called the 'tea-and-sympathy' context, which Harvey [Cox] mentioned a while ago, in which I could conceive, from the pastoral point of view, the legitimacy of something like adultery in extreme situations."

3. *CN*, March 22, 1965: Otten cites the *St. Louis Post-Dispatch*, March 14, 1965: "100 students and faculty members of the Concordia Lutheran Seminary participated in a prayer vigil for two victims of Alabama racial violence with all concerned members of all religious faiths."

4. Ibid.

5. "Jewish-Lutheran Seminar Held at Sem; Michael, Sandmel Speak," *CN*, April 5, 1965: "The seminars are part of a project in inter-religious cooperation, sponsored jointly by Concordia Seminary and the Anti-Defamation League of B'nai B'rith."

6. "Lutherans Participate in Demonstrations," *CN*, April 19, 1965, 1–2: Otten wrote that some professors and students of the LCMS "have been actively involved in recent civil rights demonstrations," egged on by the LHRAA. He also hits Concordia Teachers College, River Forest, Illinois, which joined neighboring Rosary College with four hundred "silent demonstrators" for a demonstration on April 1, 1965.

7. John Moldstad, "Those Preachers at Selma," *CN*, May 17, 1965.

8. "Students Hear Rev. Neuhaus Condemn US Vietnam Policy," *CN*, January 24, 1966. Reprint of January 1966 article in *The Torch*, the student newspaper of Valparaiso University.

9. "Clergymen United to Protest Escalation of Vietnam War," *CN*, April 18, 1966, 11. Again a reprint from March 1966 *The Torch*.

10. Otten, the anti-intellectual, turned to a conservative intellectual to combat Neuhaus: James D. Bales, "A Reply to Richard John Neuhaus on Vietnam," *CN*, December 13, 1965, 9. Bales was responding to a Neuhaus article in the *LW-R*, November 28, 1965, 3.

11. "The Revolution in the Missouri Synod," *CN*, May 30, 1966, 1. Richard John Neuhaus argues in *Una Sancta* 22, no. 3 (1965): 32–33, "The Lutheran Church—Missouri Synod CONFIRMED AN INTERNAL REVOLUTION."

12. Arnold T. Jonas, "No Heresy Trial—Quo Vadis Missouri?" *CN*, May 30, 1966, 1.

13. Neuhaus, *Una Sancta*, 32–33.

14. "Civil Disobedience and War," *CN*, November 1, 1965.

15. *CN*, March 23, 1965, 8. For proof of his claims, Otten relied on the work of southern governors like John J. McKeithen of Louisiana, who appointed a "Joint Legislative Committee on Un-American Activities."

16. August W. Brustat, "In Behalf of the Police," *CN*, April 4, 1966, 6.

17. *CN*, April 18, 1966, 5.

18. *CN*, April 5, 1965, 4.

19. *CN*, March 22, 1965, 12.

20. Article from *VOICE*, March 1965, *CN* Archives.

21. Article from *THE STANDARD BEARER*, March 1, 1965, *CN* Archives.

22. "ICCC to Meet," *CN*, May 3, 1965, 5.

23. *CN*, May 3, 1965, reprint from *Oak Leaves*, April 1, 1965.

24. "A Challenge to Lutheran Youth Officials," *CN*, March 22, 1965, 6.

25. "Lutheran Youth Officials Say Charges vs. Seeger Untrue," *CN*, April 5, 1965, 1. Otten cites Elmer Witt, who claims that the charges were investigated and dismissed by the *Milwaukee Journal*, March 13, 1965.

26. *CN* Archives, SOC file. Notes from meeting of the Executive Committee of SOC: Dr. Warren Hamula, Rev. Paul Lehenbauer, Dr. Robert Taylor, Rev. Carl Hoffmeyer, Rev. Kenneth Miller, Rev. Roy Faulstick, Rev. Walter Otten, Mr. Fred Bendewald.

27. "Identified Communist: Protests Mount vs. Seeger at Mo. Synod Youth Convention," *CN*, April 19, 1965, 1; "Youth Officials Refuse to Heed Protest," *CN*, May 3, 1965, 2.

28. *American Lutheran* 48 (May 1965).

29. *CN*, May 31, 1965, 7.

30. "A new and effective Anti-communist weapon"; advertisement on the same page, "An Answer to Pete Seeger—Folk Singer Janet Greene," *CN*, May 17, 1965, 9.

31. "Best Known of All Communist Party Entertainers," May 17, 1965, 8.

32. *LW-R*, May 9, 1965, quoted in *CN*, May 31, 1965, 5.

33. "A Shocking Administration," ibid.

34. "Conservatives to Meet in Detroit; Liberals Challenged to Defend Views," ibid., 11. The central "challenge" was to the Seeger appearance, but also to a debate on "New Mission Philosophy" and Martin Scharlemann. Otten's modus operandi was to send a letter or survey, post an article in *CN* stating that he had done so, and infer guilt from the absence of response: "The LUTHERAN NEWS editor has accepted. A reply has not yet been received from Dr. Nickel." Another example: "Harms Explains Why He Declines to Answer on LWF and Doctrine," *CN*, March 21, 1966, 9: Otten reprints letter written by Harms to Hoffmeyer at SOC in response to Hoffmeyer letter.

35. Pete Seeger, interview with author, August 6, 2001; letter from Pete Seeger, June 5, 2001.

36. "4,500 Teen-Agers Cheer Seeger," *CN*, July 26, 1965. Reprint of article from *LW-R*.

37. Herman Otten interviews.

38. Herman J. Otten, *Baal or God?* (New Haven, Mo.: Leader, 1965), 81.

39. Ibid.

40. Back cover of Otten, *Baal or God?* Otten cited Machen here, as he did elsewhere. J. Gresham Machen, *Christianity and Liberalism* (Grand Rapids: Eerdmans, 1923), 52.

41. Otten cites Merton P. Strommen's new study, *Profiles of Church Youth* (St. Louis: Concordia, 1963), a survey of LCA, ALC, and LCMS youth. "Moral revolution" and "sexplosion" are confronted in chapter 15, "The Law of God," in Otten, *Baal or God?* 76ff.

42. Otten, *Baal or God?* 81. From *Time*, October 29, 1956.

43. Ibid., iii: Machen argues that a huge gulf exists between evangelical Protestantism and the Roman Catholic Church, yet while the Catholic Church is a perversion of Christianity, "naturalistic liberalism is not Christianity at all."

44. Ibid., 6, 15. In chapter 2, "Christianity and History," Otten attacks neo-orthodoxy as a child of liberalism, not a return to Reformation theology.

45. Robert P. Scharlemann in *Communism and the Christian Faith* (St. Louis: Concordia, 1963), 7–9; Otten, *Baal or God?* 88: "Two convictions in particular are shared by Biblical Christianity and communism. . . . The second common concern is the passion for social justice. Communism shares this passion especially with the Old Testament prophets."

46. Ibid., 85–93, 96.

47. Karl L. Barth, "Doctrine," *LW* 84 (June 1965): 19.

48. LCMS, *Proceedings of the Forty-Sixth Regular Convention of the Lutheran Church—Missouri Synod* (St. Louis: Concordia, 1965). (Resolution 2-20), 99; (Resolution 2-23), 100; (Resolution 2-36), 103; (Resolution 9-02), 166; (Resolutions 9-21, 9-14, 9-21, 9-22, 9-23, and 9-24), 170–72; (Resolution 2-04: While delegates refused to change Luther's Small Catechism, which forbids "desertion" as an allowance for divorce, they did recognize that the definition of "desertion as Scriptural grounds for divorce . . . may differ in different cases"), 95; (Resolution 9-18), 169–70; (the six Mission Affirmations: The Church Is God's Mission [1-01A]; The Church Is Christ's Mission to the Whole World (1-01B); The Church Is Christ's Mission to the Church [1-01C]; The Church Is Christ's Mission to the Whole Society [1-01D]; The Church Is Christ's Mission to the Whole Man [1-01E]; and The Whole Church Is Christ's Mission [1-01F]), 79–81; (Resolutions 3-03, 3-06, and 3-06a), 104–6; (Resolution 3-11), 106–11; (Resolution 3-14), 111.

49. Ibid. (Resolution 5-41), 127; (Resolution 2-22 referred criticisms of Concordia Publishing House [CPH] to the CHP Board of Directors), 99; (Resolution 5-17), 127; (Resolutions 5-29, 5-30, 5-31, and 5-34), 128; (Resolution 5-36), 134; (Resolution 5-29: Delegates also rejected Resolution 5-35, to request President Harms to "consider evidence" in Otten's appeal case), 132–34; (Resolution 12-09), 184; (Resolution 13-04), 186; (Resolution 8-01, which addressed seven overtures), 161–62.

50. "The Right of Petition—For Unaware Laymen," *CN*, November 1, 1965; JAOP, correspondence with Waldo Werning, 1965ff.

51. RP, M-0016, Herman Otten: Case File, vols. 1–2, f.129.

52. LCMS, *Proceedings of Convention* (1965), 162–63. Resolutions 8-01 and 8-02.

53. RP, M-0016, Herman Otten: Case File, vols. 1–2, f.129.

54. Ibid.

55. "The Right of Petition—For Unaware Laymen," *CN*, November 1, 1965, 3.

56. RP, M-0016, Herman Otten: Case File, vols. 1–2, f.129. Also, Resolution 5-38, "To Amend 'Handbook' Sections 1.25 and 1.27." Braun was actually mistaken in his interpretation of Resolution 5-38: The submission of petitions to the synod was restricted not simply to "pastors, teachers and professors" but rather to "members of the Synod."

57. Ibid.

58. LCMS, *Proceedings of Convention* (1965), 135. Resolution 4-04.

59. RP, M-0016, Herman Otten: Case File, vols. 1–2, f.129.

60. "Anti-intellectualism in the Missouri Synod," *CN*, June 13, 1966, 8. Reprint of article by Rev. Wayne Saffen, University of Chicago, printed in *Lutheran Campus Pastor*, May 1966.

61. Walter Bouman, interview with author, August 8, 2001.

62. "Anti-Intellectualism in the Missouri Synod," 8.

63. "When Compromise Is Progress," *LW* 86 (August 1967): 6–7.

64. Harms was facing serious financial troubles by 1968. Synod officials were wringing their hands over the "Ebenezer fiasco," a failed effort by the Harms administration to raise millions for missions. In a June 7, 1968, letter from Martin W. Mueller, executive editor of the *LW*, to Wolbrecht, Mueller said Ebenezer failed because (1) it "violated a basic stewardship principle because it suggested a standard of giving (multiply age times dollars—a gimmick) instead of encouraging people to give in proportion to their earnings. (2) Ebenezer failed to tell people why they should evidence gratitude to God in this particular way—the needs were not accented

and dramatized, the urgency of the needs did not come through." Mueller complains, "The time is long gone when you can get people to respond to a gimmick and some generalities about doing the Lord's work." Mueller worried about new efforts by Wolbrecht and Harms to raise $1.5 million (September 1968). EOR, *LW-R.*

65. Message 1 from transcript collection of Harms telephone messages. EOR, Harms file, 200 HAR folder. Telephone Messages, 1967–1968.

66. Messages 6 and 7, 1967–1968, ibid.

67. Hadden's position is supported, albeit less stridently, by Merton P. Strommen, Milo L. Brekke, Ralph C. Underwager, and Arthur L. Johnson, *A Study of Generations: Report of a Two-Year Study of 5,000 Lutherans Between the Ages of 15–65, Their Beliefs, Values, Attitudes, Behavior* (Minneapolis: Augsburg Publishing House, 1972), 278. The authors claim that their results "are consistent in showing that clergy uniformly show higher commitment to personal and church involvement in social issues than laity do."

68. Eight percent of LCMS clergy agreed with the statement "I basically disapprove of the civil rights movement in America." Sixty-nine percent agreed with the statement "For the most part, the churches have been woefully inadequate in facing up to the civil rights issue." Seventy-eight percent agreed that "many whites pretend to be very Christian while in reality their racial attitudes demonstrate their lack of or misunderstanding of Christianity." Thirty-one percent agreed that "Negroes would be better off if they would take advantage of the opportunities that have been made available to them rather than spending so much time protesting." Twenty percent agreed that "Negroes could solve many of their own problems if they were not so irresponsible and carefree about life." And 49 percent of LCMS ministers were in "basic sympathy with Northern ministers and students who have gone to the South to work for civil rights." Jeffrey K. Hadden, *The Gathering Storm in the Churches: The Widening Gap Between Clergy and Laymen* (New York: Doubleday, 1969), 104–10.

69. Ibid., 141ff. Unfortunately, Hadden does not break down Protestantism into its denominational constituents, as he does with data on clerical views. Still, his findings are significant: While only 35 percent of clergy nationwide agreed that "Negroes would be better off if they would take advantage of the opportunities that have been made available to them rather than spending so much time protesting" (and just 31 percent of LCMS clergy), 86 percent of Protestant churchgoers agreed.

70. Ibid., 26–30, 53.

71. Ibid., 75. Twenty percent of neo-orthodox Missouri Synod Lutherans identified themselves as Democrats, while only 9 percent of conservatives did so. Perhaps more significant is the number of respondents who identified themselves as conservative or neo-orthodox (697 conservative, 44 neo-orthodox).

72. George Wallace in Dan T. Carter, *The Politics of Rage: George Wallace, the Origins of the New Conservatism, and the Transformation of American Politics* (Baton Rouge: Louisiana State University Press, 1995), 425.

73. Spiro T. Agnew address to the California Republican state convention, September 11, 1970. http://www.time.com/time/magazine/archive/1996/dom/960930/agnew.html (accessed September 27, 2010).

74. Andrew Schulze, "Force in Race Crisis," *LW* 87 (May 1968): 21.

75. J. Elmo Agrimson, "A Lutheran Approach to Social Issues," *LW* 87 (June 1968): 12.

76. "Student Power," *LW* 87 (June 1968): 3.

77. Roger Fink, "What Will the Church Do Now?" *LW* 87 (August 1968): 31.

78. The LCMS elects a synodical president but is also separated into dozens of individual districts, each of which elects its own president. LCMS district presidents are roughly analogous to bishops in more episcopal church bodies.

79. Waldo Werning, interviews with author, 2000–2002.

80. Werning, *Making Missouri Functional*, 53.

81. Ralph Bohlmann, interview with author, August 10, 2001.

82. Werning, *Making Missouri Functional*, 53.

83. James E. Adams, *Preus of Missouri and the Great Lutheran Civil War* (New York: Harper & Row, 1977), 129: The Lutheran Laymen's League (LLL) elected conservative Robert Hirsch in 1965, who soon "began hobnobbing with Jack Preus and promoting his candidacy for clergy president of Missouri." Werning memorandum, April 5, 1965: "Strategy Meeting 'Faith Forward—First Concerns.'" Participants: Rev. Karl Barth, Rev. W. W. Koenig, Dr. Harry Krieger, Dr. G. W. Lobeck, Rev. John Lutze, Rev. Ellis Nieting, Dr. Jack Preus, and Werning. JAOP, Correspondence with Waldo Werning, 1965ff.

84. Bryan V. Hillis, *Can Two Walk Together Unless They Be Agreed? American Religious Schisms in the 1970s* (Brooklyn: Carlson, 1991), 50; Waldo J. Werning, *Making Missouri Functional Again* (Fort Wayne: Biblical Renewal Publications, 1992), 57; EOR, f.662: Faith Forward–First Concerns (FF–FC), 1965, Box 17, "Districts: South Wisconsin," 1963–1967. Former president John W. Behnken agreed, speaking derisively about "academic freedom" or "exegetical freedom" at the seminary, products of the "Americanization" of the church (while also chastising the "freelance" movements causing harm to the synod). John Behnken, recorded monologue, November 11, 1965, CHI Oral History Collection.

85. Werning, *Making Missouri Functional*, 59–63; EOR, f.662 FF–FC, South Wisconsin 1963–1967.

86. Ibid.

87. Capitalization original. EOR, f.662 FF–FC, South Wisconsin 1963–1967; Werning, *Making Missouri Functional*, 54–63. Werning's own account (*Making Missouri Functional*, 54–55) reproduces the entire text of the original letter with one exception: He omits the concluding call, "CONSERVATIVES UNITE. . . ."

88. Waldo Werning interviews.

89. Waldo Werning to Wm. T. Eggers, cc to J. A. O. Preus and W. Harry Krieger, April 15, 1965. JAOP, Correspondence with Waldo Werning, 1965ff.: "If this is correct, has not the time come for the use of the tool of publicity in whatever measure we can use it?"

90. Ibid. Details of "The Letter" and how Werning and Preus decided to pull the story "at the last moment off the front page." Werning continues, "My understanding is that both Lutheran News and The Confessional Lutheran have agreed not to use any material connected with the whole movement represented by The Letter."

91. Werning, *Making Missouri Functional*, 54.

92. Rev. G. F. Barthel (Counselor Circuit 4, Milwaukee, Wisconsin) to Oliver Harms, May 17, 1965, EOR, FF–FC.

93. Oliver Harms to Rev. Kurt W. Biel (president of Western District of LCMS), April 7, 1965, ibid.

94. "Memo to My Brethren," reprint in *CN,* May 31, 1965, 5.

95. Richard Koenig, "What's Behind the Showdown in the LCMS? Conservative Reaction: 1965–1969," *Lutheran Forum* 7 (1973): 19.

96. "The Los Angeles Riots," *CN,* September 6, 1965, 10.

97. "Massive Evangelism Needed in Negro Communities" and "Communism and Racial Hatred," *CN,* September 20, 1965, 8.

98. *CN,* September 20, 1965, 4; "LCA OK's Interchurch Work in Race Relations—Supports NCC Commission on Religion and Race and Delta Ministry" and "Fourth Jewish-Lutheran Dialogue at Concordia Seminary," *CN,* November 1, 1965, 1.

99. RP, M-0016, Herman Otten: Case File, vols. 1–2, f.129, September 20, 1965. Officials in Western District moved to expel Otten's New Haven church (Trinity) from LCMS (it had been suspended from membership on April 12, 1962). The LCMS Board of Appeals, August 24, 1965, rejected the suspension and did not order Trinity to remove Herman Otten (Trinity had extended its call to Otten on January 8, 1961).

100. "A Strategy for Take-over: The Victory Is Announced," *CN,* November 1, 1965, 5.

101. "Wiederanders and Neuhaus," *CN,* April 18, 1964, 12.

102. "Chicago, December 14–15: Neuhaus, Elliot, Leuking, Lutze, Coates, Berry to Speak at Closed Race Session," *CN,* December 13, 1965, 1; "Why All the Secrecy? Another Closed Meeting with Liberals," *CN,* December 27, 1965, 3.

103. "Littell to Lecture at Concordia Seminary: Vice Chairman of Foundation for Reformation Research Charged with Having Communist Front Record," *CN,* October 18, 1965, 12.

104. "An All Time Low," *CN,* November 1, 1965, 5. Writes that *LW* has "not been known for its strong position of witnessing to the truth in recent years." He also complains that *LW* had recently run an article by Piepkorn on "What We Can Learn from the Roman Catholic Church in the Present Dialogue."

105. "Martin E. Marty Now on Lutheran Witness Board," *CN,* October 4, 1965, 1.

106. *CN,* December 27, 1965, 3: Otten attacks "Martin Marty and Dean Peerman" in their "Pen-ultimate" article in *Christian Century,* December 15, 1965, entitled "Barry as Exegete." Marty takes issue with Goldwater, who says, "Christ would not have needed a draft card because he would have been the first to offer his services to his country, to the world, and to you." Goldwater's words were in response to a student question, "Do you think Christ would have carried a draft card?"

107. J. A. O. Preus to Glen Peglau, April 10, 1967. JAOP, Peglau. Preus asked Peglau to provide money to "clear up the [Otto] Hintze account of $1500 by that time [end of fiscal year]." Hintze had purchased furniture and charged it to the school, leaving Jack in "hot water" with synodical auditors, the Board for Higher Education, and even the Board of Governors. Also J. A. O. Preus to Eugene R. Bertermann, May 5, 1967, JAOP, Peglau.

108. Frederick W. Danker, *No Room in the Brotherhood: The Preus-Otten Purge of Missouri* (St. Louis: Clayton, 1977), 188.

109. Waldo Werning to Elton Rengstorf, with handwritten note at bottom of cc to Jack Preus. JAOP, Correspondence with Waldo Werning, 1965ff.

110. J. A. O. Preus, "How Close Are Lutherans in America?" *LW* 85 (July 1966): 28–29.

111. Waldo Werning interviews. Montgomery's biography touts: "He is internationally regarded both as a theologian (his debates with the late Bishop James Pike, death-of-God

advocate Thomas Altizer, and situation-ethicist Joseph Fletcher are historic)." http://id-www. ucsb.edu/FSCF/LIBRARY/MONTGOMERY/bio.html (accessed September 27, 2010).

112. Adams, *Preus of Missouri*, 130.

113. *LW-Reporter: Great Lakes Edition*, May 8, 1966, 1.

114. *LW-Reporter: Great Lakes Edition*, May 22, 1966, 7; John W. Montgomery, *Ecumenicity, Evangelicals, and Rome* (Grand Rapids: Zondervan, 1969), 89.

115. Waldo Werning interviews.

116. EOR, Box 17, f.591, Districts: South Wisconsin, 1963–1967.

117. Waldo Werning interviews.

118. Walter Bouman, e-mail to author, July 31, 2001: "During my time at River Forest we had a faculty symposium in which various members of the theology department wrote papers about what we were teaching for discussion by the faculty. There was a significant but respectful opposition within the faculty, led by Neelak Tjernagel from the History Department. The papers were 'leaked' to Otten by the secretary of the president, Martin Koehneke. Otten printed them triumphantly as example of the false doctrine being taught and tolerated. John Warwick Montgomery mounted an attack against me in essays delivered to pastors and teachers conferences, and later published." Herman Otten disputes Bouman's account. Otten claims that his brother, Walter, was given the papers by Tjernagel before Tjernagel was to undergo a risky surgery. Tjernagel survived the surgery, but Walter Otten made copies of the papers and sent them to Herman before returning the originals to Tjernagel. "Pastors and Politics," *CN*, June 11, 2007, 9.

119. Waldo Werning to J. A. O. Preus, October 20, 1966, JAOP, Correspondence with Waldo Werning, 1965ff. Werning misnamed the Pew Charitable Trusts the "Pew Foundation."

120. "Lawrence, Celeste and family" to Herman and Grace Otten, February 10, 1966, *CN* Archives, Montgomery.

121. From *Eternity*, June 1967, *CN* Archives, Montgomery.

122. Herman Otten to John Warwick Montgomery, June 28, 1967, *CN* Archives, Montgomery.

123. John Warwick Montgomery to Herman Otten, July 3, 1967, *CN* Archives, Montgomery.

124. Montgomery, *Ecumenicity, Evangelicals, and Rome*, ii.

125. Uriah J. Fields, *The Anatomy of Mutuality* (Los Angeles: American Christian Freedom Society, 1966); *CN*, June 27, 1966, 7.

126. For information on McIntyre's Christian Admiral, see http://www.geocities.com/drakkar91/cadmiral/christia.html (accessed September 27, 2010).

127. EOR, f.1786, Herman Otten, 1966–1967. "Christian Admiral" flyer, conference held May 27—October 15, 1966.

128. Herman Otten interviews. He continued, "I've spoken, oh, I don't, a half a dozen times to International Council of Christian Churches, and they have all kinds of denominations all over the world. And what the Christian Admiral is, the building is torn down now, that was owned by the, that's where they had some of the International Council of Christian Churches meetings. And they're from, they're all small denominations. They say they come from over a hundred different countries, although in later years I think they were, people had dropped off. They always said they had over a hundred denom, no a couple hundred denominations, but

they're all these small ones, see. And I wanted Missouri Synod, and we put some resolutions in there, to have people there speaking."

129. SOC Treasurer's Report, June 30, 1966: Receipts through November 15, 1964: $3,189.40. From November 15, 1964, through June 30, 1966: $5,621.05. Disbursements: "Defense of Doctrine (Publishing): $1,025.00." Spent $1,868 on Detroit convention and $1,000 on Independent Lutheran Missions. *CN* Archives, SOC.

130. Joseph Kenny to Herman Otten, July 9, 1966, ibid.

131. Herman Otten interviews.

132. *CN* Archives, DIALOG.

133. *CN*, July 11, 1966, 11.

134. Richard John Neuhaus to Herman Otten, n.d., *CN* Archives.

135. Examples include letters to Otten from Montgomery, Werning, E. J. Otto, and Swanson. *CN* Archives.

136. EOR, f.787, Herman Otten, 1968–69.

137. Alvin Mueller and Carl Muhlenbruch, interview with August Suelflow, June 9, 1995, CHI Oral History Collection.

138. Ibid.

139. Elmer Kraemer (managing editor of *LW-R*) to Carl Hoffmeyer, July 6, 1966. Kraemer asks Hoffmeyer to respond to reports given to *LW-R* about a speech Hoffmeyer gave in Michigan on June 26, in which he urged members to withhold contributions from the synod. *CN* Archives, SOC.

140. Carl Hoffmeyer to Board of SOC, November 29, 1967. *CN* Archives, SOC.

141. Carl Hoffmeyer to SOC, December 21, 1966, *CN* Archives, SOC. Letter outlines "assignments" for members: "1. Rev. Burgdorf: The CTCR documents, especially 'Stance' and more recent ones. 2. Dr. Taylor and Rev. Otten: 'Mission resolutions.' H. Otten: If you cannot speak, you could give Taylor an outline and material for his help." Includes "Fred Rutz, financier from Cleveland Ohio." Herman Otten interviews. Otten called Baur his "fundraiser." Newsletter to SOC members, November 20, 1968: "Dr. John Baur of St. Louis has been working behind the scenes, trying to get some action started to smoke out Harms and prove that they are not straightforward in their answers to specific questions about doctrine and practice." *CN* Archives, SOC 7/13.

142. Carl Steffen, "President Harms versus Jesus Christ: A Strategy to Deceive Fools." JAOP, Correspondence with Waldo Werning, 1965ff.

143. *CN*, October 3, 1966, 1.

144. "Concerned Lutheran Laymen Meet in Oregon—Ohio," *CN*, October 3, 1966, 1: Guess had been urging such a meeting since at least October of that year. Karl Barth, interview with author, July 25, 2000: Barth remembers meeting Otten for the first time at this meeting.

145. Refers to the Law as a norm and guide for Christians, who "should daily exercise themselves in the Law of the Lord" (*Book of Concord*, VI, 4, "Third Use of the Law.")

146. Adams, *Preus of Missouri*, 132–33; Waldo Werning interviews; Hillis, *Can Two Walk Together*, 50.

147. Adams, *Preus of Missouri,* 121.

148. Herman Otten interviews. Otten on first trip to UPC: "Okay, toward the end they invited me up there, but they invited me, I had to keep my mouth shut where I was going. Well,

you can imagine how tough that is, well, I finally consented. I wasn't even supposed to tell my wife. I flew up to Chicago, I even wanted to pay my own way, I don't want to be beholden to anybody. I can't recall exactly. . . . And so we met there, of course Waldo Werning was there, Walter Maier, Karl Barth, president of Brazil, all the top leaders who had been working for Jack's election, see. And so they told me 'you gotta keep quiet.' Now I trust my misgivings at first and said, 'Now Gentlemen I have a problem with this. See, we should be out in the open, nothing secret.' Then Robert [Preus] told me, 'Well, I can see why you feel that way, but we're in a war. And in a war, you don't give the enemy your plan.'

149. United Planning Conference Agenda (LCMS Concerned Laymen meeting, Chicago, Ill., February 18, 1967), *CN* Archives, UPC.

150. Ibid.

151. Karl Barth interview.

152. Adams, *Preus of Missouri*, 133.

153. Waldo Werning interviews. Werning was on the phone so much in the months before New York, he joked, "It was a wonder my wife didn't leave me."

154. Herman Otten interviews.

155. United Planning Conference Agenda, *CN* Archives, UPC. James Adams, interview with author, 10 July 2000.

156. LCMS, *Proceedings of the Forty-Seventh Regular Convention of the Lutheran Church—Missouri Synod* (St. Louis: Concordia, 1968): Support for the LHRAA (Resolution 9-02), 149. On caring for the "poor, the hungry, and the homeless" Resolution 9-04), 149; "To Support Open Housing" (Resolution 9-08), 150; "To Encourage Inter-Lutheran Welfare Agencies" (Resolution 9-11), 151; "To Encourage Fairness in Business and Employment" (Resolution 9-12), 151; "To Express Concern for War and International Crisis" (Resolution 9-14), 151.

157. Ralph Bohlmann interviews. Bohlmann thinks that the "concerted attempt" to elect delegates first began in 1967: "And what happened was the far right that had supported Preus, they never quit. They haven't since that time. They have discovered that you can organize the national conventions and the national synod rather easily. You can't do it at a district level. But at the synod, the national level you can. And you can kind of, you know, there are probably some very nice people that say, this is how we serve God, we elect, we get our people in there, we'll keep it orthodox. But it has become a power play, so that you have a power politics living on in the synod since '67 right on to 2001. By power, I mean it's a concerted attempt to elect delegates, it's very structured, very end justifies the means, tremendous publicity efforts of which *Christian News* is one."

158. Paul Zimmerman to Oliver Harms, July 18, 1967, JAOP.

159. Chet Swanson to Lyndon Baines Johnson, n.d., complaining about inefficiencies in Johnson's "War on Poverty," *CN* Archives, Swanson. On "concerns," Karl Barth interview.

160. Waldo Werning to Edgar J. Otto, March 27, 1967, JAOP, Correspondence with Waldo Werning, 1965ff.

161. Karl Barth interviews.

162. Waldo Werning to Edgar J. Otto, March 27, 1967, JAOP, Correspondence with Waldo Werning, 1965ff.

163. Walter "Pat" Wolbrecht to *LW-R* editor calling it the "Ebenezer Fiasco." EOR, Box 55, f.2067, Publications: *Lutheran Witness*/Correspondence, 1961–1963.

164. LCMS, *Proceedings of Convention* (1967), 110. Resolution 4-32.

165. LCMS, *1967 Statistical Yearbook* (St. Louis: Concordia, 1968), 242. Average annual giving per communicant was $80.87 in 1956, $109.67 in 1966, and $119.56 in 1967.

166. Ibid., 261. Average annual giving per communicant to the synod was $13.48 in 1964, $12.80 in 1967.

167. Ibid. Synod's budget was $24,639,686 in 1966, $24,343,538 in 1967. The 1967 amount equals, adjusted for inflation, $25,354,236 in 1967. So, in constant dollars, synod's budget declined by approximately 4 percent from 1966 to 1967.

168. Pat Wolbrecht to Martin Mueller, April 14, 1968, EOR, Box 55, f.2067, Publications: *Lutheran Witness*/Correspondence, 1961–1963.

169. "Witness and Reporter Operations," "Synodical Districts Analysis of Witness and Reporter Operations," January 31, 1968, EOR, *LW*. South Wisconsin, Barth's district, had the largest deficit to the synod for *LW* and *LW-R* expenses: $64,289 deficit. The English District, of comparable size, had a $1,000 deficit.

170. Waldo Werning interviews.

171. Thomas A. Baker, *Watershed at the Rivergate: 1,400 vs. 250,000* (Sturgis, Mich.: T. Baker, 1964), 62.

172. John H. Tietjen, *Memoirs in Exile: Confessional Hope and Institutional Conflict* (Minneapolis: Fortress Press, 1990), 6–7.

173. Herman Otten, interviews with author, 2000–2002; Bohlmann interviews (with respect only to Scharlemann's desire for the job); Tietjen, *Memoirs*, 49: Tietjen says that Bohlmann was "upset at being denied the election," having received the most nominations for the position (100). Also in Baker, *Watershed*, 58. Bohlmann demurs, insisting that rather than coveting the position, he thought himself unqualified to lead a seminary at such a young age.

174. Tietjen, *Memoirs*, 9.

175. "Smoke screen" in Adams, *Preus of Missouri*, 12. On Tietjen and the "divine call," see Tietjen, *Memoirs*, 31.

176. Ralph Bohlmann interview in "A Warrior of God, a Man of Peace: The Life and Times of Jacob Preus," video recording (St. Louis: Lutheran Church—Missouri Synod, 1995).

177. Waldo Werning interviews. Karl Barth interview: "A lot of lay people read his paper," said Barth. "When it came time to vote, they went his way."

178. Herman Otten interviews.

179. Ibid., Werning interviews.

180. Herman Otten interviews.

181. Herman Otten interviews; Waldo Werning interviews; Chet Swanson, telephone interviews with author, 2000–2002.

182. Edwin Weber, interview with author, July 2000.

183. Waldo Werning interviews; Herman Otten interviews.

184. Herman Otten interviews.

185. Ibid.; Adams, *Preus of Missouri*, 134–36.

186. Ibid., 137, 139.

187. Tietjen, *Memoirs*, 3.

188. Adams, *Preus of Missouri*, 137.

189. EOR, Harms, Sermons and Addresses.

190. LCMS, *Proceedings of Convention* (1970), 20.

191. Mueller/Muhlenbruch interview. Muhlenbruch: "I've heard it said that if it had not been for Pat Wolbrecht's speech against politicking, Dr. Preus may not have been elected." "It's he, with his speech, got Dr. Preus elected." Mueller: "Wolbrecht was one of the great politicians. . . . I think you're very right." Muhlenbruch: "If that same speech had been given by one of the laymen, it would have been well-received." The problem was that many considered Wolbrecht to be the liberal power behind Harms: "Pat made it clear that Ollie Harms just could not eat the red meat and get in there" to fix the problems at the seminary; anonymous interview.

192. "The Matter of Politics," EOR, Swanson.

193. Waldo Werning interviews.

194. LCMS, *Proceedings of Convention* (1969), 20.

195. J. A. O. Preus interview.

196. Adams, *Preus of Missouri*, 140.

197. LCMS, *Proceedings of Convention* (1969), 20. "President's Report," July 12, 1969.

198. "President's Report," July 12, 1969.

199. Waldo Werning interviews; Herman Otten interviews.

200. Waldo Werning interviews.

201. Adams, *Preus of Missouri,* 142.

202. Ibid., 141–42.

203. Chet Swanson to J. A. O. Preus, July 20, 1969, EOR, Swanson.

204. J. A. O. Preus to Chet Swanson, August 5, 1969, ibid.

205. Herman Otten interviews; *CN,* June 14, 1969, 35.

206. Herman Otten interviews. Some of the conversations through 1972 may have been recorded by Glen Peglau, then conveyed to Otten.

Chapter Three

1. "Focus on Denver," *LW* 87 (August 1968): 3.

2. Ray Holsten (executive director of the Lutheran Benevolent Association) to Edgar C. Rakow, July 23, 1969, about "politicking" at the convention, cc to Wolbrecht with handwritten message. EOR, Wolbrecht.

3. Robert Preus interview in "A Warrior of God, a Man of Peace: The Life and Times of Jacob Preus," video recording (St. Louis: Lutheran Church—Missouri Synod, 1995).

4. Frederick W. Danker, *No Room in the Brotherhood: The Preus-Otten Purge of Missouri* (St. Louis: Clayton, 1977), 41–42.

5. James E. Adams, *Preus of Missouri and the Great Lutheran Civil War* (New York: Harper & Row, 1977), 147.

6. "Social Action and Welfare: Not Many 'Maybe' Answers," *LW* 87 (July 1969): 16–17.

7. "Shift to Conservatism," *LW* 87 (October 1968): 3.

8. Martin Mueller to J. A. O. Preus, EOR, f.2076, Publications: *LW-R* Correspondence, 1969.

9. "Mission to the Whole Society," *LW* 89 (February 1970): 6–8.

10. Statement of the Council of Presidents, October 3, 1969, signed by J. A. O. Preus. JAOP, Council of Presidents.

11. John H. Tietjen, *Memoirs in Exile: Confessional Hope and Institutional Conflict* (Minneapolis: Fortress Press, 1990), 25.

12. Martin Marty, e-mail to author, June 26, 2002.

13. Ralph Reinke to Pat Wolbrecht, October 15, 1969, about "continued decline in subscription levels of the Reporter." JAOP, Wolbrecht.

14. Reported in a questionnaire submitted to J. A. O. Preus from Jim Adams. JAOP, Jim Adams. In a September 4, 1969, meeting between Jack Preus and Martin Mueller, Mueller asked that Preus not "shut them out," but rather inform them ahead of time of official meetings and events. "Minutes," EOR, *LW-R.*

15. J. A. O. Preus to Martin Mueller, November 21, 1969, JAOP, *LW-R.* Preus refers to the column saying, "I'm getting a little static on some of Omar's material in having to do with poronographic [*sic*] movies as it comes out in the Reporter."

16. In *Spire*, November 6, 1969. Copy of article in JAOP, *LW-R.*

17. J. A. O. Preus to Harry Marks, JAOP.

18. Herman Otten interviews.

19. Adams, *Preus of Missouri*, 124.

20. Ibid., 144–49; article in *Chicago Sun-Times*, October 9, 1969, JAOP, Executive Director. The "gag order" restricted Wolbrecht to speaking only when directed to do so by the Board or Preus.

21. Ibid., 149.

22. J. A. O. Preus to Rev. Hilgendorf, October 10, 1969; Hilgendorf to Preus, October 2, 1969, JAOP, Executive Director. Herodias was daughter to Herod, who granted her request by beheading John the Baptist. He then had John's head delivered to her on a platter (Matthew 14:1-12).

23. J. A. O. Preus interviews.

24. Several letters labeled "PERSONAL AND CONFIDENTIAL" between Preus and Philip A. Draheim, attorney at law, Stolar, Heitzmann, and Eder, strategizing on ways to get rid of Wolbrecht, 1969–1971, JAOP, Executive Director.

25. Herman Otten to J. A. O. Preus, March 19, 1977, JAOP, Otten/CN.

26. Chet Swanson to J. A. O. Preus, July 20, 1969, EOR, Swanson.

27. Herman Otten to J. A. O. Preus. JAOP, Otten/CN.

28. Otten to Preus, August 22, 1969, EOR, f.1787, Herman Otten, 1968–1969.

29. Herman Otten interviews.

30. EOR, f.1787, Herman Otten, 1968–1969.

31. Minutes of Council of Presidents meeting, October 2–3, 1969, ibid.

32. Herman Otten to J. A. O. Preus, March 19, 1977, LCMS Office of the President, JAO Preus Administration Supp. II, Box 28, f.05 "Blackmail."

33. Waldo J. Werning, *Making the Missouri Synod Functional Again* (Fort Wayne: Biblical Renewal Publications, 1992), 114.

34. Herman Otten interviews; Herman Otten to Council of Presidents, November 1969: "Some of you have told us that you regretted signing the repudiation, but to the best of our knowledge no signer has taken his name from it. One of the signers told us how sorry he was for the repudiation and yet when talking with liberals he leaves them with the impression that he still supports it. A signer tells conservatives he regrets being forced into a position where he

had to sign the statement, and yet the same signer tells liberals he backs the statement." EOR, f.1787, Herman Otten, 1968–1969; *CN* Archives.

35. Some letters were copied to the Council of Presidents, others sent only to Preus, who responded sympathetically to most. JAOP, *Christian News* (reaction to C/P repudiation, 1969).

36. Chet Swanson to J. A. O. Preus, October 28, 1969, EOR, Swanson.

37. Danker, *No Room in the Brotherhood,* 42.

38. J. A. O. Preus interviews.

39. Adams, *Preus of Missouri,* 168.

40. Herman Otten interviews.

41. J. A. O. Preus to Goetz, November 4, 1969, EOR, f.1787, Herman Otten, 1968–1969. Preus included a judgment on Herman's brother, Walter: "Your letter to Walter Otten is fine, but of course it will bring you in for additional criticism, because you can never say anything that will please him."

42. "Minutes," EOR, *LW-R.*

43. J. A. O. Preus interviews.

44. J. A. O. Preus to Mr. and Mrs. John F. Bergmann, October 14, 1969, JAOP, Personal Correspondence.

45. J. A. O. Preus to Ed Steyer, October 13, 1969, JAOP, Personal Correspondence.

46. Preus attributed the leaks to Wolbrecht in an October 22, 1969 note. JAOP, Executive Director.

47. EOR, f.1787, Herman Otten, 1968–1969.

48. Danker, *No Room in the Brotherhood,* 42.

49. Karl Barth interview.

50. Marcus Lang, telephone interview with author, July 27, 2001.

51. Ibid.; 2000–2002.

52. Marcus Lang interview.

53. Herman Otten interviews.

54. Adams, *Preus of Missouri,* 165.

55. Chet Swanson, telephone interviews with author, 2000–2002.

56. Ralph Bohlmann, interview with author, August 10, 2001.

57. Werning, *Making Missouri Functional,* 113–15.

58. Waldo Werning interviews.

59. Werning, *Making Missouri Functional,* 116. From memo to J. A. O. Preus, March 24, 1970.

60. Ibid. From letter to Preus, December 14, 1970.

61. Ibid., 117. From letter to Preus, May 5, 1975.

62. Waldo Werning to Herman Otten, n.d., JAOP, Balance, 1970–5/71.

63. J. A. O. Preus to Martin Mueller, November 17, 1969, EOR, f.2076, Publications: *LW-R* Correspondence, 1969.

64. LCMS, *1969 Statistical Yearbook* (St. Louis: Concordia, 1970), 275; LCMS, *1970 Statistical Yearbook* (St. Louis: Concordia, 1971), 279: Overall contributions to the synodical budget increased by $300,000 between 1969 and 1970 but fell in constant dollars and on an "average per communicant" level from $12.29 in 1969 to $12.25 in 1970. (Note: Contributions to the synodical budget peaked in 1964 at $13.48 per communicant and dropped steadily thereafter.) This while contributions "per communicant" increased from $122.22 in 1969 to $123.87 in 1970.

65. Fred Rutz to J. A. O. Preus, September 29, 1969, EOR, f.2076, Publications: *LW-R* Correspondence, 1969.

66. Ibid.

67. Fred Rutz to J. A. O. Preus, February 10, 1970, JAOP, Rutz.

68. Roy H. Guess (petroleum exploration geologist, Casper, Wyoming) to Martin Mueller, October 2, 1969, EOR, *LW-R;* EOR, f.2076, Publications: *LW-R* Correspondence, 1969.

69. J. A. O. Preus to Roy Guess, cc to Mueller, October 10, 1969, ibid.

70. Martin Mueller to Roy Guess, October 16, 1969, ibid.

71. Richard Koenig, "What's Behind the Showdown in the LCMS? Conservative Reaction: 1965–1969," *Lutheran Forum* 7 (February 1973): 21.

72. Lester Kinsolving, "Chairman Jao Takes a Hard Line," *Seattle-Post Intelligencer*, April 26, 1970. Reprinted in Herman Otten, ed., *A Christian Handbook on Vital Issues: Christian News 1963–1973* (New Haven, Mo.: Leader, 1973), 692.

73. Paul Zimmerman, interview with author, August 7, 2001.

74. Walter Bouman interviews. Herman Otten clarifies that Walter Otten later filed a twenty-page paper to the Concordia–River Forest Board of Regents on "why Walter Bouman should not be granted tenture," but disputes that it was a "formal charge of false doctrine." "Pastors and Politics," *CN*, June 11, 2007, 9.

75. Adams, *Preus of Missouri,* 160; Werning, *Making Missouri Functional,* 112.

76. F. Dean Lueking, interview with author, January 5, 2003.

77. Adams, *Preus of Missouri,*160.

78. Herman Otten to Bertwin Frey (president of English District), March 3, 1970. *CN* Archives; EOR, f.1789, Herman Otten, June–October 1970.

79. J. A. O. Preus to Herman Otten, May 15, 1970, ibid.

80. EOR, f.1789, Herman Otten, June–October 1970. "Dear Marty" letter from J. A. O. Preus, July 9, 1970: "I hope this does the trick. At least at my end, until there is further motion from New Haven, I am satisfied with your explanation."

81. Scharlemann's conversion to the conservative camp is the subject of much speculation. Author of the controversial paper challenging inerrancy in 1958, Scharlemann was brought low at the synodical convention in Cleveland in 1962, which forced him to publicly apologize for having authored the essay. By 1970 Scharlemann was collaborating with the conservative camp.

82. Tietjen, *Memoirs,* 17–18.

83. "Lutheran Faction Here Urges More Freedom in Beliefs," *St. Louis Globe-Democrat*, February 2, 1970; Otten, *Christian Handbook,* 761.

84. Adams, *Preus of Missouri,* 149.

85. Waldo Werning interviews: "Jack would tell Jungkuntz that 'boy, they're trying to fire you.' Then he would go into the meeting and tell them that he wanted to fire Jungkuntz, then come out and say, 'boy, there was nothing I could do.'"

86. Bryan V. Hillis, *Can Two Walk Together Unless They Be Agreed? American Religious Schisms in the 1970s* (Brooklyn: Carlson, 1991), 52. Hillis mistakenly calls this a "faculty response."

87. "A Call to Openness and Trust," reprinted in Otten, *Christian Handbook,* 760–61.

88. "LCMS 'Moderates' Not Retracting Liberal Theology," *CN*, October 25, 1971; Otten, *Christian Handbook,* 762–63.

89. Kinsolving, "Chairman Jao Takes a Hard Line"

90. Phyllis Kersten, "Mission to the Whole Society," *LW* (February 1970): 6–8. Preus actually called for ecumenical efforts to combat "white, middle-class backlash. . . . Maybe the only voice the poor will have left is the church. It is time for the clergy of this area [St. Louis] to stick very closely together and to resist what is apt to become a major trend in our country."

91. Robert Preus to Chet Swanson, February 22, 1971, RP, f.15, Balance Inc/*Affirm*, January–March 1971. Preus discusses Herb Mayer in *Concordia Theological Monthly*, February 22, 1971. He calls Mayer a "man of limited abilities" and tells Swanson that he had talked with "Jack" about bringing change "with a new CENSOR immediately."

92. Roy Larson, "Seven Lutheran Congregations Form a New Denomination," *Chicago Sun-Times*, November 2, 1971, EOR, Box 29, f.1040, Districts: South Wisconsin, 1963–1967. FAL counted 8,000 members.

93. A handwritten note from Werning in the foreword of "Blueprint for Winning the Confessional Battle" reads, "The program was arranged by Waldo Werning." Erich H. Kiehl and Waldo J. Werning, eds., *Evangelical Directions for the Lutheran Church* (n.p., 1970). JAOP, Waldo Werning, Board for Missions.

94. "Blueprint for Winning the Confessional Battle" given to "Congress for Evangelical Lutherans, Chicago, August 1970," JAOP, Waldo Werning, Board for Missions.

95. Kiehl and Werning, *Evangelical Directions*, 166.

96. Francis A. Schaeffer, "Truth versus the New Humanism and the New Theology," in ibid., 21–29.

97. Richard Klann, "Shaping Society—Social Action," in ibid., 30–34.

98. Francis A. Schaeffer, "A Protestant Evangelical Speaks to His Lutheran Friends in a Day of Theological Crisis," in ibid., 143–50.

99. Kiehl and Werning, foreword to ibid., n.p.

100. Ralph Bohlmann interviews.

101. List of founding members and CODE OF REGULATIONS of BALANCE, INC, Article V, Membership, RP, f.15, Balance Inc/*Affirm*, January–March 1971. Founding members included Rev. Marcus T. Lang; Dr. Edwin Weber; Dr. Robert Preus, President; Dr. Walter Forster; Al Wipperman; Lyle Kiel; Glen Peglau; Fred C. Rutz, Vice President and Treasurer; and Rev. Paul Schnelle, Secretary. Trustees included Rev. Eldor Mueller, Hyman Firehammer, Marcus Braun, Rev. Paul Schnelle, Rev. Albert F. Jesse, Fred C. Rutz, and George Mohr.

102. "Meeting of Trustees and Officers of Balance, Inc.," June 26, 1970, RP, f.15, Balance Inc/*Affirm*, January–March 1971.

103. Herman Otten interviews.

104. Minutes, June 26, 1970, RP, f.15, Balance Inc/*Affirm*, January–March 1971. See also minutes of August 7, 1970, meeting of "Officers and Board of Trustees, Balance, Inc.," in O'Hare American, where thanks are made to Fred Rutz and his foundation for paying for legal fees and other donations ($1,400), ibid. Rutz gave another $1,000 in April 1971. "Income statement to 4/13/71. Preus Copy," ibid. Also, Balance, Inc. income statement: "Income from 1/28/71 to 2/9/71. Preus Copy," ibid.

105. Adams, *Preus of Missouri*, 164.

106. Danker, *No Room in the Brotherhood*, 113.

107. Robert Preus to "Brother [William] Eggers," October 14, 1970, RP, f.14, Balance Inc/*Affirm*.

108. Ibid.

109. Al Tessmann to Robert Preus, October 28, 1970, RP, f.15, Balance Inc/*Affirm*, January–March 1971.

110. Walter A. Maier II, telephone interview with author, August 2001.

111. *Affirm* 1, no. 6 (November 1971). On Swanson's authorship, see "Missouri Synod President Preus in Dispute with Conservatives," *CN*, August 7, 1978; Herman Otten, ed., *The Christian News Encyclopedia, Christian News 1973–1983* (Washington, Mo.: Missourian Publishing, n.d.), 1449.

112. Edgar Runge (chairman of South Carolina Pastors Conference) to J. A. O. Preus, December 21, 1971, JAOP Supp. II, Box 35. The conference expressed concern that he was addressing Resolutions 2-21 and 5-24 in *Affirm*.

113. J. A. O. Preus to Edgar Runge, December 27, 1971, ibid.

114. J. A. O. Preus to Chet Swanson, December 1, 1971, JAOP, Chet Swanson, 1971–1973.

115. J. A. O. Preus to Chet Swanson, December 20, 1971, ibid.: "I may still use that avenue if the situation requires it. . . . I don't care to have Herman Otten put me on the spit." Again he tells Swanson, "You are my good and loyal friend."

116. Ralph Bohlmann interviews.

117. Ibid.

118. H.J. Hilst was paid $18,004 in fiscal year 1972 by Balance, Inc. "FINANCIAL REPORT of Balance Inc/*Affirm*," RP, f.19, Balance Inc/*Affirm*: January–April 1973. Some remember that Hilst volunteered his time and was only reimbursed for expenses (anonymous interview), while Swanson remembers Hilst as "one of the paid people." He also believed Hilst "spent too much" money. Swanson was on the finance committee of Balance, Inc. Chet Swanson interviews.

119. Paul Zimmerman interview.

120. Ralph Bohlmann interviews.

121. Anonymous sources referred to him as "the pipeline." See Werning, *Making the Missouri Synod Functional,* 169.

122. Chet Swanson interviews; Herman Otten interviews; Tom Baker, interview with author, July 28, 2001.

123. Tom Baker reports that August Suelflow, late director of the Concordia Historical Institute, was disturbed when compiling the Preus brothers' historical record that nothing existed from Henry Hilst. Tom Baker interview.

124. Quote from Werning, Waldo Werning interviews; Tom Baker interview; Jack Cascione, interview with author, August 7, 2001.

125. Waldo Werning interviews.

126. Ibid.

127. Swanson tried to get Preus to publicly release the names of delegates to the Milwaukee convention. Synod Secretary Herbert Mueller informed Swanson of Preus's decision that "no names are to be released except upon authorization of President Preus." Herbert Mueller (secretary of LCMS) to Chet Swanson, February 16, 1971, JAOP, Chet Swanson, 1971–1973.

128. Waldo Werning, Marcus Lang, Herman Otten, and anonymous sources confirm that Preus, through Hilst, distributed delegate lists to Otten. Waldo Werning interviews; Marcus Lang interview; Herman Otten interview; anonymous interviews.

129. Herman Otten interviews.

130. Waldo Werning interviews.

131. Adams, *Preus of Missouri*, 195.

132. Chet Swanson interviews.

133. Chet Swanson to Henry Hilst, J. A. O. Preus, Zimmerman, and A. H. Tessmann, JAOP, Chet Swanson, 1971–1973. Swanson writes, "Drs. JAOP and PAZ [Zimmerman] divide the DCP list of contacts and call them. . . ."

134. Undated, handwritten note by Robert Preus, RP, f.18, Balance Inc/*Affirm*, 1972. "Call Jack and Paul Z (Paul is Tzar). Henry [Hilst] should be in constant contact."

135. Zimmerman calls Baker a "Johnny come lately" and insists Baker did not know the inner workings of the movement in the early 1970s. Zimmerman knows and confirms, however, that Hilst compiled lists of potential nominees from "contact men" in each district, often leaving district presidents out of the loop. Paul Zimmerman interview.

136. Tom Baker interview.

137. Adams reports that Scharlemann "actively sought the presidency." Adams, *Preus of Missouri*, 172.

138. Tietjen, *Memoirs*, 29, 30–31, 36.

139. LCMS, *Proceedings of the Forty-Ninth Regular Convention of the Lutheran Church—Missouri Synod* (St. Louis: Concordia, 1971), "President's Report," 56. Full transcripts of the interviews are available in JAOP, FFC; excerpts in Tietjen, *Memoirs*, 35–56, and Danker, *No Room in the Brotherhood*, 96–105.

140. Tietjen, *Memoirs*, 36.

141. LCMS, *Proceedings of Convention* (1971), 165–66. Resolution 5-26.

142. Danker, *No Room in the Brotherhood*, 87.

143. LCMS, *Proceedings of Convention* (1971), 122: "To Direct the Board of Control of Concordia Seminary, St. Louis, to Act."

144. Tietjen, *Memoirs*, 58; LCMS, *Proceedings of Convention* (1971), 119.

145. Ibid., 117–20. Resolution 2-21.

146. Ibid., 37. In Tietjen, *Memoirs*, 61.

147. J. A. O. Preus interviews.

148. J. A. O. Preus to William Fackler, September 10, 1970, JAOP, Balance, 1970–5/71.

149. J. A. O. Preus to Waldo Werning, May 12, 1972, JAOP, Board for Missions Correspondence. Werning had a list of questions for Kretzmann and demanded "yes" or "no" answers. He wanted Preus to compel Kretzmann to answer. Preus responds, "I would much prefer that you would make your request directly to the CTCR and have the members of your board who join you in this concern make it directly. Otherwise, I am afraid the whole thing will be very much misunderstood and used against me. Therefore, please go back to the board and have the members of the board support you in a formal way."

150. Hillis, *Can Two Walk Together*, 72–73.

151. Ibid.

152. "Mission Board's Chief Executive Resigns in Protest Against Board," *LW*, April 28, 1974, 1. JAOP.

153. David L. Mahsman, "A Time to Heal," *LW*, May 1997, 23. Hillis puts the number at thirteen of eighteen. Hillis, *Can Two Walk Together*, 74.

154. Waldo Werning interviews.

155. Werning insists that he had good cause to fire Mayer, who, Werning claims, had lied to the Board for Missions. Will Sohns apparently discovered this on a flight with Mayer to India. Waldo Werning interviews.

156. Danker, *No Room in the Brotherhood*, 87.

157. Ibid.

158. John W. Behnken, *Brief Statement of the Doctrinal Position of the Missouri Synod* (St. Louis: Concordia, 1932), 3. Also Todd, *Authority Vested*, 3.

159. LCMS, *Proceedings of the Forty-Fifth Regular Convention of the Lutheran Church—Missouri Synod* (St. Louis: Concordia, 1963), 105–6. "Resolution 9 and Synodically Adopted Doctrinal Statements," Resolution 3-17.

160. Jacob A. O. Preus, "A Statement," n.p., 1971; Danker, *No Room in the Brotherhood*, 76–86; Otten, *Christian Handbook*, 792–96.

161. Danker, *No Room in the Brotherhood*, 76–86.

162. Otten, *Christian Handbook*, 792–96.

163. J. A. O. Preus interview with Betty Medsger of *Washington Post*, in Tietjen, *Memoirs*, 33.

164. Paul Zimmerman interview.

165. "Extracts from Report of the Synodical President to the Lutheran Church—Missouri Synod in Compliance with Resolution 2-28 of the 49th Regular Convention," *LW*, September 3, 1972, 19–26; Otten, *Christian Handbook*, 800–807.

166. Ibid.; *LW*, September 3, 1972, 19–26.

167. Tietjen, *Memoirs*, 117.

168. Danker, *No Room in the Brotherhood*, 106. Reference to "The War Is On," *CN*, March 13, 1972; Otten, *Christian Handbook*, 791.

169. Waldo Werning interviews.

170. Chet Swanson to Bob Jones, August 24, 1970, RP, f.15, Balance Inc/*Affirm*, January–March 1971. The letter was a response to Lester Kinsolving's description of Jones as "president-owner of E. Carolina's unaccredited, hyperfundamentalist, rigidly regimented, thoroughly segregated and adamantly anti-Catholic Bob Jones University." Swanson carbon copied the letter to Senator Strom Thurmond, Rev. Billy Graham, Roy Guess, and Jack Preus.

171. Robert Preus, handwritten note, n.d., RP, f.15, Balance Inc/*Affirm*, January–March 1971. Unsigned, but unmistakably Robert Preus's draft (handwritten corrections).

172. J. A. O. Preus to William Fackler, September 10, 1970, JAOP, Balance, 1970–5/71.

173. J. A. O. Preus to Duane E. Imig, April 27, 1971, ibid. He furthermore remarked, "Although I have nothing to do with Balance or its fund raising program, I must say that I am grateful that there are some people in the church who are somewhat interested in supporting the position of our church."

174. Robert Preus to J. A. O. Preus, March 31, 1971, RP, f.15, Balance Inc/*Affirm*, January–March 1971; JAOP, Balance, 1970–5/71. J. A. O. Preus to Robert Preus, April 27, 1971, ibid.: "Dear Big: Please reply to this letter and give him some satisfaction." Jack Preus to Duane Imig, April 27, 1971, ibid., again denying relationship. Undated letter, Robert Preus to Duane Imig, ibid.: "I feel I should reply to some of the innuendos and allegations you said in your letter. The Pres. of the Synod has no connection with Balance, Inc. This fact was made clear by me in a letter to the *Lutheran Witness-Reporter* when a certain Rev. Koenig from Massachusetts made unfounded allegations and criticisms similar to yours."

175. Herman Otten to J. A. O. Preus, July 14, 1970, JAOP, Herman Otten.

176. J. A. O. Preus to Chet Swanson, September 2, 1970, JAOP, Chet Swanson, 1971–1973.

177. Herman Otten to J. A. O. Preus, November 24, 1970, with cc to Robert Preus, John Baur, Waldo Werning, Larry Marquardt, and Glen Peglau, JAOP, Herman Otten.

178. C.W. Greinke to J. A. O. Preus, October 8, 1970, JAOP, Glen Peglau.

179. J. A. O. Preus to C.W. Greinke, October 19, 1970, ibid.

180. Herman Otten interviews.

181. *Missouri in Perspective*, April 25, 1977, copy in JAOP, Otten/CN.

182. Chet Swanson to J. A. O. Preus, November 7, 1973, JAOP, Chet Swanson, 1971–73.

183. J. A. O. Preus to Chet Swanson, July 2, 1971, ibid.; Chet Swanson to J. A. O. Preus, June 3, 1971, ibid. Preus stayed with Swanson while in Cincinnati in July 1971 and other times: "As to housing, we hope that you will do as Walter Maier did and make our home your base while in Cincinnati." Still, Preus had to be careful, even with friends like Swanson. Chet Swanson to J. A. O. Preus, December 22, 1970, ibid., apologizing for having reproduced and distributed a private letter Preus sent him on December 1. It was not the first time.

184. John Baur to Robert Preus, November 9, 1970, RP, M-0016, Herman Otten: Case File, vols. 1–2, f.129.

185. Chet Swanson to Herman Otten, November 18, 1972, *CN* Archives, Swanson.

186. Ibid.: "I am in touch—and have been for many years—with Presbyterians, Methodists, Catholics, Baptists, etc., who are as concerned as you and I are with social gospel."

187. J. A. O. Preus to Chet Swanson, October 6, 1970, JAOP, Chet Swanson, 1971–1973.

188. J. A. O. Preus to Swanson, April 2, 1971, ibid.

189. Chet Swanson to J. A. O. Preus, January 29, 1971, ibid.

190. J. A. O. Preus to Chet Swanson, April 27, 1971, ibid.: "I agree with you completely relative to the role of the liberals. I have never tried to make friends with them and have no expectation of doing so." Swanson had written (referenced in Preus letter) that "I have formed a distinct impression that you have few friends in that spectrum [liberals]."

191. Chet Swanson to J. A. O. Preus, January 11, 1970, ibid.

192. J. A. O. Preus to Chet Swanson, March 4, 1971, ibid.

193. Chet Swanson to "Various Clerics and Laymen in LCMS," March 1971, ibid.

194. Karl Barth interview in "A Warrior of God, a Man of Peace."

195. Packet of bundled letters with accompanying cover note, Chet Swanson to J. A. O. Preus, January 9, 1971, JAOP, Chet Swanson, 1971–1973.

196. Chet Swanson to Marcus Lang, February 5, 1971, ibid.

197. Robert Preus to Balance, December 9, 1971, RP, f.16, Balance Inc/*Affirm*, April–December 1971.

198. Henry Meier to Robert Preus, February 7, 1972, RP, f.18, Balance Inc/*Affirm*, 1972: "Responses to date for membership have been very nominal with most of the few hundred dollars of funds being the direct result of personal solicitations on the part of Chet Swanson."

199. Memorandum from Bill Eggers, dated "May '72," RP, f.17, Balance Inc/*Affirm*, 1972.

200. Bill Eggers to Robert Preus, May 14, 1972, RP, f.18, Balance Inc/*Affirm*, 1972.

201. Chet Swanson to Henry Meier, November 1, 1972, ibid.

202. Minutes of Balance, Inc., meeting, October 14, 1972, ibid.

203. W. C. Dissen to Robert Preus, November 14, 1972, ibid.

204. Waldo Werning to Robert Preus, November 7, 1972, ibid.: $18,000 was coming from "our friend in Casper, Wyoming," into Balance and Werning wanted to make sure it did not all go into *Affirm*. Waldo Werning interviews—Werning confirms that "our friend" was Roy Guess.

205. Minutes of Balance, Inc., meeting, October 14, 1972, RP, f.18, Balance Inc/*Affirm*, 1972. Donations by September 1972: Fred C. Rutz, $1,801.27; Leonard Schoenen, $1,000.00; Alfred Tessmann, $1,000.

206. Handwritten note to self by Robert Preus, ibid.: "Call Phil Giessler $55,000 from 3 donors. Follow with Jack." Continues, "Call Jack and Paul Z (Paul is Tzar). Henry should be in constant contact."

207. C. A. Swanson to Balance, Inc. Finance Committee, October 1, 1972, ibid. By September 1972, *Affirm* had taken in only $22,300.

208. Chet Swanson to Robert Preus, November 1, 1972, RP, DCP: "Perhaps some of you feel that a letter from JAOP to CAS (along the lines I suggested re 721023-2a) is not wise. But, I believe you think otherwise."

209. Chet Swanson, "Mailings to DCP-LCMS," January 31, 1973, ibid. Proposed overtures included "Overture: To Welcome Rev. Herman Otten into LCMS Ministerium."

210. Chet Swanson, press release, February 12, 1973, ibid. Swanson announced DCP as a "conservative conglomerate of persons and programs which support" the candidacy of J. A. O. Preus and "his continued efforts to remove teaching and practices which are contrary to the Synod's stated position."

211. This after releasing his own series of press releases to the secular media. Chet Swanson, "1973 AD HOC DOCTRINAL CONCERNS PROGRAM GROUP," ibid.

212. Marcus Lang interview.

213. Chet Swanson to J. A. O. Preus, October 29, 1972, JAOP, Chet Swanson, 1971–1973.

214. Chet Swanson to J. A. O. Preus, October 23, 1972, ibid.

215. Chet Swanson to Marcus Lang, November 2, 1972, ibid.: Swanson urged Lang to read current issues of *The Presbyterian Layman* and *Forum Letter,* cc to Robert Preus, Zimmerman, JAOP, Tessmann, and Hilst.

216. Chet Swanson to Robert Preus, November 4, 1972, RP, DCP.

217. Chet Swanson to Marcus Lang, November 2, 1972, RP, f.18, Balance Inc/*Affirm*, 1972.

218. J. A. O. Preus to Chet Swanson, November 13, 1972, RP, DCP; JAOP, Chet Swanson, 1971–1973.

219. Chet Swanson to Herman Otten, November 18, 1972, RP, DCP.

220. Chet Swanson to Herman Otten, cc to Phil Giessler, November 18, 1972, RP, DCP.

221. Chet Swanson to Henry Hilst, J. A. O. Preus, Paul Zimmerman, and Al Tessmann, n.d., RP, f.18, Balance Inc/*Affirm*, 1972.

222. Adams, *Preus of Missouri*, 165–66.

223. Ibid., 166. Adams reports that Marvin Mueller, DCP chief in southern Illinois, would "neither confirm or deny" the rumor.

224. Chet Swanson to J. A. O. Preus, November 18, 1972, *CN* Archives, Swanson.

225. "Urges 'Peaceful Reorganization' of Synod," *Badger Lutheran*, November 12, 1970; Otten, *Christian Handbook*, 755–56.

226. J. A. O. Preus to Herman Otten, February 26, 1970, RP, f.1788, Herman Otten, January–May 1970: Preus read and privately supported Christian News. "I want to thank you also for the wonderful support which you have been giving me through various letters which I read recently in *Christian News*. It would be a great joy if more people would express their support in public. I get a lot of letters in private but what we need, of course, is a barrage of letters sent to key newspapers and other groups." J. A. O. Preus to Chet Swanson, January 4, 1971, JAOP, Chet Swanson, 1971–1973.

227. Paul Zimmerman interview: Zimmerman says that the seminary "took its revenge" on Otten.

228. Herman Otten interviews.

229. Ibid.; Chet Swanson to J. A. O. Preus, July 20, 1971, JAOP, Chet Swanson, 1971–1973: "But, perhaps, it is just as well H.O. is outside LCMS."

230. Herman Otten interviews.

231. Chet Swanson to J. A. O. Preus, October 28, 1969, JAOP, Chet Swanson, 1971–1973.

232. Marcus Braun to Herman Otten, cc to J. A. O. Preus, February 17, 1970, cc to JAOP, *CN*. Braun suggested that the 5–5 tie by the LCMS Board of Appeals on November 11, 1960, could be interpreted as an Otten victory and that Otten take the issue up in civil courts.

233. Partial transcript of committee debate, ibid.

234. J. A. O. Preus to Chet Swanson, February 8, 1971, JAOP, ibid.

235. J. A. O. Preus to Theodore F. Nickel, September 8, 1971, ibid., regarding a letter he and Paul Zimmerman were crafting to send to Otten referencing the committee rejection of his claims at the 1971 convention: "As you can see from the enclosed letter from Otten, he has both Paul and me on the spit on this matter and we have to be extremely careful in the way in which we answer." "On the spit" was likely a reference to the heavy-hitters Otten employed in pressuring Preus after the convention. Swanson and Tessmann led the charge, while Tessmann tried to enlist Werning, Walter Maier, and Robert Preus in the effort. J. A. O. Preus to Chet Swanson, January 18, 1972, EOR, f.1791, Otten/Herman, 1972. Preus suggested a meeting to discuss the Otten situation: "Let's talk about this when we get together." A. H. Tessmann to Otten, March 4, 1972, with cc to Waldo Werning, Walter A. Maier, II, Robert Preus, Harry Huth, and Eugene Klug; John Baur to J. A. O. Preus, February 29, 1971, ibid.; J. A. O. Preus to John Baur, March 10, 1971, ibid.

236. Paul Zimmerman to J. A. O. Preus, February 11, 1972, EOR, f.1790, Herman Otten, 1971.

237. Chet Swanson to J. A. O. Preus, July 20, 1971, JAOP, Chet Swanson, 1971–1973. Swanson again served as Otten's advocate: "In regard to *CN*, I wanted to point you to another example of Herman trying to be a reconciling agent among the conservative 'factions.' I think you are aware that I am often in this role. But you may not realize how frequently and effectively H.O. takes up this cue. About a year ago (more or less) I encouraged H.O. to avoid favoring any one group (at the time he was beginning to support FAAL and Sola Scriptura) to the almost exclusion of Balance, Inc. and other groups. He responded to my advice very positively and, I feel, has done a very creditable job in this domain in the past year. . . . As to getting H.O. his day in court within LCMS, it appears that the Appeals channel has been exhausted. Hence, I am suggesting he consider starting back at the beginning. I don't know how he'll take my suggestion but I felt I should offer it. If you have any recommendations, I'd be delighted to receive them.

(Private or public as you desire.)" Finally, Swanson added, "But, perhaps, it is just as well H.O. is outside LCMS."

238. Chet Swanson to J. A. O. Preus, June 29, 1972, ibid. Swanson was promoting a "black layman" named John H. McCants.

239. J. A. O. Preus to DeWitt Robinson, March 17, 1970, JAOP, ABLC.

240. Clemonce Sabourin to J. A. O. Preus, October 10, 1970, ibid.

241. J. A. O. Preus to DeWitt Robinson, March 17, 1970, ibid.

242. J. A. O. Preus to Joseph Lavalais, October 19, 1970, ibid.

243. Will Herzfeld to J. A. O. Preus, February 2, 1971, JAOP, Otten/*Christian News*. Otten was taking Herzfeld to task for pursuing "financial independence for Black Churches." Herzfeld warned Preus: "Not once have I tried to use my personal knowledge of you or the confidences that we have shared to hurt you. Pete [Albert Pero] and I both share a fondness for you as a °person, and a °drinking buddy. But if you are going to let Otten call the shots, you might be able to get rid of us a lot sooner than ever you could anticipate. (no threat—just a factual read-out) You said you were moving toward the middle—where are you moving from? If you are moving from the right, just keep on moving and we'll have a beautiful free church, better hurry though, cause some of us Blacks cannot wait too much longer. (no pun intended)." (*Asterisks included in letter.*)

244. Clemonce Sabourin to J. A. O. Preus, October 10, 1970, JAOP, ABLC. Sabourin accused Pero, "Brewster, and Harold Beverly" of reverse racism: "I fear that the men involved have become as hardened in their racism as most of our white racists. The pity of it is that while talking to those from whom they seek financial help, they use all the pious talk they have learned from whites, but while talking to disgruntled Negroes they use language that is designed to evoke support that springs from hatred. Can this be why they do not want white men in their meetings?"

245. J. A. O. Preus to Joseph Lavalais, October 19, 1970, JAOP, ABLC: "The Lutheran Church—Missouri Synod," Preus continued, "is most anxious to have all of the black pastors work together in peace and harmony in order to carry the gospel both to their own people and to all people throughout the world."

246. JAOP Subject Files, Box 2: Black Churchmen, Expenses (Special Account—President), 1971–1972.

247. Clemonce Sabourin to J. A. O. Preus, October 10, 1970, JAOP, ABLC.

248. Adams, *Preus of Missouri*, 154.

249. Ibid., 156. Preus's sermon was entitled "The Power of Prayer in the Space Age."

250. Herman Otten to J. A. O. Preus, September 25, 1971, EOR, f.1790, Herman Otten, 1971: "Some loyal Lutherans in the St. Louis area are disturbed about the front page story in the September 25 ST. LOUIS LUTHERAN titled: 'Dr. Preus says—SOCIAL MINISTRY AFFIRMATIONS POINT IN RIGHT DIRECTION.' Is this story correct? Do you support the Social Ministry Affirmations and take issue with The Federation of Authentic Lutherans for opposing these resolutions. [*sic*] FAL spokesmen tell us that you have said that some FAL leaders 'lie, are not telling the truth, and are guilty of unethical tactics.'"

251. J. A. O. Preus to Herman Otten, October 7, 1971, ibid.: Preus said that he refused to reply to "anonymous allegations."

252. Adams, *Preus of Missouri*, 154.

253. J. A. O. Preus interview.

254. Herman Otten interviews. Otten says that *he* will not tolerate adultery: "I believe that if a pastor's wife runs away from him, or she's guilty, then he can stay in the ministry. But if he's the guilty party, I mean you can serve the Lord, but not as a Pastor."

255. Handwritten note from Roland Wiederaenders to J. A. O. Preus (titled "JAOP/RPW— 8/31/72"): "This man called you again, Dr. Preus. I told him you were on vacation until next week and he plans to call you then. . . . I really don't feel we are doing the right thing by always telling him you are in a meeting, on the phone, or not available every time he calls. He's going to get wise—and angry and who knows what he will do. I think he is probably capable of doing just about anything which could be damaging to the church or even harmful to individuals."

256. To protect confidentiality, names and file will not be listed. JAOP. It was not the only time Otten would threaten action against what he considered adulterous clergymen. Another such accusation was brought to the attention of Victor Constien, then chair of the synod's Division of Parish Services. Otten wanted action taken against a pastor who, Otten was informed, had received an "unscriptural" divorce. The name of the accused will not be listed. Herman Otten to Victor Constien, April 16, 1979; Victor Constien to Herman Otten, April 19, 1979, JAOP, Otten/CN, separate file labeled "Lying/Slander."

257. Adams, *Preus of Missouri*, 159.

258. Herman Otten to Robert Preus, n.d. (1975–1976?), *CN* Archives, Robert Preus: "Jim Adams was here to interview me on this book he's writing on Jack for Harper and Row. He wants to know 'What makes Jack tick?' He noted that in his interview with Jack that he kept saying 'if I run again.' Adams wants to know who the conservatives plan to run in '77. It seems that Marty might have had something to do with this book. Adams says the libs have evidence of a direct tie between Jack and me. He mentioned some evidence for a phone call from Jack's private line to me shortly before we went to press on the day Wolbrecht was fired. The libs figure it was Jack who called us right after it happened and this is why we were able to get it in our paper just before we went to press. I still haven't figured out how this happened but it seems to me that Glen had something to do with it."

259. Waldo Werning to Jim Adams, June 18, 1973, JAOP Subject Files, Box 1: Adams, Jim (*Post-Dispatch*).

260. J. A. O. Preus to Herman Preus, May 21, 1971, ibid. Herman Preus was then on the faculty at Luther Seminary (ALC) in St. Paul, Minnesota. See also J. A. O. Preus to Martin Hauser, April 29, 1971, ibid.

261. J. A. O. Preus to Jim Adams, May 21, 1971, ibid.

262. J. A. O. Preus to Jim Adams, June 3, 1971, ibid.

263. J. A. O. Preus to Jim Adams, May 21, 1971, ibid. Preus continued, "You and I are both aware of the fact that certain things have been reported to you of an internal nature which have not been printed when they would be detrimental to the image of one side in the discussions that are going on within the church, while, on the other hand, matters have been reported which had no news value whatsoever but which can be construed in a way detrimental to those on the other side. This naturally does not make one confident as to the objectivity of certain reporters."

264. Chet Swanson to Ben Kaufman (Religion Editor of *Cincinnati Enquirer*), October 18, 1972, cc to Jim Adams, JAOP, Chet Swanson, 1971–1973. Swanson writes, "You indicated during our chat with Dr. Zimmerman that you were beginning to feel that the 'liberal' and 'orthodox' labels were not very helpful. Both sides are claiming to be orthodox and even the so-called

liberal side was sounding pretty orthodox to you." Zimmerman tells Kaufman and Swanson that "the label 'moderate' is only accurate if "a full religious spectrum is used."

265. Adams, *Preus of Missouri*, 157; William Hecht to Jim Adams, January 9, 1976, JAOP, Subject Files, Box 1: Adams, Jim (*Post-Dispatch*).

266. J. A. O. Preus to Clayton Carlson, February 1, 1977, ibid.

267. *New York Times*, June 11, 1972; Kurt E. Marquart, *Anatomy of an Explosion: A Theological Analysis of the Missouri Synod Conflict* (Fort Wayne: Concordia Seminary, 1977), 90: "Faced with the loss of accreditation, the Concordia Seminary faculty and administration acknowledged this week that the school's future as a viable academic institution depended on the Lutheran Church—Missouri Synod rejecting its conservative leader, the Rev. Dr. Jacob A.O. Preus, or in revising church laws to check his power. . . . Many faculty members say privately that the ideal solution for the seminary is the defeat of Dr. Preus."

268. George Loose to congregation in "Newsletter of Hope Lutheran Church, Pompano Beach, Florida," April 1972, in Otten, *Christian Handbook*, 833.

269. S. A. Hein to J. A. O. Preus, July 5, 1972, JAOP, Concordia Seminary: "Lay responses made up 19% of the total of which 1/3 showed definite signs of clergy coaching (citing constitution, theological jargon, etc.)."

270. Arthur Carl Piepkorn, *Report of the Synodical President to the Lutheran Church—Missouri Synod (In Compliance with Resolution 2-28 of the Forty-Ninth Regular Convention of the Synod)* (St. Louis: Concordia, 1972), 21, 24, 87 (hereafter referred to as *Blue Book*); Hillis, *Can Two Walk Together*, 55; Otten, *Christian Handbook*, 800–809.

271. Piepkorn, *Blue Book*, 147–48; Hillis, *Can Two Walk Together*, 56.

272. H. P. Eckhardt, *Fact Finding or Fault Finding? An Analysis of President J. A. O. Preus' Investigation of Concordia Seminary* (St. Louis: Concordia Seminary, 1972); Otten, *Christian Handbook*, 810–11; Hillis, *Can Two Walk Together*, 56–57.

273. "The War Is On," *CN*, March 7, 1972; Otten, *Christian Handbook*, 791.

274. Chet Swanson to Robert Preus, May 25, 1972, RP, f.17, Balance Inc/*Affirm*, 1972.

275. Chet Swanson to Ben Kaufman, cc to Jim Adams, October 18, 1972, JAOP, Chet Swanson, 1971–1973.

276. *CN*, June 14, 1999, 9.

277. Herman Otten interviews. Otten refused to disclose the source of funding for publishing and distribution of the *Christian Handbook*.

278. "Summary of Interview" with various professors, JAOP, Concordia Seminary.

279. Hillis, *Can Two Walk Together*, 57; *Convention Workbook for the 1973 Convention* (St. Louis: Concordia, 1973), 100.

280. H. P. Eckhardt, *Exodus from Concordia: A Report on the 1974 Walkout by the Board of Control, Concordia Seminary, St. Louis, Missouri* (St. Louis: Concordia College, 1977), 40.

281. Danker, *Preus of Missouri*, 106; Hillis, *Can Two Walk Together*, 57.

282. Art Beck to J. A. O. Preus, December 4, 1972; Art Beck to John Tietjen, cc to J. A. O. Preus, January 11, 1973; J. A. O. Preus to Art Beck, July 20, 1973, JAOP, Art Beck.

283. *Proceedings of Convention* (1973), 17–18; Hillis, *Can Two Walk Together*, 58; Karl Barth interview.

284. J. A. O. Preus interview.

285. Tietjen, *Memoirs*, 146–47.

286. *Proceedings of Convention* (1973), 20, 163, Resolution 5-01, "To Retain Bylaw 2.129b (Prior Consent to Serve)."

287. *Proceedings of Convention* (1973), 21. Preus received 606 votes on the first ballot, Kohn 340.

288. Tietjen, *Memoirs*, 148.

289. *Proceedings of Convention* (1973), 27.

290. Tietjen, *Memoirs*, 147.

291. *Proceedings of Convention* (1973), 52. Otto's majority was 57 percent, 596 votes out of 1,050.

292. George Loose, interview with author, July 17, 2002.

293. Tietjen, *Memoirs*, 145.

294. Adams, *Preus of Missouri*, 2.

295. *Proceedings of Convention* (1973), 30–31, 111–15, Resolution 2-12, "To Understand Article II of the Synod's Constitution as Requiring the Formulation and Adoption of Synodical Doctrinal Statements."

296. *Proceedings of Convention* (1973), (Resolution 2-12), 30–31, 111–15, "To Understand Article II of the Synod's Constitution as Requiring the Formulation and Adoption of Synodical Doctrinal Statements"; (Resolution 3-01), 36, "To Adopt 'A Statement,'" 127–31, 137.

297. Ibid., 133–39. Resolution 3-09, "To Declare Faculty Majority Position in Violation of Article II of the Constitution."

298. Ibid. (Resolution 3-09), 133–39, "To Declare Faculty Majority Position in Violation of Article II of the Constitution"; 39–41 (the resolution received 574 of 1,025 votes); 43–45, 140–42.

299. Tietjen, *Memoirs*, 157–5; Eckhardt, *Exodus from Concordia*, 59; *Proceedings of Convention* (1973), 45.

300. Luke 23:34: "Then Jesus said, "Father, forgive them; for they do not know what they are doing. And they cast lots to divide his clothing."

301. "Nobody ever accused that entire faculty of false doctrine." J. A. O. Preus interview.

302. J. A. O. Preus interview. Karl Barth agreed with Preus's sentiment; Karl Barth interview.

303. *Proceedings of Convention* (1973), 202–3, 206, 116–17. Resolution 9-11, "To Work Toward Equal Rights for Women," and Resolution 9-22, "To Continue Efforts to Combat Racism." Two others, affirmations of synodical ministries, might be construed as similar: Resolution 9-10, "To Support [Synodical] Welfare Agencies," and Resolution 9-13, "To Work Toward Prisoner Rehabilitation and Prison Reform."

304. Ibid., 107–8, 110, 185. Resolution 1-23, "To Facilitate Gospel Proclamation Among Jews" (no action taken); Resolution 1-25, "To Intensify Mission to Minorities" (no action taken); Resolution 1-26, "To Make Fuller Use of Minority Representation in the Mission of the Church" (no action taken); Resolution 1-27, "To Plan and Implement Programs for the Elimination of Racism in the Church" (no action taken); Resolution 2-08, "To Develop Worship Materials That Reflect Equality of Persons Before God" (no action taken); Resolution 6-28, "To Improve Our Ministry to Women" (no action taken). Even statements on conservative social issues did not receive attention: Resolution 2-18, "To Denounce Euthanasia," and Resolution 2-19, "To Reaffirm Synodical Position on Abortion," were both disregarded.

305. Alvin Mueller/Carl Muhlenbruch interview: August Suelflow commented that Otto was a "man of action." Muhlenbruch retorted that, unfortunately, "he had myopic vision. His way was the only way. He was as autocratic as they come. He had no use for laymen. . . . He was useful. He was an ally. But he was absolutely rude."

306. Tietjen, *Memoirs*, 179–80.

307. Ibid., 182; Hillis, *Can Two Walk Together*, 68.

308. Tietjen, *Memoirs*, 184.

309. *CN*, January 14, 1974, 8; Danker, *No Room in the Brotherhood*, 3.

310. Hillis, *Can Two Walk Together*, 68; Danker, *No Room in the Brotherhood*, 205; Eckhardt, *Exodus from Concordia*, 102. The student body vote was 274 in favor of the boycott to 92 against.

Chapter 4

1. *Missouri in Perspective* 1 (September 9, 1974): 1.

2. Bryan V. Hillis, *Can Two Walk Together Unless They Be Agreed? American Religious Schisms in the 1970s* (Booklyn: Carlson, 1991), 65–66.

3. "Official Notices: Constitutional Rulings," *LW*, September 16, 1973, 383; *Missouri in Perspective* 1 (October 22, 1973): 1.

4. LCMS, *1973 Statistical Yearbook* (St. Louis: Concordia, 1974), 289; LCMS, *1974 Statistical Yearbook* (St. Louis: Concordia, 1975), 299; LCMS, *1975 Statistical Yearbook* (St. Louis: Concordia, 1976), 223. Adjusted for 2002 dollars, synod's 1965 budget topped $138 million; 1973 budget, $98 million; 1974 budget, $88 million; 1975 budget, $72 million. Actual numbers: 1965 budget, $24 million; 1973, $24 million; 1974, $24 million; 1975, $21 million.

5. Herman Otten to J. A. O. Preus, n.d. (c. 1974), JAOP, Herman Otten.

6. Hillis, *Can Two Walk Together*, 79–80.

7. "From the President: Meeting of Insurgents Deplored," *LW*, June 3, 1974, 4; *LW* June 16, 1974, 24; Hillis, *Can Two Walk Together*, 80.

8. "President's Report," in LCMS, *Proceedings of the Fifty-First Regular Convention of the Lutheran Church—Missouri Synod* (St. Louis: Concordia, 1975), 59.

9. Ibid., 34–35. Resolution 5-02A, "To Deal with District Presidents Who Have Ordained or Who Have Authorized Ordination of Persons Who Are Not Properly Endorsed," *Proceedings of Convention* (1975), 122–24.

10. Ibid., 36–37. Resolution 3-06, "To Declare the Synod's Position on Evangelical Lutherans in Mission (ELIM)," ibid., 96–99.

11. Ibid., 145–47. Resolution 6-08A, "To Initiate Action for the Continued Development of the Synodical Higher Education System."

12. Ralph Bohlmann, interview with author, July 10, 2001: "And I think ever since Ozzie [Hoffmann] was defeated in '73, there has been no real moderate political organization of any kind in this church."

13. David L. Mahsman, "A Time to Heal," *LW*, May 1997, 23; Tietjen, *Memoirs*, 269.

14. Tietjen, *Memoirs*, 269.

15. Danker, *No Room in the Brotherhood*, 356.

16. Karl Barth interview in "A Warrior of God, a Man of Peace: The Life and Times of Jacob Preus," video recording (St. Louis: Lutheran Church—Missouri Synod, 1995).

17. For a brief history of FAL, see http://www.wels.net/about-wels/our-history (accessed September 27, 2010); for LCR, see http://www.lcrusa.org/ (under construction October 5, 2010) or http://en.wikipedia.org/wiki/Lutheran_Churches_of_the_Reformation.

18. Barth in "Warrior of God."

19. *Missouri in Perspective*, April 25, 1977, 1; JAOP, Otten/*CN*.

20. Chet Swanson, telephone interviews with author, 2000–2002.

21. Tom Baker, interview with author, July 28, 2001. Both Swanson and Baker remembered that Larry Brown, another early supporter, left the movement with Gebauer.

22. *Missouri in Perspective* 1 (October 22, 1973): 1; JAOP.

23. J. A. O. Preus interview.

24. J. A. O. Preus to Fred Rutz, October 31, 1975, JAOP, Fred Rutz.

25. Fred Rutz to J. A. O. Preus, January 20, 1976, ibid. Rutz continued his close relationship with Otten, ghost-writing articles for *Christian News* at least through 1977. Fred Rutz to Herman Otten, December 23, 1977: "Dear Herman: Attached you will find three articles for the Christian News which I wish you publish in the order they are numbered." *CN* Archives, Fred Rutz 7/13. Rutz helped finance the construction of Otten's Camp Trinity, and almost built Otten a house. Herman Otten interviews.

26. "FRED C. RUTZ, Individually, as a Delegate to The Lutheran Church—Missouri Synod, and as a representative of Zion Evangelical Lutheran Congregation U.A.C. of Painesville, Ohio, and THE FRED C. RUTZ FOUNDATION, Plaintiffs, vs. J. A. O. Preus, and THE LUTHERAN CHURCH—MISSOURI SYNOD, Defendants," JAOP, Fred Rutz. Apparently Rutz in 1975 was concerned about losses of "millions of dollars" by synod and offered Preus to have someone look into it (on June 13, 1975, and again on November 29, 1975). Preus refused and would not allow Rutz to examine the records. Plaintiffs wanted to look at handling of the Pension and Welfare Funds from January 31, 1970, to January 3, 1978, and also records relating to investment in the Brazilian mining industry, indebtedness incurred in 1962 and 1967, purchase and demolition of the Commerce Building in St. Louis, salaries and expenses of all synod officials from 1966 to date, the $1.3 million loss in operations for fiscal year 1978, and Mission records from 1970 to 1978. Included in Preus's Rutz file was a detailed list of Rutz's actions, including over twenty "threats" Rutz had issued to Preus.

27. Chet Swanson to Balance, January 1973, RP, f.19, Balance Inc/*Affirm*: January–April 1973.

28. "Crossroads" in Herman Otten, ed., *The Christian News Encyclopedia, Christian News 1973–1983*, vol. 2 (Washington, Mo.: Missourian Publishing, n.d.), 1196.

29. "News Release: 2/12/73," RP, f.19, Balance Inc/*Affirm*: January–April 1973.

30. "Crossroads," *CN Encyclopedia* 2, 1196.

31. Herman Otten interviews. Swanson similarly argues that DCP had "tens of thousands of people," although he made "no effort to keep track of members." Chet Swanson interviews.

32. Chet Swanson to Balance, September 27, 1975, RP, Balance Inc/*Affirm*.

33. Ibid.

34. Chet Swanson to DCP Council, January 1973, RP, f.19, Balance Inc/*Affirm*: January–April 1973.

35. Chet Swanson to J. A. O. Preus, November 7, 1973, ibid.

36. Chet Swanson to Herman Otten, November 18, 1972, *CN* Archives, Swanson.

37. Chet Swanson to Jim Adams, February 23, 1976, JAOP, Chet Swanson, 1971–1973.

38. Waldo Werning to J. A. O. Preus, Ellis Nieting, Wilbert Sohns, and Ervin Lemke, June 13, 1977, JAOP, Correspondence with Waldo Werning.

39. Karl Barth, interview with author, July 25, 2000.

40. Werning to Otten, October 2, 1974. *CN* Archives, Waldo Werning.

41. Undated and unsigned letter in Werning's handwriting (and file), *CN* Archives, Waldo Werning. Another example in letter from Waldo Werning to Herman Otten, November 1, 1977, ibid.: "Enclosed are several folders publicizing the Congress on the Lutheran Confessions which will be held at the Fort Wayne Seminary next January 4–6, 1978. . . . You may reproduce the folder in any way you see fit. When you write any news articles on it, please add Dr. Ralph Bohlmann, President of the St. Louis Seminary, to the list of speakers."

42. Waldo Werning to Herman Otten, n.d., ibid.

43. Waldo Werning, interviews with author, 2000–2002.

44. LCMS, *Proceedings of the Fiftieth Regular Convention of the Lutheran Church—Missouri Synod* (St. Louis: Concordia, 1973), Resolution 1-06, "To Reaffirm Our Church's Mission," 102–3.

45. Waldo Werning to J. A. O. Preus, February 11, 1975, JAOP, Waldo Werning, Board for Missions. See also Waldo Werning to J. A. O. Preus, February 28, 1975, ibid.: "They obviously used a tactic which makes it impossible for me to report now without making a big case out of their sins. . . ."

46. Waldo Werning interviews.

47. Waldo Werning to J. A. O. Preus, Ellis Nieting, Wilbert Sohns, and Ervin Lemke, June 13, 1977, JAOP, Correspondence with Waldo Werning.

48. "Pitfalls of Conservatives: Mixing Church and State," in Otten, *Christian Handbook*, 254. January 4–6, 1972.

49. LCMS, *Proceedings of the Forty-Ninth Regular Convention of the Lutheran Church— Missouri Synod* (St. Louis: Concordia, 1971), 23, 20, 61, 191–93. Resolution 9-07, "Social Ministry Affirmations." The Affirmations stated, in part, that the synod pledged itself to "work for the control and elimination of crime and injustice," support "those programs in public and private sectors that seek to eliminate the causes of poverty and hunger; we seek comprehensive medical care for all; and we support all efforts to sensitize legal, social, financial, and educational structures to provide justice and fairness for all." It also promoted "programs that lead to the elimination of racist and separatist attitudes" and called on people to "avoid the practice of applying stereotypes to ethnic and social groups that result in people being polarized rather than reconciled." Finally, it called on the synod to "use in responsible ways those channels that are open to it to influence other structures and institutions such as government, business, and labor, to sensitize them to the task of improving the quality of life at every level." A handful of conservatives attempted to amend the Affirmations. One rejected amendment read, "We support the efforts of individual Christians but reject the thought that the church should support such programs as a church." Another stated, "We call on the church, as a corporate entity, to refrain from establishing or maintaining positions on secular [social, economic, and political] issues past, present, or future; and we express ourselves against joining any other body, denomination, council, or group which has a different doctrinal basis or is expressly associated with corporate positions on secular affairs."

50. J. A. O. Preus in "Pitfalls of Conservatives: Mixing Church and State," in Otten, *Christian Handbook*, 254.

51. LCMS, *Proceedings of Convention* (1971), 61: "Of particular concern in this area is the ongoing problem of combating racism in our own nation and church. We dare not allow this evil and demonic spirit to devour us."

52. Will Herzfeld to Herman Otten, September 9, 1975, JAOP, Otten/CN; Herman Otten to Will Herzfeld, September 12, 1975, EOR, f.1793, Herman Otten, 1975.

53. "Political Conservatives and Historic Christianity," in Otten, *Christian Handbook*, 223–24, March 12, 1973.

54. Ralph Moellering to Herman Otten, January 8, 1973, EOR, f.1792, Herman Otten, 1973.

55. Paul Zimmerman to Herman Otten, November 10, 1971: "I am basically reluctant to engage in further conversation with you inasmuch as it seems to me that you have not dealt as a Christian brother." EOR, f.1790, Herman Otten, 1971.

56. LCMS, *Proceedings of Convention* (1973), 216. Resolution 11-20, "To Refer the Herman Otten Case to the President of Synod for Resolution." Delegates did not vote on the resolution, but referred it to the Board of Directors under omnibus Resolution 4-47, "To Refer Unfinished Business," 160–61. Preus reported to the synod in 1975 that he was carrying on "correspondence relating to this matter" with Otten. LCMS, *Proceedings of Convention* (1975), 64.

57. Ibid., 171. Resolution 9-10, "To Advise the Rev. Herman Otten to Apply to the Faculty of Concordia Seminary, St. Louis, for Certification into the LCMS Ministerium." Also JAOP, Otten/CN.

58. Herman Otten to J. A. O. Preus, December 30, 1974, ibid. *CN* was "informed" of the recent Christmas party of LCMS staff and former employees, an "elaborate Christmas party," where a "good number of mixed drinks were available, liquor flowed rather freely, and . . . a dance followed the expensive dinner. You are supposed to have been present. . . . Some seem to think that the affair was paid for by the LCMS and question whether such a party should be paid for by 'mission' funds." J. A. O. Preus to Herman Otten, January 9, 1975, ibid.: synod paid for the food, laymen paid for the liquor.

59. Several drafts of letters to Herman Otten from J. A. O. Preus, November 7, 1975, EOR, f.1793, Herman Otten, 1975.

60. Herman Otten to J. A. O. Preus, November 24, 1975, ibid.

61. Waldo Werning calls Robert's decision to accept the presidency of Springfield the "source of the conflict" between Jack and Robert. Waldo Werning interviews.

62. "Officers, Trustees, Voting Members and Committees, Balance, Inc. 1973," RP, Balance Inc/*Affirm*. The editorial committee included Robert Preus and W. J. Hoffman (both officers of Balance), and Swanson and Marcus Braun (both trustees of Balance). *Affirm*'s chief editor was W. T. Eggers (assistant treasurer of Balance).

63. Questions were raised in November 1973 during a series of complaints issued by George Sommermeyer, member of the CCM, who argued that Balance predated Denver and was aiming to seize political control of the synod. Marcus Lang answered Sommermeyer that Balance did not predate Denver (he later admitted in interviews that it did) and that it was not political, but rather had "as its objective the support of Synod and the upholding of her historic and constitutional theological position. It is ELIM that is dissenting from Synod's resolutions and her doctrinal positions." Robert Preus wrote the same thing to Sommermeyer and "TO

ALL MEMBERS OF THE COUNCIL OF PRESIDENTS, TO ALL MEMBERS OF THE COMMISSION ON CONSTITUTIONAL MATTERS, and TO ALL MEMBERS OF THE BOARD OF DIRECTORS—LCMS," denying that Balance was political. RP, f.20, Balance Inc/ *Affirm*, 1973.

64. "This charge is false. Balance, Inc.'s primary activity has been the decision to publish Affirm." ibid.

65. Rreport of Balance Inc/*Affirm* for fiscal year 1972, RP, f.19, Balance Inc/*Affirm*, January–April 1973: Of $77,517 in receipts to Balance, $41,277 went to *Affirm*. Almost half that amount, $18,004, went to H. J. Hilst, and $2,734 went to Cleveland Doctrinal Concerns.

66. J. Barclay Brown to Robert Preus and Gebauer, November 21, 1972, RP, f.18, Balance Inc/*Affirm*, 1972.

67. J. A. O. Preus to Robert Preus, March 18, 1974, JAOP, Robert Preus.

68. Karl Barth interview.

69. Robert Preus to Herman Otten, handwritten note (presumably 1974): "All goes well here at the seminary. . . . They could walk off any time." Also, handwritten note on scratch paper, Robert Preus to Herman Otten, n.d.: "The libs had their own plans and time table for attempting to close down the sem and then blame the Board for it, and Hinchey was privy to this. You might also mention that there were names of prospective students on file at Concordia Seminary after Hinchey and most of the faculty left. Such a list has never shown up to this day. Here are other files that were just not there." CN Archives, R. Preus, 7/12.

70. Robert Preus to Herman Otten, handwritten note, n.d., ibid: "I enjoy reading CN every week. I hope you have room for this in your FORUM section. Please caption it: 'The Living Bible is not the Bible.' Thanks. Robt. Preus."

71. Robert Preus to Herman Otten, handwritten note, n.d., ibid.: "Could you send me [John] Baur's address? I have lost it. Would you send him this assignment from Affirm? 1,000 or 1,500 words on 'Dissent, Disobedience and Rebellion.' The nature of Baur's article is obvious. He has full freedom to say anything that comes to mind on the subject. We just thought Affirm needed some good Bauresk rhetoric on the important subject." Also, "Would you please send Christian News to my son, Rolf at Concordia College . . . ? He needs it a lot. MIP is apparently all over the place." Also, Robert Preus to Herman Otten, May 16, 1977, ibid.: "This is a copy of some resolutions that the Southern District are bringing into the Synod apparently trying to revise the Handbook so that Seminex people can get into the Synod without going through the present colloquy thing. You may want to print it just to let people know what is going on."

72. Herman Otten to Robert Preus, n.d., ibid.: references Jim Adams, who "wants to know who the conservatives plan to run in '77."

73. Waldo Werning argues that Robert Preus merged the two dominant conservative groups, Balance, Inc. and the Continuation Committee. Werning, who served as Preus's development director at Fort Wayne, believes that Preus became the leader of the "inner core" by 1982. Waldo Werning interviews.

74. Ibid.

75. Herman Otten to J. A. O. Preus, March 17, 1977, LCMS Office of the President, JAO Preus Administration Supp. II, Box 28, f.05 "Blackmail"; RP, M-0016, Herman Otten: Case File, vols. 3–4, f.131.

76. Handwritten notes of phone call with Herman Otten, written by Robert Sauer, March 17, 1977. LCMS Office of the President, JAO Preus Administration Supp. II, Box 28, f.05 "Blackmail." "The Peglau information will be included," Otten told Sauer.

77. Herman Otten to J. A. O. Preus, March 19, 1977, JAOP, Otten/CN.

78. Herman Otten to J. A. O. Preus, March 19, 1977, LCMS Office of the President, JAO Preus Administration Supp. II, Box 28, f.05 "Blackmail"; RP, M-0016, Herman Otten: Case File, vols. 3–4, f.131.

79. William H. Hecht to Herman Otten, July 7, 1977, ibid.

80. LCMS Office of the President, JAO Preus Administration Supp. II, Box 28, f.05 "Blackmail."

81. Preus took 544 votes of 1,097 cast on the first ballot (546 needed for election) and 596 on the second. LCMS, *Proceedings of the Fifty-Second Regular Convention of the Lutheran Church—Missouri Synod* (St. Louis: Concordia, 1977), 25–26; Tom Baker interview; Chet Swanson interviews.

82. Fred Rutz to Herman Otten, June 28, 1977, CN Archives, Rutz 7/13.

83. Marie Meyer, interviews with author, 2001–2002; LCMS, *Proceedings of Convention* (1977), 38.

84. Richard "Dick" Korthals to J. A. O. Preus, "Monday P.M. [July 18: written on Ramada Inn Convention Center, Dallas, stationery]," JAOP, Robert Preus.

85. J. A. O. Preus to Richard "Dick" Korthals, August 5, 1977, ibid.

86. Marie Meyer to J. A. O. Preus, July 22, 1977, JAOP, Marie Meyer; Marie Meyer interviews.

87. J. A. O. Preus to Marie Meyer, August 5, 1977, ibid.

88. Marie Meyer interviews. Preus may have used a harsher invective to describe Robert. She recalls being shocked that a man would talk about his brother so openly that way.

89. W. A. Schroeder to Robert Preus, August 2, 1977, RP, Balance Inc/*Affirm*.

90. Robert Preus to W. A. Schroeder, September 20, 1977, ibid.

91. J. A. O. Preus to Syle Stuehrenberg, July 12, 1977, Ralph Bohlmann Files, Unprocessed, Preus Misc. Files, Box 24.

92. Ihno Janssen to J. A. O. Preus, September 29, 1977, JAOP, Balance/*Affirm*.

93. J. A. O. Preus to Robert Preus, William Eggers, and E. J. Otto, October 10, 1977, ibid.

94. Marcus Lang to J. A. O. Preus, September 11, 1977, ibid.

95. J. A. O. Preus to Marcus Lang, September 16, 1977, ibid. Eugene Fincke, the *Affirm* candidate, was defeated by twenty votes for treasurer by Norman Sell. For the Board for Higher Education, Elmer Moeller defeated *Affirm* candidate Herbert Wians by twenty-one votes. LCMS, *Proceedings of Convention* (1977), 57–58.

96. "Christian News and 'Preus of Missouri,'" CN, April 18, 1977; Otten, CN *Encyclopedia* 2, 1447–48.

97. "Missouri Synod President Preus in Dispute with Conservatives," CN, August 7, 1978; Otten, CN *Encyclopedia* 2, 1449.

98. "Investigate Christian News," CN, January 1, 1979; Otten, CN *Encyclopedia* 2, 1448.

99. "Missouri Synod President Preus in Dispute with Conservatives"; Otten, CN *Encyclopedia* 2, 1449.

100. Herman Otten to J. A. O. Preus (unsigned), December 16, 1978, JAOP, Otten/CN.

101. The West German church is the *Selbstandige Evangelisch-Lutherische Kirche.*

102. J. A. O. Preus to Herman Otten, December 15, 1978, JAOP, Otten/*CN.*

103. Marie Meyer interviews.

104. "President Preus Says AAT Bible Published During Liberal Period," *CN,* February 5, 1979; Otten, *CN Encyclopedia 2,* 1450.

105. Herman Otten to Victor A. Constien, April 16, 1979. JAOP, Otten/*CN,* "Lying/ Slander."

106. Herman Otten interviews.

107. Victor A. Constien to Herman Otten, April 19, 1979, JAOP, Otten/*CN,* "Lying/Slander." The pastor's name has been removed. Herman Otten interviews. Otten insists that the remarks about Hoffmeyer in Constien's letter were Preus's doing.

108. Waldo Werning to Herman Otten, July 6, 1978, *CN* Archives, Werning, 7/12. Information sent to Otten with the request, "We would appreciate if you would find it possible to reproduce it in <u>Christian News</u> and provide some publicity"; Waldo Werning to Herman Otten, June 1, 1978, ibid.

109. Marie Meyer interviews.

110. J. A. O. Preus to Herman Otten, January 17, 1979, JAOP, Otten/*CN*; RP, M-0016, Herman Otten: Case File, vols. 3-4, f.131; *CN* Archives, J. A. O. Preus.

111. Kurt Marquart to Marie Meyer, March 28, 1979, JAOP, Otten, Herman/*CN.*

112. J. A. O. Preus to Kurt Marquart, April 19, 1979, ibid.

113. J. A. O. Preus to Herman Otten, June 20, 1979, ibid.

114. "Preus and Doctrinally Divided COP," *CN,* March 14, 1977; Otten, *CN Encyclopedia 2,* 1223.

115. J. A. O. Preus to Herman Otten, June 20, 1979, JAOP, Otten/*CN.*

116. J. A. O. Preus to Herman Otten, April 6, 1978, ibid.

117. Herman Otten to J. A. O. Preus, May 4, 1979, ibid. Otten writes, "We are also willing to publish any evidence you have to support your charge that we are a liar, character assassinator, and slanderer." J. A. O. Preus to Herman Otten, May 14, 1979, ibid.

118. Herman Otten to J. A. O. Preus, June 23, 1979, ibid.

119. E. A. Weise to J. A. O. Preus, May 8, 1978, JAOP, Balance/*Affirm.* Weise was West Coast Regional Chairman of DCP-LCMS. He wrote, "Synod, in convention at Anaheim in 1975, very specifically <u>ex</u>cluded AFFIRM/DCP from Resolution 3-06, which properly labeled ELIM-MIP-PIM as divisive."

120. J. A. O. Preus to E. A. Weise, June 5, 1978, ibid.

121. "Affirm's Future," *Affirm* 7, no. 5 (May 1, 1978). Also Andrew Simcak Jr. to Balance, May 4, 1978, JAOP, Balance/*Affirm:* "The editor has been delaying publication [of <u>Affirm</u>] until debts can be paid. The situation is extremely serious. Please help."

122. J. A. O. Preus to E. J. Otto, May 3, 1978, Ralph Bohlmann Files, 7/17/00, Preus Misc. Files, Box 24. Preus also warned Otto not to allow the seminary to "yield on its library policy," and to continue banning Seminex students from making use of the facility. "The solution to the Seminex problem," he wrote, "is that they go out of business." He added, "The greatest service we can render them and our own church is to remain firm on this matter. . . . We only give them aid and comfort by a weak and vacillating library policy."

123. Handwritten note from Martin Scharlemann to Ralph Bohlmann, March 29, 1979, ibid. Scharlemann wrote Bohlmann, "My approach has been that I was this Seminary's agent for

in-put at the request of the Chairman of the Board. And until I am notified otherwise, that will continue to be my interpretation of the relationship."

124. J. A. O. Preus to Walter Otto, May 24, 1978, JAOP, Balance/*Affirm*. Also J. A. O. Preus to Vernon Harley, June 23, 1978, ibid; RP, f.21, Balance Inc/*Affirm*, 1974–84: "However, the point that I am most concerned about is the matter of electioneering on the part of Affirm. This does not produce the best officers and it tends to anger a great many people who are just as orthodox as those who are not on the Affirm list. It makes them appear to be liberals and they do not like this. I have heard this from scores of them and I wish that Affirm could understand that in designating somebody they are also taking a slap at somebody else. This is not right."

125. Walter A. Forster to J. A. O. Preus, July 19, 1978, JAOP, Balance/*Affirm*; RP, f.21, Balance Inc/*Affirm*, 1974–1984.

126. J. A. O. Preus to Walter Forster, August 16, 1978, JAOP, Balance/*Affirm*; RP, f.21, Balance Inc/*Affirm*, 1974–1984.

127. William Eggers to J. A. O. Preus, May 10, 1978, ibid.

128. Herman Otten interviews. Otten cautions that while he believes Eggers was forced out, he may have chosen to leave following his divorce to spare Balance the disgrace.

129. Robert Preus to William Eggers, September 18, 1979, Ralph Bohlmann Files, 7/17/00, Preus Misc. Files, Box 24.

130. Marcus Lang, telephone interview with author, July 27, 2001.

131. Waldo Werning interviews.

132. Agenda for DCP national meeting, February 1–2, 1980, JAOP, Balance/*Affirm*.

133. Marcus Lang interview.

134. Waldo Werning interview; Jack Cascione, interview with author, August 7, 2001; Marcus Lang interview; Tom Baker interview (Lang, Baker, and Cascione only acknowledged that Preus was pushed out, not that Hilst and Firehammer were present); anonymous interview.

135. Waldo Werning interviews.

136. J. A. O. Preus, "TO THE CONGREGATIONS OF THE LUTHERAN CHURCH—MISSOURI SYNOD, October 24, 1980, JAOP, Balance/*Affirm*.

137. Walter Maier Jr. to Board of Directors, LCMS, October 31, 1980, JAOP, Balance/*Affirm*.

138. Tom Baker interview; Chet Swanson interviews.

139. Herman Otten interviews.

140. Ralph Bohlmann interviews.

141. LCMS, *Proceedings of the Fifty-Fourth Regular Convention of the Lutheran Church—Missouri Synod* (St. Louis: Concordia, 1981), 25–27. Bohlmann was elected on the fourth ballot with 722 votes to 388 for Charles Mueller.

Conclusion

1. Ralph Bohlmann, interview with author, August 10, 2001.

2. Sauer was elected on the third ballot with 548 votes of 1,007 cast. LCMS, *Proceedings of Convention* (1981), 32.

3. "Gerhardt W. Hyatt, 69, Dies; Ex-Chief of Army Chaplains," *New York Times*, August 31, 1985.

4. J. A. O. Preus interview.

5. Notes from "Art" conversation with Adams, April 1977, EOR, f.1795, Otten, 1976–1978.

6. Robert Preus to Ralph Bohlmann, January 31, 1984, Ralph Bohlmann files, Robert Preus; Bohlmann interviews.

7. Robert Preus to Ralph Bohlmann, April 3, 1984, Ralph Bohlmann files, Robert Preus.

8. Bohlmann was defeated at the synod's 1989 convention by the movement's newest standard-bearer, A. L. Barry.

9. Paul A. Zimmerman, *A Seminary in Crisis: The Inside Story of the Preus Fact Finding Committee* (St. Louis: Concordia, 2007), 7, 10, 143. See also Zimmernan's interview on Issues, Etc., February 7, 2007: http://wittenbergmedia.org/audio/The_Battle_for_the_Bible_in_the_LCMS_-_Zimmerman.mp3 (accessed September 27, 2010).

10. Daniel Preus, "The Lutheran Church—Missouri Synod Holiday from History," April 7, 1999. http://www.confessionallutherans.org/papers/dantalk.htm (accessed September 27, 2010).

11. Daniel Preus, interviews with author, July 2000.

12. Waldo Werning to Herman Otten, August 23, 1989, *CN* Archives, Werning 7/12.

13. Otten's handwritten transcription of phone conversation with Waldo Werning, November 5, 1990, ibid.

14. Werning, *Making the Missouri Synod Functional Again,* 169.

15. Ibid., 63, 118, 85, 138. "During the years from 1965 to 1969 when J. A. O. Preus was elected President of the Synod, I was leader of the "Conservative" movement or party of the right" (63).

16. Ibid., 113.

17. Ibid., 80–81, 105. Werning describes the synod's official attempt to justify a politics that was tearing it apart, even in 1988. The LCMS Council of Presidents recognized a "Ministry of Influence" presumably equivalent to other spiritual gifts, concluding that "there is such a thing as wholesome politics as well as evil or destructive politics in the church." It warned against use of "election lists," arguing that "a responsible Ministry of Influence will not seek to be 'a party of power' in the Church. Instead, it will seek to live under the only power, which is the Word. . . . The power in the Church, therefore, is not, nor ever shall be, politics, persons, programs, presidents, District or Synodical staff, political groups or cliques." It is, instead, "the Word of God."

18. J. A. O. Preus interview.

19. LCMS, *1972 Statistical Yearbook* (St. Louis: Concordia, 1972), 288.

20. The LCMS reported membership of 2,337,349 at the end of 2008. "Congregations report more 'specialized ministries,' " *LW-R.* http://www.lcms.org/pages/rpage.asp?NavID=16031 (accessed September 27, 2010).

21. Southern Baptist Convention membership in 1960 was 9,485.276. LCMS, *1960 Statistical Yearbook* (St. Louis: Concordia, 1962), 285. Membership in 2001 was roughly 15.9 million. http://www.sbc.net/aboutus/default.asp (accessed September 27, 2010).

22. Synod's budget in 1970 was $24,630,384, while giving was $196,534, 555. LCMS, *1970 Statistical Yearbook* (St. Louis: Concordia, 1971), 279. Synod's budget in 1980 was $24,582,394 from total contributions of $399,898,631. LCMS, *1980 Statistical Yearbook* (St. Louis: Concordia, 1981), 221.

23. LCMS, *1972 Statistical Yearbook,* 288; LCMS, *1992 Statistical Yearbook* (St. Louis: Concordia, 1993), 252.

Bibliography

Manuscript Collections

Atlantic District of the Lutheran Church—Missouri Synod, Bronxville, N.Y.
Christian News Archives, New Haven, Mo.
Concordia Historical Institute (Archives of the LCMS), St. Louis, Mo.
    Ralph A. Bohlmann Papers
Executive Office Records
    J. A. O. Preus Papers
    Robert Preus Papers

Interviews (personal, telephone, and e-mail)

James Adams
Tom Baker
Karl Barth
Paul Behling
Ralph Bohlmann
Walter Bouman
Larry Burgdorf
Jack Cashione
Victor Constien
John Damm

Marvin Huggins
Marcus Lang
George Loose
F. Dean Lueking
Walter A. Maier II
Kurt Marquart
Martin E. Marty
Marie Meyer
Richard John Neuhaus
Herman Otten
Albert "Pete" Pero
Daniel Preus
Pete Seeger
Art Simon
Chester "Chet" Swanson
Kathryn Weidemann
Waldo Werning
Paul Zimmerman
Several anonymous sources, 2000–2002

Oral Histories

Concordia Historical Institute, St. Louis, Mo.
    John Behnken
    Alvin Mueller and Carl Muhlenbruch
    J. A. O. Preus
    Edwin Weber

Studies

Barnhart, Melody Ruth. "Heresy vs. Orthodoxy: The Preus/Tietjen Controversy." M.S. thesis, University of North Texas, 1991.

Burkee, James Christian. "Pastors and Politics: The Conservative Movement in the Lutheran Church—Missouri Synod, 1956–1981." Ph.D. diss., Northwestern University, 2003.

Greising, Jack Howard. "The Status of Confessional Conservatism: Background and Issues in the Lutheran Church—Missouri Synod." Ph.D. diss., St. Louis University, 1972.

Hayes, Laurie Ann Schultz. "The Rhetoric of Controversy in the Lutheran Church—Missouri Synod with Particular Emphasis on the Years 1969–1976." Ph.D. diss., University of Wisconsin Madison, 1980.

LaBore, Richard Donald. "Traditions and Transitions: A Study of the Leadership of the Lutheran Church—Missouri Synod During a Decade of Theological Change, 1960-1969." Ph.D. diss., St. Louis University, 1980.

Neeb, Larry W. "Historical and Theological Dimensions of a Confession Movement within the Lutheran Church—Missouri Synod." D.Min. thesis, Eden Theological Seminary, 1975.

Shaud, James Howard. "A Study in Idolatry: An Evaluation of the Doctrine of the Word in the Recent Lutheran Church—Missouri Synod Controversy, Based on Owen Barfield's Theory of the Idolatry of a Literal Consciousness," Ph.D. diss., Syracuse University, 1981.

Stevens, Leland Robert. "The Americanization of the Missouri Synod as Reflected within the 'Lutheran Witness.'" Ph.D. diss., Saint Louis University, 1987.

Todd, Mary. "'Not in God's Lifetime': The Question of the Ordination of Women in the Lutheran Church—Missouri Synod." Ph.D. diss., University of Illinois at Chicago, 1996.

Wilke, Wayne William. "Changing Understanding of the Church-State Relationship: The Lutheran Church—Missouri Synod, 1914–1969." Ph.D. diss., University of Michigan, 1990.

Periodicals

Affirm
American Lutheran
Badger Lutheran
Christian Century
Christianity Today

The Cresset
Der Lutheraner
Dialog
The Lutheran
Lutheran Forum
Lutheran Layman
Lutheran News (1962–1968)
Christian News (1968–present)
Lutheran Witness
Lutheran Witness-Reporter
McCall's
Missouri in Perspective
National Review
The New American
Playboy
The Seminarian
The Springfielder
St. Louis Lutheran
St. Louis Post-Dispatch
The Torch
Una Sancta

Synodical Reports, Statistics, and Minutes

LCMS. *Proceedings of Convention* [convention action and minutes].
    1938–2001.
LCMS. *Statistical Yearbook* [compilation of synodical and American reli-
    gious data]. 1938–2000.
LCMS. *Workbook* [reports and memorials to the convention]. 1938–2001.

Published Works: Primary Sources

Adams, James E. *Preus of Missouri and the Great Lutheran Civil War.* New York: Harper & Row, 1977.

Baker, Thomas A. *Watershed at the Rivergate: 1,400 vs. 250,000.* Sturgis, Mich.: T. Baker, 1973.

Behnken, John W. *This I Recall.* St. Louis: Concordia, 1964.

Danker, Frederick W. *No Room in the Brotherhood: The Preus-Otten Purge of Missouri.* St. Louis: Clayton, 1977.

Eckhardt, H. P. *The English District: A Historical Sketch.* N.p.: English District of the Synod of Missouri, Ohio, and Other States, 1946.

_____. *Exodus from Concordia: A Report on the 1974 Walkout by the Board of Control, Concordia Seminary, St. Louis, Missouri.* St. Louis: Concordia College, 1977.

Graebner, Alan. *Uncertain Saints: The Laity in the Lutheran Church—Missouri Synod 1900–1970.* Westport, Conn.: Greenwood, 1975.

Kiehl, Erich H., and Waldo J. Werning, eds. *Evangelical Directions for the Lutheran Church.* N.p., 1970.

Koenig, Richard. "What's Behind the Showdown in the LCMS? Missouri Turns Moderate: 1938–65." *Lutheran Forum* 7 (1973): 19–20, 29.

_____. "What's Behind the Showdown in the LCMS? Conservative Reaction: 1965–1969." *Lutheran Forum* 7 (1973): 18–21.

Lueking, F. Dean. *A Century of Caring: The Welfare Ministry Among Missouri Synod Lutherans, 1868–1968.* St. Louis: LCMS Board for Social Ministry, 1968.

_____. *Grace Under Pressure: One Congregation's Testimony.* Richmond: Skipworth, 1979.

_____. *Mission in the Making: The Missionary Enterprise Among Missouri Synod Lutherans, 1846–1963.* St. Louis: Concordia, 1964.

Machen, J. Gresham. *Christianity and Liberalism.* Grand Rapids: Eerdmans, 1923.

Marquart, Kurt E. *Anatomy of an Explosion: A Theological Analysis of the Missouri Synod Conflict.* Fort Wayne: Concordia Seminary, 1977.

Marty, Martin E. *Church Unity and Church Mission.* Grand Rapids: Eerdmans, 1964.

_____. *The New Shape of American Religion.* New York: Harper & Row,
1959.

McCarthy, Joseph. *McCarthyism—The Fight for America.* New York:
Devin-Adair, 1952.

Meyer, Carl S., ed. *Moving Frontiers: Readings in the History of the Lutheran
Church—Missouri Synod.* St. Louis: Concordia, 1964.

Montgomery, John W. *Crisis in Lutheran Theology: The Validity and Relevance of Historic Lutheranism vs. Its Contemporary Rivals.* Vol. 1.
Minneapolis: Bethany Fellowship, 1967.

_____. *Ecumenicity, Evangelicals, and Rome.* Grand Rapids: Zondervan,
1969.

Neuhaus, Richard John. *America Against Itself: Moral Vision and the Public
Order.* Notre Dame: University of Notre Dame Press, 1992.

Otten, Herman. *Baal or God?* New Haven, Mo.: Leader, 1965.

_____. ed. *A Christian Handbook on Vital Issues: Christian News 1963–
1973.* New Haven, Mo.: Leader, 1973.

_____, ed. *Christian News Encyclopedia.* Vol. 1 (1973–1983). Washington,
Mo.: Missourian Publishing, n.d.

_____, ed. *Christian News Encyclopedia.* Vol. 2 (1973–1983). Washington,
Mo.: Missourian Publishing, n.d.

_____, ed. *Crisis in Christendom: Seminex Ablaze.* New Haven, Mo.:
Lutheran News, 2004.

Pieper, Franz. *Brief Statement of the Doctrinal Position of the Missouri
Synod.* St. Louis: Concordia, 1932.

Piepkorn, Arthur Carl. "What Does 'Inerrancy' Mean?" *Concordia Theological Monthly* 36 (September 1965): 577–93.

*Report of the Synodical President to the Lutheran Church—Missouri Synod
(In Compliance with Resolution 2-28 of the Forty-Ninth Regular Convention of the Synod).* St. Louis: Concordia, 1972.

Root, E. Merrill. *Collectivism on the Campus: The Battle for the Mind in
American Colleges.* New York: Devin-Adair, 1955.

Scharlemann, Robert P. *Communism and the Christian Faith.* St. Louis: Concordia, 1963.

Schulze, Andrew. *Race Against Time: A History of Race Relations in Lutheran Church—Missouri Synod.* Valparaiso, Ind.: Lutheran Human Relations Association of America, 1972.

Speaking the Truth in Love—Essays Related to A Statement. Chicago: Willow, n.d.

Stormer, John A. *None Dare Call It Treason.* Florissant, Mo.: Liberty Bell, 1964.

Suelflow, August R., ed. *Heritage in Motion: Readings in the History of the Lutheran Church—Missouri Synod, 1962–1995.* St. Louis: Concordia, 1998.

Tietjen, John H. *Fact Finding or Fault Finding? An Analysis of President J. A. O. Preus' Investigation of Concordia Seminary.* St. Louis: Concordia Seminary, 1972.

_____. *Memoirs in Exile: Confessional Hope and Institutional Conflict.* Minneapolis: Fortress Press, 1990.

Werning, Waldo J. *Making the Missouri Synod Functional Again.* Fort Wayne: Biblical Renewal Publications, 1992.

_____. *Renewal for the 21st Century Church.* St. Louis: Concordia, 1988.

Weyl, Nathaniel. *The Jew in American Politics.* New Rochelle, N.Y.: Arlington, 1968.

Zimmerman, Paul A. *A Seminary in Crisis: The Inside Story of the Preus Fact-Finding Committee.* St. Louis: Concordia, 2007.

Published Works: Secondary Sources

Ahlstrom, Sydney E. *A Religious History of the American People.* New Haven: Yale University Press, 1972.

Ammerman, Nancy Tatom. *Baptist Battles: Social Change and Religious Conflict in the Southern Baptist Convention.* New Brunswick, N.J.: Rutgers University Press, 1990.

"Born Again! The Year of the Evangelicals." *Newsweek,* October 25, 1976, 68.

Bridston, Keith R. *Church Politics*. New York: World, 1969.

Brinkley, Alan. *Voices of Protest: Huey Long, Father Coughlin, and the Great Depression*. New York: Vintage, 1983.

Capps, Walter H. *The New Religious Right: Piety, Patriotism, and Politics*. Columbia: University of South Carolina Press, 1990.

Carter, Dan T. *The Politics of Rage: George Wallace, the Origins of the New Conservatism, and the Transformation of American Politics*. Baton Rouge: Louisiana State University Press, 1995.

Crawford, Alan. *Thunder on the Right: The "New Right" and the Politics of Resentment*. New York: Pantheon, 1980.

Cromartie, Michael, ed. *No Longer Exiles: The Religious New Right in American Politics*. Washington, D.C.: Ethics and Public Policy Center, 1990.

Diamond, Sara. *Spiritual Warfare: The Politics of the Christian Right*. Boston: South End, 1989.

Dickinson, Richard C. *Roses and Thorns: The Centennial Edition of Black Lutheran Mission and Ministry in the Lutheran Church—Missouri Synod*. St. Louis: Concordia, 1977.

D'Souza, Dinesh. *Falwell Before the Millennium: A Critical Biography*. Chicago: Regnery Gateway, 1984.

Findlay, James F., Jr. *Church People in the Struggle: The National Council of Churches and the Black Freedom Movement, 1950–1970*. New York: Oxford University Press, 1993.

Forster, Walter O. *Zion on the Mississippi: The Settlement of the Saxon Lutherans in Missouri, 1839–1841*. St. Louis: Concordia, 1953.

Friedland, Michael B. *Lift Up Your Voice Like a Trumpet: White Clergy and the Civil Rights and Antiwar Movements, 1954–1973*. Chapel Hill: University of North Carolina Press, 1998.

Gallup, George, Jr., and David Poling. *The Search for America's Faith*. Nashville: Abingdon, 1980.

Glock, Charles Y., and Rodney Stark. *Religion and Society in Tension*. Chicago: Rand McNally & Company, 1965.

Hadden, Jeffrey K. *The Gathering Storm in the Churches: The Widening Gap Between Clergy and Laymen*. New York: Doubleday, 1969.

Hartz, Louis. *The Liberal Tradition in America: An Interpretation of Political Thought Since the Revolution.* New York: Harcourt, Brace, Jovanovich, 1955.

Herberg, Will. *Protestant—Catholic—Jew: An Essay in American Religious Sociology.* Garden City, N.Y.: Anchor/Doubleday, 1960.

Hillis, Bryan V. *Can Two Walk Together Unless They Be Agreed? American Religious Schisms in the 1970s.* Brooklyn, N.Y.: Carlson, 1991.

Himmelstein, Jerome L. *To the Right: The Transformation of American Conservatism* Berkeley: University of California Press, 1990.

Hunter, James Davison. *Culture Wars: The Struggle to Define America.* New York: Basic, 1991.

Huntington, Samuel P. *Political Order in Changing Societies.* New Haven: Yale University Press, 1968.

Hutchinson, William R., ed. *American Protestant Thought in the Liberal Era.* New York: University Press of America, 1968.

Kersten, Lawrence. *The Lutheran Ethic: The Impact of Religion on Laymen and Clergy.* Detroit: Wayne State University Press, 1970.

Kristol, Irving. *Neo-Conservatism: The Autobiography of an Idea, Selected Essays 1949–1995.* New York: Free, 1995.

Leonard, Bill J. *God's Last and Only Hope: The Fragmentation of the Southern Baptist Convention.* Grand Rapids: Eerdmans, 1990.

Liebman, Robert C., and Robert Wuthnow. *The New Christian Right: Mobilization and Legitimation.* New York: Aldine, 1983.

Lipset, Seymour Martin, and Earl Raab. *The Politics of Unreason: Right-Wing Extremism in America, 1790–1970.* New York: Harper & Row, 1970.

Marsden, George M., ed. *Evangelicalism and Modern America.* Grand Rapids: Eerdmans, 1984.

_____. *Religion and American Culture.* Fort Worth: Harcourt, Brace, Jovanovich, 1990.

_____. *Understanding Fundamentalism and Evangelicalism.* Grand Rapids: Eerdmans, 1991.

Marty, Martin E. *A Nation of Behavers.* Chicago: University of Chicago Press, 1976.

_____. *The Public Church: Mainline-Evangelical-Catholic.* New York: Crossroad, 1981.

McGreevy, John T. *Parish Boundaries: The Catholic Encounter with Race in the Twentieth-Century Urban North.* Chicago: University of Chicago Press, 1996.

Mintz, Frank P. *The Liberty Lobby and the American Right: Race, Conspiracy, and Culture.* Westport, Conn.: Greenwood, 1985.

Mundinger, Carl S. *Government in the Missouri Synod: The Genesis of Decentralized Government in the Missouri Synod.* St. Louis: Concordia, 1947.

Nelson, Jeffrey S. *The Theology of Inexpedience: Two Case Studies in "Moderate" Congregational Dissent in the Lutheran Church—Missouri Synod.* New York: University Press of America, 1998.

Noll, Mark A. "Common Sense Traditions and American Evangelical Thought." *American Quarterly* 37, no. 2 (Summer 1985): 216–38.

Ribuffo, Leo P. "God and Contemporary Politics." *Journal of American History*, March 1993, 1515–33.

_____. *The Old Christian Right: The Protestant Far Right from the Great Depression to the Cold War.* Philadelphia: Temple University Press, 1983.

Rudnick, Milton. *Fundamentalism and the Missouri Synod: A Historical Study of Their Interaction and Mutual Influence.* St. Louis: Concordia, 1966.

Scherer, Ross P., ed. *American Denominational Organization.* Pasadena: William Carey Library, 1980.

Simon, Merrill. *Jerry Falwell and the Jews.* Middle Village, N.Y.: Jonathan David, 1984.

Stark, Rodney, and Charles Glock. *American Piety: The Nature of Religious Commitment.* Berkeley: University of California Press, 1968.

Stark, Rodney, Bruce D. Foster, Charles Y. Glock, and Harold E. Quinley. *Wayward Shepherds: Prejudice and the Protestant Clergy.* New York: Harper & Row, 1971.

Steinfels, Peter. *The Neoconservatives: The Men Who Are Changing America's Politics.* New York: Simon & Schuster, 1979.

Stelzer, Ronald W. *Salt, Light, and Signs of the Times: The Life and Times of Alfred M. (Rip) Rehwinkel*. New Haven, Mo.: Lutheran News, 1993.

Stevens, Leland Robert. "Trends in the Missouri Synod as Reflected in *The Lutheran Witness*, 1882–Early 1990s." *Concordia Historical Institute Quarterly* 69, no. 2. (Summer 1996): 88–101; no. 3. (Fall 1996): 116–32; no. 4 (Winter 1996) 165–82.

Stout, Harry S., and D. G. Hart, eds. *New Directions in American Religious History*. New York: Oxford University Press, 1997.

Strommen, Merton P. *Profiles of Church Youth*. St. Louis: Concordia, 1963.

Strommen, Merton P., Milo L. Brekke, Ralph C. Underwager, and Arthur L. Johnson. *A Study of Generations: Report of a Two-Year Study of 5,000 Lutherans Between the Ages of 15–65, Their Beliefs, Values, Attitudes, Behavior*. Minneapolis: Augsburg Publishing House, 1972.

Todd, Mary. *Authority Vested: A Story of Identity and Change in the Lutheran Church—Missouri Synod*. Grand Rapids: Eerdmans, 2000.

Trilling, Lionel. *The Liberal Imagination: Essays on Literature and Society*. Garden City, N.Y.: Doubleday, 1953.

Weber, Max. *The Sociology of Religion*. Boston: Beacon, 1922.

Wentz, Abdel Ross. *A Basic History of Lutheranism in America*. Philadelphia: Fortress Press, 1964.

Wills, Garry. *Under God: Religion and American Politics*. New York: Simon & Schuster, 1990.

Wuthnow, Robert. *The Restructuring of American Religion: Society and Faith Since World War II*. Princeton: Princeton University Press, 1988.

Correspondence

Letter from Anti-Defamation League (ADL). June 21, 2001.

Press Release

The Lutheran Church—Missouri Synod Board for Communication Services, 2001–2002.

Video Recording

"A Warrior of God, a Man of Peace: The Life and Times of Jacob Preus." St. Louis: Lutheran Church—Missouri Synod, 1995.

Internet Sources

Beschloss, Michael. Interview by Jim Lehrer, "Barry Goldwater," *News-Hour with Jim Lehrer,* PBS, May 29, 1998. For Hypertext, http://www.pbs.org/newshour/bb/remember/1998/goldwater_5-29.html

Christian Admiral, http://www.geocities.com/drakkar91/cadmiral/christia.html

Concordia Theological Seminary, www.ctsfw.edu

Evangelical Lutheran Church in America, www.elca.org

Evangelical Lutheran Synod, www.evluthsyn.org

Lutheran Church—Missouri Synod, www.lcms.org

Lutheran Churches of the Reformation, www.lcrusa.org

United States Department of Commerce, Bureau of Economic Analysis, http://www.bea.doc.gov/

United States Department of Commerce, United States Census Bureau, http://www.census.gov/

Index

Pieper, Franz, 32, 39
  Brief Statement, 24, 29, 84, 124
Piepkorn, Arthur Carl, 23, 25, 35, 54,
  62, 77, 147–48
Ping Pong Club, 105
Preus, David, 155
Preus, J. A. O., ix–x, 3–5, 7, 9–10, 12,
  15, 23, 40–41, 44–46, 49, 74–75,
  79–80, 86, 90–113, 116–23, 125–48,
  151–82
Preus, Robert, 3, 15, 23, 40, 81–82,
  86, 96, 112, 114–16, 119, 126, 128,
  130–32, 156, 159–60, 163–65, 167,
  174, 176, 178, 180–82

Rehwinkel, Alfred "Rip," 32–33, 37, 57
religious right, xiv, 2–3, 11
Repp, Arthur, 30–2, 34–36, 81, 88, 97,
  147–48
Republican, xiii–xiv, 5, 10–11, 43, 82
Ribuffo, Leo, 13
Rutz, Fred, 38–40, 46, 81, 85, 87, 107–
  8, 114–15, 128, 131, 155–56, 164–66

Saffen, Wayne, 62, 69
Sauer, Robert, 164, 166, 177
Scharlemann, Martin, 24, 32–33, 35–36,
  42, 44, 65, 67, 88–89, 110, 119,
  146–48, 171, 173
  1958 Essay, "The Inerrancy of Scrip-
  ture," 42
Schaeffer, Francis, 113
Schoedel, William, 31
Schulze, Andrew, 25–26, 48, 57, 59, 73
Seeger, Pete, 61–63, 66–68, 74, 76
Seminex. *See* Concordia Seminary-in-
  Exile
social gospel, 42, 52, 59, 85, 125, 128,
  136
Social Ministry Affirmations, 138, 161
Sohns, Wilbert, 113
Southern Baptist Convention, xi, 183
State of the Church Conference, 40–43,
  45, 56, 58, 61, 81, 83, 85, 170

"A Statement of Scriptural and Confessional Principles," 123–25, 140–42,
  145, 179
Stephan, Martin, 178
Stormer, John, 17, 64
Student Nonviolent Coordinating Committee (SNCC), 59
Stuenkel, Omar, 84, 98, 110, 112, 132
Swanson, Chester, 79, 81, 87, 90, 94,
  101–2, 105, 114, 116, 119, 126–36,
  139, 142, 155–58, 164, 166, 168,
  175–76, 179
Synodical Conference, 40

Tessmann, Al, 114, 116, 128, 130,
  132–33
Tietjen, John, ix, 28, 62, 88–89, 96–97,
  104, 110, 115, 119–22, 125, 140–54,
  181
Todd, Mary, 2, 5
Trilling, Lionel, 18
Trinity Lutheran Church (New Haven,
  Missouri), 37, 55, 67, 84, 114

United Planning Conference, 84–87,
  89–91, 105, 107, 127, 163

Valparaiso University, 39, 50, 75, 109
Vietnam War, 5, 13, 53, 57–58, 60,
  66, 70, 72, 78, 93, 96, 98, 106, 112,
  137

Wallace, George, 13, 72
Walther League, 61–63, 67–68
Walz, Jeff, xiii
Weber, Edwin, 90, 98, 144, 155, 165–66
Werning, Waldo, xv, 55, 73–75, 79–81,
  85–88, 90, 92–93, 105–7, 109, 112–
  14, 117–18, 122–23, 128, 131, 139,
  158–60, 164, 170, 175, 180–82
Wiederaenders, Roland, 55, 94, 98, 116,
  127, 138
Wisconsin Evangelical Lutheran Synod
  (WELS), 12, 40, 112, 129

Printed at Repro India Ltd.

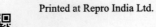